WHAT
WOMEN
WANT
MEN
TO KNOW

BARBARA DE ANGELIS, Ph.D.

WHAT WOMEN WANT MEN TO KNOW

The Ultimate Book About Love, Sex, and Relationships for You — and the Man You Love

HYPERION

NEW YORK

To the one I waited for all these years,
in honor of Love that does not flee from the face of fire,
but joyfully submits,
knowing that, through grace,
it will be transformed into gold.

Library of Congress Cataloging-in-Publication Data

De Angelis, Barbara.
    What women want men to know : the ultimate book about
love, sex, and relationships for you—and the man you love /
Barbara De Angelis.—1st ed.
        p. cm.
    ISBN 0-7868-8994-2
    1. Man-woman relationships. 2. International relations. 3. Love.
    4. Sex. I.Title.

HQ801 .D435 2001
306.7—dc21
                                                        2001024362

ISBN-13: 978-0-7868-8994-5

FIRST MASS MARKET EDITION

10   9   8   7   6   5

CONTENTS

ACKNOWLEDGMENTS

I would like to express my deep love and gratitude to the following people:

First, to the thousands of women who, over the past twenty years, have attended my seminars, called me on the radio, written me letters, and trusted me with your secrets: This is the book you've been asking for.

To Harvey Klinger, my dear friend and literary agent: Eleven books later, and we're still together—that's a successful relationship for us both! Thank you for being a strong and steady presence in my life, and for always believing in me.

To Leslie Wells, my editor at Hyperion: Thank you for your patience and trust that I will deliver what I promise. You are the most enthusiastic cheerleader!

To my business partner, Bob Marty: I'm so glad you finally showed up. Thank you for restoring my faith in co-creation, and being a true friend.

To my assistant, Alison Betts: No words are adequate to express my gratitude for the blessing of your presence in my life. You are the sister and the daughter I never had, and yet you take care of me like the most nurturing mother. You alone know what it took to make this book happen. Thank you for always knowing who I am, and for being there in ways I wouldn't even know how to ask for.

To Andres Garcia, Alison's husband: Thank you for sharing your wife with me so generously, and for helping her take care of my family.

To Ruth Cruz: Thank you for your loving service, your pure heart, and your tender care of me, Bijou, Shanti, and Luna.

Special thanks to: Lucinda Faraldo, for the sweet and open way you love and support me; *Jedd Rabon*, for a gift too precious ever to repay; *Marilyn and Joe Herst*, for taking care of me at a very tender time—you are true examples of great, spiritual souls; *David Steinberg*, for all the wisdom you share that continues to help me learn compassion, patience, and trust.

To my true friends on the spiritual path, whose unwavering loyalty and love, now more than ever, is priceless:

Amanda Kamsler: Thank you for being my protector and never letting go of my hand. The only good thing about your being on the other side of the world is that whenever I need you I can call you in the middle of my nighttime, and you're up because it's daytime in Australia.

Pam Kear: Even though we're far apart, I feel you with me always. You love me with so much compassion and kindness, and every day I thank God that we met.

Timothy Lehman: You are my soul brother, and so much more. Thank you for teaching me to be in the moment, for always being there to listen to my heart, and for being such a wise, ancient friend.

Vidura Barrios: You always give me sweetness, laughter, and love.

Sandra Crowe: For reminding me, as I remind you, that we both deserve the best, and for a reunion too miraculous to believe.

To my dear friend Robyn Todd: You are the sister I never had, and we both know you showed up just in time. I could never have imagined how much I would need you, or how much you would be there for me always. Thank you for a million moments of love and support.

To those who guide me in mystical ways with their gifts, I offer my humble thanks:

Jane Miller, for always keeping my vision on the highest, for encouraging me to find the strength to hold the door open so light could peek through, and for teaching me how to have faith until the darkness passed.

Margaret Sweet, for your continuing wisdom and clarity always shared in the sweetest way.

Judy Hevenly, for being a true angel.

Barbara Reeder, for being a visionary and a friend, and reminding me of my reason for being here.

Dr. Sat Kaur Khalsa, for your continued guidance and untiring support.

To Mom and Dan: Thank you for always believing in me and, over and over again, offering me unconditional love.

To Walter Muller and Mariarosa Ortega de Muller: You are like a second set of parents to me. Thank you for welcoming me so quickly into your hearts, for recognizing the purity and dedication of my love, and for being there for me whenever I have needed you. *Te quiero mucho*.

To my little fur angels, Bijou, Shanti and Luna: You are the most faithful and loving companions on this earth. I see you sleeping beside me even as I write this, reminding me that God shows me His love every day through you.

And to you whom I've given my whole heart: This book is for you.

INTRODUCTION

A Message to Women

I wrote this book for you, and for the man you love. I believe that it is a book every woman has always wished existed, a book she could give to her mate that would effectively explain all the things she wanted him to know about loving her. *"Read this,"* she would say, *"and you will understand me."*

How many times have I myself wished for such a book: times when it was clear that, once again, I had failed to successfully convey my needs to my partner; times when, no matter how hard I tried, I could not convince him that if only he would make one small gesture or handle a situation a bit differently, things would be so much easier between us; times when my attempt to communicate what I wanted and why it was important to me resulted in him concluding that I was simply too needy rather than being motivated to do something that would make me happy. In these, and so many other moments, I would sigh, as all women have undoubtedly sighed for thousands of years, and wish there was some way I could get through to him, some way to make him understand.

If you are a woman reading this, you know this sigh well. It is the sigh that whispers, *"I just want him to care enough to really see who I am."* It is the primal need to be known, to be valued, to be accepted just as you are. Of course, we all have tasted this experience of another soul truly knowing ours. Ironically, it is the bond we have with other women—our girlfriends, our sisters, our colleagues—where the very kind of deep comprehension of who we are and what we are trying to say happens effortlessly, and almost instantaneously.

Does the following story sound familiar?

You are sitting across from a girlfriend at lunch, and early on in the conversation you start to explain a problem you are having in your relationship, or something your mate did that upset you. Within moments of your initial remarks, your friend seems to understand exactly what you mean. She nods her head sympathetically, shows concern for all the right issues, and even finishes your sentences with the perfect words. And as you look at her gratefully, something inside you sighs with relief and exclaims: **"YES! That's exactly how it is.... You know just how I am feeling!"**

The conversation continues, and within ten minutes, you and your girlfriend have agreed on solutions to a whole list of issues that you and your husband have argued over, with no resolution, for ten years. You're amazed at how effortless the discussion is, how completely she comprehends your emotions, your reactions, your needs. You shake your head in frustration, knowing that if you try to bring up these same topics with your mate, his response will be quite different: thinly veiled irritation; eye-rolling; sighs of weary exasperation; and numb, emotionless stares, as if you were not speaking English but Swahili, so therefore he has no idea what you are talking about!

As you finish your lunch, you thank your friend for being so supportive. And then you say the words that, at some point, we have all found ourselves saying to other women in our lives: **"If only my husband could understand me like you do...! It's too bad that you're a woman—otherwise we'd be perfect for each other!"** *And your friend nods in agreement, for once again, she understands exactly what you mean...*

After countless experiences like this one, after decades of working with men and women trying to help them understand one another, it was time for me to write *What Women Want Men to Know*. Actually, people have been asking me to write a book like this for over ten years. Ever since 1990, when I wrote my first best-seller, *Secrets About Men Every Woman Should Know*, women and men as well have begged me to create its counterpart—**a book that would explain women to men.** In my seminars, on my television and radio shows, through my fan mail, and whenever they would meet me on the street or in an airport, literally thousands of people have made the same kinds of comments:

"I've tried to explain why I am the way I am to my boyfriend, but he just doesn't get it. I know if you explained it, he would listen!"

"Why can't my husband understand that if he just did certain simple things, I would be so happy? Please write a book telling men what we want and why we want it!"

"My best girlfriend understands me PERFECTLY. If men could eavesdrop on what women say to each other, they would become experts on loving us!"

"Every time I try to talk to my husband about sex, he gets defensive. Could you please write the nitty-gritty stuff about women and sex for men to read like you did for women to read in your book Secrets About Men?*"*

"My wife complains that I'm not intimate enough, but whenever I ask her to explain what she means, her answers leave me confused, and I have no idea what she's talking about. I really do want to make her happy, but I need help figuring her out."

What Women Want Men to Know is my response to these requests for help from both sexes: It presents all the things women wish men knew about understanding us and loving us. Over the past twenty-five years, I have worked with tens of thousands of women, listening to what they wanted and needed from the men in their lives, and hearing their frustrations in not always being able to get these needs met. I've also worked with tens of thousands of men, discovering how they look at love, sex, and intimacy, and how mystified they often are about us as women. I've learned how to translate for women what men want and how they feel, as I did in *Secrets About Men*. And now, in this book, I've translated for men what women want, how we feel, and what we've been trying to tell them about loving us.

Why Men Need This Book

Before we go on, there's something very important that I need to share with you, something I reiterate to men in the next section: *I love men!* I have loved men my whole life, and despite a very substantial collection of heartaches and disappointments, I have never stopped loving them or given up on them or on relationships. So this book is *not* about what's wrong with men; it is not designed to chastise or criticize them for not knowing how to love us properly. **Rather, its intention is to invite men to see and understand women as they never have before**. I have a reputation for knowing how to get through to my male readers, students, and seminar attendees, and I worked very hard in writing this book to express information in a way I hope men will really hear. You see, I understand how difficult it is for men to go where we want them to go emotionally, to open up to the kind of intimacy we crave, and to understand the heart and soul of women. And it is out of that love and compassion that I approach working with men, and it is out of that love and compassion that this book is written.

Recently, I bumped into an old friend in a health food store. I asked how she and her husband were doing, and we spent a few moments catching up on each other's lives. "What are you working on these days?" she questioned. "A new book called *What Women Want Men to Know*," I replied.

"Really? That's fabulous!" she said excitedly. "I can't wait to get it and give it to Donald. I mean, he's a great guy, but, well, he's still a man, right?"

A male customer happened to be standing next to us during this exchange, and when he heard my friend's comments, he shot us a nasty look, as if to say, "You women just love putting men down." As he walked by shaking his head, my girlfriend and I exchanged a smile, because we knew that his interpretation of what had occurred was totally incorrect—she hadn't been putting her husband down at all. She adores her husband. Rather, she'd been describing a reality most women naturally understand—*that even the best men are still MEN, not women, and for that reason alone, they can use a little help understanding the females in their lives*.

The harsh truth is this: **Just because men love us does not mean they can know us.** They inhabit a very different world than we do, and as we will see throughout this book, our world often appears mysterious, confusing, and contradictory to them.

I think this is why often even the best-intentioned man who deeply loves his partner appears to simply not persist at trying to understand her. *To put it bluntly, many men just give up, not because they don't care, but because they feel they are certain to fail at gaining any glimmer of true cognition of our complex nature, and since men don't like failing, they often opt for not trying at all.*

I wrote *What Women Want Men to Know* to make it easier for men to try to succeed at understanding and loving us, to make them better boyfriends and better husbands, better companions and better lovers. And I wrote this book to make it easier for you to succeed at expressing your needs, explaining your nature, and sharing your heart with the man you love.

How to Use This Book for Yourself

First and foremost, this book is for you as a woman to read. It wasn't written just to help men understand you—*it is an invitation for you to know and understand yourself more than you ever have before*. After all, if you don't quite understand why you feel the things you feel, do the things you do, and need the things you need, you will have a difficult time explaining these parts of your being to the men in your life. And if we are honest, we must confess that sometimes we wonder about ourselves as women: Are we "normal"? Is what we expect and hope for "too much"? Are our men right when they accuse us of being "too sensitive, too needy"? In truth, we don't always know and fathom ourselves as deeply as we claim to, and this lack of knowledge results in the destructive habits of self-criticism, self-doubt, and low self-esteem.

What Women Want Men to Know will reveal to you and to the men who read it that there are intelligent, loving reasons behind all the things you do and feel. There is a reason we call a man five times until we get through; a reason we feel terrible when he shuts down when we try to find out what's bothering him; a reason we love to plan time with our mate, and become anxious when he avoids committing to scheduling in advance. The reason is *not* that we are neurotic, or weak, or insecure. The reason, simply put, is that we are women, and what drives us and defines us is uniquely different from what drives and defines men. As you will see in the following chapters, **our needs and behaviors as women only ap-**

pear to be mysterious or confusing when we don't understand our true nature.

This is one of my purposes in writing this book, so that as women we can understand ourselves more and judge ourselves less, so that we can honor and celebrate our unique capacity to feel deeply, to love with uninterrupted focus, and to cherish connection over separation. When you have this kind of confidence and deep comprehension of yourself as a woman, you will have a much better chance of being able to communicate your needs and emotions to the man in your life. Of course, this still isn't a guarantee that you will always get the response you want, but at least you will have an advantage in that you will be able to give men something they appreciate and feel comfortable with when addressing a problem: *a logical explanation.*

Here's what I mean: Imagine that you're trying to communicate to your husband why you would like him to commit to planning more specific activities in advance with you and your children on the weekends, rather than always waiting until the last minute. You feel his resistance to this idea, his rebellion against feeling pinned down, and he responds by saying, "I don't get what the big deal is about. Why do you always want to have things planned out all the time? Why can't you be more spontaneous?"

Think for a moment—what would your answer be? Do you actually know *why* planning things in advance is so important to you, not just logistically but emotionally? Would you know how to express this to him? Much of the time, we aren't sure why we want and need the things we do, and we reply to a man's reluctance with vague statements like: *"I can't explain it,"* or *"Isn't it enough that I tell you it's important to me?"* or, when we are really frustrated, *"Just forget it—you obviously don't care about how I feel."*

Believe it or not, your man *is* listening, but he is probably listening from his head, and not from his emotions. Your lack of what he considers a logical explanation leaves him to conclude, consciously or unconsciously, that there is no logical explanation for these needs of yours, that they are just another example of the way women get needy or whiney, and are never satisfied. **Without information that can satisfy his brain, your partner may have a difficult time opening his heart to doing what it takes to make you happy. Instead, he will often dismiss your needs or requests as whimsical, irrational, and not deserving of serious attention**.

Throughout this book, I've not only detailed what women want regarding love, intimacy, communication, and sex but WHY we want it, WHY it is important to us, WHY, because of who we are as women, certain kinds of behaviors from our male partners fulfill our most profound and essential needs. These explanations are just as important for you to understand as they are for men, and the information you'll gain will make it much easier for you to successfully communicate with the person you love. So before you give this book to the man you love, please read and understand it for yourself!

How to Share This Book with Men

Earlier, I said that I wrote this book for you as a woman. And of course I also wrote it for men: any man who wants to be more successful at loving, pleasing, and living harmoniously with a woman. If you are presently in a relationship with a man and are reading these words right now, I must warn you about a temptation that will be difficult to resist—the temptation to thrust this book under his nose when he comes home tonight, or the next time you see him, and say: **"Here...READ THIS! It explains everything I've been trying to tell you for years. Better yet, MEMORIZE IT!"**

As enticing as this scenario might sound, it probably won't be particularly effective in getting your loved one to want to read this book, and will only serve to alienate him further from the possibility. How do I know this? Men who've been the "victims" of my enthusiastic female fans and ended up cringing at the very sound of my name have confessed it to me, sometimes years later, when they finally recover from the trauma of hearing *"Barbara says..."* every five minutes!

I met such a man only a few weeks ago. I was waiting in line at a coffee store when I was approached by a friendly-looking guy in his thirties. "You're Barbara De Angelis, aren't you?" he asked. I told him I was, and he began to smile.

"I just had to come up to you," he replied, "because I used to really hate you." Noticing the look of distress on my face, he quickly continued. "I was in a relationship for two years with a woman who worshiped you. You were like her guru. She had ordered every tape and video you've made, she owned every book you ever wrote, and all I heard day and night was 'Barbara said this' and 'Barbara thinks this about that,' most of which, by the way, was that I was screwed up. Whenever we'd have an argument, I felt like I was in a fight with two people—my girlfriend and you! By the time we broke up, I was furious at you, and blamed you for all of my problems.

"I went through a year of disappointing dating experiences. Then, several months ago, a male friend of mine told me he'd just read a fantastic book about how to choose the right partner called *Are You the One for Me?* He read me a few passages on the phone one night, and everything he said made perfect sense and explained some of the mistakes I'd been making. 'This sounds terrific,' I told him. 'Can I borrow the book?' He agreed to lend it to me, and the next evening at the gym, he handed me a well-worn copy of *Are You the One for Me?*—with your picture on the cover!

You can imagine my surprise when I found out this great book was written by the woman who had ruined my relationship with my girlfriend.

"Well, in spite of my prejudice, I did go home and read it. And of course I loved the book, and had to admit that my ex-girlfriend had been right—your stuff is great. I even called her up that week to tell her she wouldn't believe whose book I was reading, and we had a really good conversation. So when I saw you here, I just had to come over and tell you that I don't hate you anymore, and that actually, I think you're wonderful!"

I gave this man a big hug, and thanked him for his delightful story. Would you be surprised if I told you that I've heard this same tale in different versions many times? It seems my readers, usually the female ones, sometimes use my books as intellectual weapons, and I become an unwitting ally in their attack on their partner's behavior. Of course this approach never works, and I always feel regretful when I hear about it.

So here's my request to you: **If you are going to share this book with the man in your life, PLEASE SHARE IT LOVINGLY.** Don't shove it at him along with a sarcastic comment; don't give it to him in the middle of an argument; don't leave it on his pillow with a note attached that says: "You need this!" Come from a positive, instead of a negative, place, as if you've discovered a great treasure and want him to know about it, and he will be much more open to hearing what I have to say.

Here are some suggestions for getting your partner to read *What Women Want Men to Know:*

- Ask him to read the "Message to Men" that follows this section. It sets the tone for the whole book, and will hopefully make him want to continue reading!

- Give him a copy as a gift with a note that says: *"Because I love you and always want to have a fabulous relationship and a great sex life..."* For extra emphasis, include some lingerie with another note: "I can't wait to wear this for you," so he gets the idea that he will be rewarded for reading the book!

- Read him small sections, particularly the ones marked *For Men*, and ask him what he thinks of the information. This will allow him to slowly become interested in the material.

- Let him know you're reading the book so you can do a better job of expressing yourself to him, and give him an example of what you've learned. Then he won't feel you're saying *he* is the only one who needs the book.

- Arrange for one of your girlfriends to give him the book.

- Read him hot tips from the sex section while you're lying in bed, and then go back to reading. This will get him intrigued, and maybe even more ... !

- Leave the book in the bathroom with your favorite pages marked. Do not remove it for several weeks!

Perhaps you're already thinking: "My partner will NEVER read this." My response is: Don't be so sure. I worked hard to make this book user-friendly for men, to explain things in ways that will make it easy for them to want to read more. Men know I like them, and often they can accept feedback and suggestions from me that they can't from their own wife or girlfriend. My hope is that receiving this information about you *from me* will help the man you love finally hear what you've been trying to tell him for a long time. One thing is certain—any man who reads this book will know that my intention in writing it *is to make his love life easier, less intense and dramatic, and more hassle-free.* And no man can argue with those results!

How else can you share this book with men?

- *Give it to the boyfriends or husbands of your female friends*— you know they need it, and your girlfriends will love you for it.

- *Send it to your former lover.* Although your relationship with him is over, you will be doing a service to the next woman he is with. And if you are still interested in him, maybe it will reopen some doors.

- *Give it to your male friends who just can't seem to make a relationship work.* Their future partners will thank you one day!

- *Give it to your father.* It's not too late, and your mother will be grateful that you cared.

- *Give it to your son if he is old enough to appreciate it.* Don't you wish someone would have taught your mate this information when he was starting to date?

Getting the Most out of This Book

The information in this book was compiled from a combination of sources. The majority comes from several decades of working with tens of thousands of women and hearing what they wish men knew about them. As in all of my books, I've also added my own experiences from relationships into the mix, along with those of my close friends and acquaintances. In addition, I include hundreds of responses from a questionnaire I distributed to women over the past year.

Still, with all of this input, the best I can do in these chapters is to generalize about the way women are. All of us are unique and different. And while many women will find the descriptions of how we think and feel, and why we do the things we do, accurate, others may, at times, read what I've written and say, "I'm not that way at all." The truth is I know many men who have more of the "female" characteristics and motivations I describe (straight men as well as gay men), and on the flip side, I know many women who demonstrate more of what might traditionally be called "male" habits. I know men who are the ones in a relationship desperately needing attention and reassurance, and women who are shut down and hate talking about feelings.

The bottom line is that all things don't apply to everyone. I am attempting to communicate what I've heard and learned over the years without being accurate to every subgroup. So the best way for you to read this book is to take what feels pertinent and valuable to you, and don't worry about the rest. And of course *What Women Want Men to Know* isn't *everything* women want men to know—to complete that task I would have to write volumes! I have tried to include the information I felt was most important and useful.

I hope this book will be everything you want it to be. I hope that after reading it you will love and honor yourself more and judge yourself less. I hope it will open the doors of clarity and communication between you and the man you love. I hope it will give you the words you need to say so that your partner can understand you from the inside out. I hope it will be a source of comfort, strength, and inspiration, reminding you that you are not alone on your journey. Most of all, I hope this book brings you many steps closer to creating the kind of loving, fulfilling, and passionate relationship you've always dreamed of.

A Message to Men

*What if I told you that by doing a few simple things,
you could get the woman you love to stop acting
in some of the ways that drive you crazy?
What if you knew some magic words to say that would
work in seconds to make a woman feel like you were the
most wonderful mate she could ever imagine?
What if I taught you some secret techniques that would
make your partner want to have more sex with you?*

Do I have your attention yet, guys? Does any of this sound interesting? If so, you've come to the right place, and you're reading the right book!

Let me alleviate any suspicions you may have and say from the start what this book is *not*:

It's *not* a "chick book," written just for women, that I hope your wife or girlfriend will somehow convince you to read.

It's *not* a thinly disguised condemnation of men, explaining how it's all your fault.

It's *not* chapter after chapter of instructions to follow that will make you feel as if you have no power in your relationship and are just obeying orders.

It's *not* a book designed to make you more like a woman, and less like a man.

I wrote *What Women Want Men to Know* to help you feel more successful, more powerful, and more in control of your love life. I wrote it so you could have more of the things you want in relationships, and less of the things you don't want. It's a book written specifically with you in mind, a book written to make your life easier.

I've spent the past twenty years working with tens of thousands of people, about half of them men. Men of all ages and from all backgrounds have opened up and shared with me what frustrates them in their relationships, what confuses them about women, and what they want in the areas of love and sex. I've been listening carefully, and here's some of what I've heard men want:

- You want to feel successful in your relationship, like you're doing a good job and not messing it up.

- You want less hassle, stress, and drama.

- You want more peace, calm, and harmony.

- You want frequent and passionate sex with your partner.

- You don't want to have to emotionally process all the time and feel as though you're always "working on things."

- You want your mate to criticize you less and appreciate you more.

- You want to feel like you're making your woman happy.

This book is designed to help you achieve these goals. How? *By understanding more about why women are the way they are, and learning some simple, practical ways you can communicate with us and relate to us that will make you and your partner happier and more satisfied in every way.*

Now I have some really great news for you:

You know all of the stuff you hate about how women can get? Our neediness, our clinginess, our insecurities, the feeling you have that no matter how much you do or give, it's never enough for us? I want you to know that so much of this is *avoidable*. Perhaps a woman has tried to explain: "If only you'd do *x* or *y*, it would make such a huge difference," and you've thought to yourself, "Yeah, right." But I'm here to tell you that this is the most important secret about women you will ever discover:

> *When you learn just a few simple things to do and say to the woman in your life, you'll prevent her from having the very kinds of emotional reactions that you dislike.*

Does this sound too good to be true? Well, it isn't. I wrote *What Women Want Men to Know* to offer you the information you need, presented logically, clearly, and to the point, for creating the kind of relationship with a woman that is fun, enjoyable, satisfying, and much less work than you could ever imagine.

Are you convinced that this book is worth reading yet? I hope so!

The More You Know, the More Powerful and Successful You Are

Recently I gave a lecture to a large group and included some of the material you will be reading in this book. During the question-and-answer session, a man stood up and said defiantly, "I'm what you might call a macho sort of guy, and I'm having a hard time with this. It sounds like what you want is for me to basically think like a woman; act like a woman; in other words, to become a woman."

"Why do you think I want you to become like a woman?" I asked him.

"Well, if I'm always trying to figure out what my wife wants, and remembering her three basic needs like you talked about, and do this and that little thing to make her happier, aren't I becoming like a woman?"

"Let me ask you a question," I replied. "Do you own a car?" The man nodded. "Is it a nice car that you'd like to keep for a while?"

"Yes," he said proudly. "Actually it's only a few months old."

"Okay, so did you read the manual when you got the car?"

"Sure," he said.

"And the manual taught you how to operate the car properly, what kind of gas to use in order to run the vehicle efficiently, what warning signs to look for that might indicate you're having problems, when to get checkups so the car can last for a long time, how to service the car so it doesn't break down, and stuff like this, right?"

"Right," he answered.

"So," I said to him with a mischievous smile, "by learning about your car and understanding how it works, were you becoming like your car? Do you feel more like a car since you read the manual? When the dealer who sold you the vehicle gave you the manual, did you become defensive and say, 'Hey, do you want me to become like a car?' "

The audience laughed, and the man laughed along with them, because he couldn't argue with my logic.

"See, your car is very valuable to you," I explained. "It's an investment, so you want to protect that investment and learn everything you can about making sure the car works perfectly. Now, I notice you're sitting next to a woman who appears to be very happy with everything I'm saying, so I assume it's your wife?"

"Yeah, she made me come tonight." He grinned.

"Well, guess what? She's your investment, and a more expensive one than the car, I might add! So why not learn all you can about her, how to keep her 'running properly,' so to speak, and then you'll get the most out of your investment... and more enjoyable rides too!"

The audience applauded enthusiastically, and the man thanked me and sat down, kissing his wife, who was, I'm sure, thrilled that she had dragged him to my seminar.

I admit I like using car analogies with men, because they are effective in getting the point across—that learning more about that which is valuable to you is your way of protecting and taking care of what is yours. **Educating yourself about what is important to you is a way to make yourself more powerful as a man, not less powerful.**

In areas of your life other than your intimate relationships, you probably find it easier to be open to learning and improving yourself. For instance, you'd never be defensive or reluctant about reading the manual for your new car, or your new VCR, or your new cell phone. In the same way, if you had to make an important presentation for work to a new client, you'd want to learn everything you could about him and his company to ensure that you'd make a good impression—you'd never say to your boss: *"I don't need any help figuring out what to say. Stop telling me what to do all the time."* And if you're a golfer, or if you play tennis, or participate in any other sport, you read and learn everything you can about how to master that sport—you'd never stubbornly insist that you didn't need any help, that learning from other people would make you a wimp.

You know where I'm going with all of this, right? Your intimate relationship is your most important and valuable investment. **The more you learn about women and about love, the better you'll become as a husband or lover, and the more control you will have over your love life.**

While flying to New York recently, I was seated next to a gentleman of Asian-American descent who is a consultant to large corporations and business executives on understanding and operating successfully within the Asian culture. He is considered an expert in his field, and companies pay him a lot of money to train their staffs in how to relate to their business counterparts in Japan, China, Singapore, and other Pacific Rim countries. This man told me fascinating stories about companies that tried to take their businesses overseas without educating themselves about the cultural differences, and ran into problem after problem. "It's amazing," he explained to me, "how comprehending the differences between cultures, and learning just a few simple tips for effective communication and behavior, can be the key to billions of dollars of profit, and the difference between success and failure."

As I listened to this very intelligent man, I couldn't help but think about the work I do, and when he was finished with his story, I said, "Well, it seems that we're in the same profession."

"Really?" he replied. "Are you a cross-cultural consultant too?"

"In a way," I responded with a smile. "I teach men and women how to understand each other."

The man laughed and said: "Then I have no doubt your job is harder than mine!"

Just as, until they undergo the proper education, this man's clients can't be expected to understand their business associates from a totally different culture, so too *you can't be expected to understand women just because you love us!* Why? Because as you already know too well, men and women are very different. Besides, the truth is that as women, we don't always understand ourselves, and if we can't figure out why we are the way we are, how in the world can we expect you to understand us? As you'll see when you read *What Women Want Men to Know*, it wasn't just written for men in order to help you understand women—it was written to help us as women understand ourselves, so we can communicate more precisely and more effectively with you about what we want and need in ways you can actually hear us.

Why This Book Has Found Its Way to You

If you are reading these words right now, chances are that this book was given to you by a woman who loves you. Perhaps it was your wife, your lover, a close friend, your ex-girlfriend, your sister-in-law, but definitely someone who wants you to be happy and successful in your relationships.

If your partner gave you this book:

She isn't saying that you are the problem.

She isn't saying she is upset with you.

She isn't saying that you aren't doing it right.

She isn't complaining or making you feel wrong.

She isn't implying that she's perfect and you're the one who's messed up.

She isn't insinuating that it's all your fault.

She isn't alleging that you're stupid and can't figure this stuff out for yourself.

If your wife or girlfriend gave you this book, she is simply saying that she loves you. She wants things to be better, she wants your relationship to last, she wants to make you happy, and she feels you might get some information from this book that will help you act in ways that will allow her to be more of what you want her to be! Be happy that someone cares about you this much and is reaching out rather than shutting down.

If someone other than your partner gave you this book, know that she, or he, is a true friend who wants the best for you.

If you found your own way to this book, it is because you love women and want to make your relationships with them easier, full of more joy and less stress. I applaud you for being a man of vision. If you are already involved with someone, she is lucky indeed to have a man who cares enough to want to become a better partner and lover. And if you haven't found your true love yet, believe me, she is going to be happy and grateful when she meets you.

Perhaps at this point in your reading, despite how much sense all of this is (hopefully!) making, you hear a familiar, rebellious voice in your head that says:

"Jeez, another of my wife's books. She's always trying to 'fix' me, like I'm screwed up or something. I'm sure it's going to tell me that all the problems in our relationship are my fault, that I need to change. I don't need this! Why should I listen to some other woman I don't even know telling me what to do? What a waste of time."

Here's my response:

This book is going to make you feel smarter and more competent, not stupid and incompetent.

It's going to make you feel less out of control, and more in control.

It's going to give you more power over your life, not ask you to give up your power.

And the small amount of time you spend reading it will be nothing compared to the amount of time you will save because you will be having less arguments, less hassles, and less unhappy moments.

What You Need to Know About Me

Here are some things I'd like you to know about me:

First of all, **I love men.** I have loved them all my life. If I didn't, I'd have written a book titled *Men: Who Needs Them?* or *It's All His Damn Fault,* rather than *What Women Want Men to Know!* Instead, I wrote this book because I realize that although men continue to make sincere efforts to figure us out, it's not always a simple matter for you to understand the woman in your life. And perhaps it will be easier to hear about what women want and need regarding love, sex, and intimacy from me, a woman you don't know but one who has talked to thousands of other women, rather than hearing it from your own partner.

So think of me as a translator, a mediator of sorts in a peace process, sitting across the table from you and saying, *"Look, if you want to get such and such results in your relationship with your wife, I suggest you try doing this, because I can guarantee she will not only love it, but will complain less,"* or *"I know her request for such and such seems silly, and you can't imagine that something so trivial will make a difference, but trust me—I've talked to her—and it will,"* or *"If you want to avoid turning her into an emotional wreck, I propose you work on eliminating this certain phrase from your vocabulary, because whenever she hears it, she's going to overreact and you won't like the outcome."* Do I believe the information I'm going to share with you in the following chapters can make an enormous difference in your love life? You bet I do. Give it a chance, and I think you'll be pleasantly surprised.

Second, this book is written by me, a woman, about what women want men to know. Isn't that the way it should be? If you're going to learn about what women want you to know in the areas of communication, intimacy, love, and sex, shouldn't your guide *be* a woman? What good is it hearing what some other man *thinks* about what women want? Naturally I am biased, but I do believe that this book contains information you'd never learn if it was written by a man. Women have confided in me, and told me things about themselves, about their needs, and about sex that I am sure they would never have revealed to a man. I think you will be intrigued by what they have to say.

Third, if you're thinking, *"Why did you just write about what men are supposed to learn and do differently? It seems so one-sided. What about women? Shouldn't they be trying to understand our needs, and make us happy too?"* Well, I couldn't agree with you more. That's why several years ago, I wrote *Secrets About Men Every Woman Should Know*. It taught women all about men's likes and dislikes regarding love, sex, communication, and suggested ways women could adjust their behavior in and out of the bedroom to improve their relationships with their husband or boyfriend. Millions of women read *Secrets*, and when they shared it with their partners, the men concluded that I was, indeed, their ally. So each time you read something in the following chapters that makes you want to say, "But what about what SHE does wrong?," just remember—it's all in the other book!

How to Get the Most out of This Book

It was a challenge to write this book so that both women and men could feel I was talking directly to them. There are sections in which I am explaining certain things to women about themselves, and hoping that you're reading this information as well. Then you will notice specific places where I make a point just for men. **The best way to read the book is from start to finish,** knowing that *everything* I've included in *What Women Want Men to Know* is designed to make you a lot smarter about women, love, and sex.

If you haven't done so already, please go back and read the "Message to Women" at the beginning of the book. It's just as much a message to you as it is to women, and you will find it helps to set up the rest of the chapters.

As I remind women in their Message, every female is unique and different, and so at best, all of what you read will be generalizations. This is where you come in: *If you're in a relationship, I strongly suggest that you discuss the material in this book with your partner*:

- Ask her if a particular point accurately describes her feelings.

- Invite her to comment on what I say or what other women expressed.

- Let her know what specific suggestions you'd be willing to try, and ask if these would make a difference to her.

Having these kinds of discussions will give you much valuable information about your wife or girlfriend. You'll also find these conversations effortless and stress-free, compared with ones you've had in the past, because you will both be able to start your dialogue from the common ground of this book, rather than just your own opinions, and thus it will feel less adversarial and more like you're both on the same side. Best of all, your partner will LOVE it that you are showing interest in her feelings, wanting her input, and that you care enough to ask.

I need to take a moment and say what this book is *not* about. *It's not about deeply wounded women with severe emotional problems who have shut down their feelings, suppressed their needs, and cut themselves off from their hearts.* If you are presently or have been with a woman like this, you may find that nothing I say about how women behave applies to her. That's because in order to defend herself from further pain, she's built walls of protection around herself, and detached from her ability to feel. Men who make a habit of choosing emotionally unavailable women will be unable to relate to much of this book, and if you suspect you might be in that category, consider reading *Are You the One for Me?*, which will help you understand more about the patterns that prompt you to end up in unhealthy relationships.

I have a confession to make: I wrote this book secretly hoping my own partner would memorize every page, drink in each word, and digest every bit of information about me as a woman. I hoped he would enthusiastically try out every suggestion and explore each technique, intent on doing all he could to become the man of my dreams. If your wife or girlfriend gave you *What Women Want Men to Know*, guess what—she's secretly hoping the same thing that I am!

Of course, what I am describing is how a *woman* would read a similar book, how a *woman* would approach pleasing a man, how a *woman* views improving herself, how a *woman* views love. Did you know that we are that way—focused on loving you twenty-four hours a day? Well, you'll learn about it in the chapters that follow.

So how *will* you read this book as a man? What will you do with what you discover in these pages? Only you have the answers to these questions.

But I'll confess another secret: *If my sweetheart only takes a few important things from this book, it will be enough.* I will be grateful that he was interested enough to spend the time to read about me, that he was committed enough to try to understand the tenderness of my heart, that he cared enough to consider ways in which he could make me feel more safe, more valued, more loved.

Your woman feels the same way. If, by reading what I offer here, you learn to appreciate her a little more fully, listen a little more closely, and love her a little more sweetly, she will be happy—and it will be enough.

Thanks for trusting me to take you on this journey into the heart and soul of a woman. I promise you it will be worth it....

PART

I

WHAT WOMEN
WANT MEN TO KNOW
ABOUT US

I begin this book with an admission to men on behalf of the women you love and the women who love you:

We want men to understand us, to truly grasp why we are the way we are and why we need the things we do.

And we feel frustrated and upset when it appears that you don't understand us.

But the truth is—and here's the admission—we do not always fully understand ourselves, either.

Why is it, for instance, that at one moment a woman can seem to be so strong and competent, and the next so fragile and insecure?

What is it about us that makes us feel like a powerful goddess when we are at our best, and like a helpless little girl at our worst?

Why can we be the most enthusiastic cheerleader, the most stalwart supporter, the most loyal protector, the most wise adviser to everyone else—but not always to ourselves?

What does it mean that we can do a million things at once and seem to be handling it all effortlessly until suddenly, in one moment, we collapse under the weight of too much responsibility and just want to crawl under the covers?

Where does our ability to love so deeply come from?

Why is it that we so easily sacrifice our own needs in order to fulfill those of others?

Why do we seem to require more time, attention, and reassurance from men than they require from us?

Why are we the way we are?

We know men ask themselves these questions about us. And whether we readily admit it or not, we have the same questions about ourselves. The good news is that there *are* answers, reasons that, as women, we feel what we feel, and do what do. These answers are contained in the pages that follow, and are meant to enlighten women as well as men, as they shed light on the mystery of our nature, of our mind and our heart, of our desires and our longings.

Allow me, for a moment, to take you into the heart of a woman, and, through the following stories, reveal our own struggle to understand ourselves:

You know the man you love is going through a hard time in his life, contemplating making some difficult business decisions. Lately, he's been anxious and distracted, and you want so badly to help in some way. One night after dinner you bring up the subject of his dilemma, sharing some thoughts you've had about the challenges he faces, suggesting steps he could take to resolve his problem. As you begin to talk to him, a tense look appears on his face, and with each new idea you present his frown gets worse and worse. Suddenly, you feel him pull away, as if you've just been shut out entirely.

"What's wrong, honey?" you ask with concern.

"I just want to handle this situation myself," he replies curtly. "I don't need your advice."

"But I'm only trying to help," you explain.

"Why don't you let me figure it out my own way? Don't you trust me?" he answers, obviously angry. "I hate when you get bossy and controlling like this." And he leaves the room.

You stand there watching your husband walk away, your heart pounding and tears filling your eyes. You want to run after him, but you can't find the right words to explain how you feel, how all you wanted to do was to support him. Instead, your efforts have made things even worse. You feel like such a failure. And a part of you wonders: **"Is he right? Am I controlling like he says?"**

————————

A long weekend is coming up, and you want to spend it with your boyfriend. You had hoped he would mention it by now, but he hasn't, and you are starting to worry. One night while talking with him on the phone, you bring up the subject: "Have you thought about the holiday weekend?"

"Not really," he responds.

"Well," you continue tentatively, "I was hoping we could be together, maybe even go away somewhere."

Your boyfriend becomes very quiet, and after a few moments says in a flat voice: "Let's see how the week goes."

How the week goes? What does he mean by that, you think to yourself. You begin to feel a little panicky. "Don't you want to spend time with me?" you ask him in a shaky voice.

"Of course I do," he replies with growing irritation, "but why do we have to plan everything? Can't you be more spontaneous? You're so insecure all the time!"

You don't know how to answer him. You just know that you'd feel so much better if you were sure you could look forward to seeing him that weekend, but you've already told him that, and there doesn't seem to be anything else to say. The conversation ends, and as you get off the phone, you have an ache in your chest that won't go away. You wonder: **"Is he right? Am I too insecure?"**

————————

Your husband has left on a business trip. When he arrives at the airport in his destination city, he calls briefly to check in and *let you know he is going out for dinner with a client. That night as it's time for bed you lie there waiting for the phone to ring. You try his hotel room a few times, but get no answer. You leave several messages, and you wait, and you wait, but he doesn't call. By now, it's two in the morning, and you're terribly anxious and worried. Where could he be, and why hasn't he called? What could keep him from wanting to say good night to you? You finally fall into an uneasy sleep.*

The next morning, you get up feeling hopeful, expecting to hear from your husband, but still, nothing. You try to make excuses for him, but you're having a hard time convincing yourself: "If he was really tired last night, he could at least have called this morning." As the hours go by with no word from him, your worry turns to paranoia, and your mind proceeds to parade its worst fears before you. "Maybe something is really wrong," you imagine. "Maybe he got sick; or maybe he's deliberately avoiding me." And then the worst fear of all: Could he be there with another woman?

Finally, that evening, your husband calls, and to your great surprise, acts as though everything is fine. "Why didn't you call me last night or this morning?" you ask in an anxious voice. "I was so worried!"

"I had just talked to you when I arrived, and after dinner I was exhausted and just collapsed into bed," he answers, his voice expressing bewilderment that you are upset at all. "And this morning I was focused on getting ready for my meeting. Then I went from one event to another. I figured we would talk sometime today."

You try to explain why you were so agitated at not hearing from him, but it doesn't come out right, and you're afraid you sound too desperate and clingy. Your husband listens, and you know by his response that he is annoyed. "Do I have to check in with you every five minutes?" he says sharply. "Why do you fall apart just because I don't call you for twenty-four hours?"

The conversation ends on a bad note, and when you hang up the phone, you feel awful. All you had wanted to do was let him know how much you missed him. Why couldn't he understand how worried you'd been? Was it that unreasonable for you to have been concerned when he didn't call or answer his phone? Or could it be that he was right: "Is something wrong with me?" you wonder. "Am I really too needy?"

———————

Most women reading these stories will resonate with the experiences and emotions described because, whether to a lesser or greater extent, we've all had these feelings at one time or another. We wonder if our reactions to our partner are justified or if they are overreactions. We question whether our needs are legitimate or excessive. *"Am I normal?"* we ask ourselves.

As for men, well, I suspect that many of you reading these stories will probably have a very different response, something like: "Here are three perfect examples of the way women overreact and drive men nuts!" And you're right—these scenarios are typical of the kinds of things women do and feel that men simply don't understand, and therefore, often categorize as undesirable female behavior.

It is easy to condemn something when we don't understand it. When not seen with eyes of wisdom and deep comprehension, a woman's unique and beautiful characteristics can appear as something else not so beautiful to men, and even to ourselves. But when you learn the inner secrets of a woman's nature, suddenly what appeared to be confusing becomes clear, what seemed unacceptable becomes appreciated, what was challenging becomes endearing.

When I prepared to write this section of the book, my goal was simple. I was looking for a few basic truths about who women are that would help us and the men we love understand our feelings and our behavior. In my research I asked women:

"What are the things you want the man you love to understand about you as a woman at the deepest level of your being?"

"What do you need to explain to your partner about your female nature that is very basic to you, yet, you suspect, so different from the way he experiences the world as a man?"

In the chapters that follow, I've done my best to summarize these basics about who women are, why we are that way, and what we want men to know about loving us. The first few chapters focus on three characteristics, the ones I believe are essential to understand in order to truly understand women. So much of why women do what we do, feel what we feel, and say what we say has its source in these truths. They are:

The Three Basic Truths About Women

1. **Women put love first.**
2. **Women are creators.**
3. **Women have a sacred relationship with time.**

Chapters 4, 5, and 6 present *the three secret needs every woman has* as a once-and-for-all response to men's question: "Is there really something I can do that will make her stop complaining and be happy?" (Yes, there is!) And finally, Chapter 7 details "Seven Myths Men Believe About Women and Why They Are Absolutely Wrong"!

CHAPTER ONE

Women Put Love First

A few months ago, a male friend I hadn't heard from in a while called to tell me he was in a new relationship with a woman he'd been seeing for six months. Brian had dated a lot in his life but had never really been seriously involved with anyone, so this was big news. I asked him how it was going, and he answered that things were great, but he had some concerns about his girlfriend.

"What kind of concerns?" I asked him.

"Well, Lori is really terrific, very sweet and affectionate," he began, "but I'm worried that something's wrong with her, like maybe she has psychological problems. That's why I am calling you—to get your feedback."

"Tell me what she does that makes you think she has psychological problems," I prompted him.

"To begin with, she says she thinks about me all the time; she calls me during the day just to tell me she misses me; she plans special things for us to do weeks in advance; and she always wants to talk about us and how well we get along. Then last week," he continued in a very serious voice, "she told me that our relationship is the most important thing in her life!"

"And what do you conclude from all of this?" I asked him, trying to hide the fact that I was smiling on the other end of the phone.

"Well, if she's so focused on me like that, I think she obviously must be neurotic and insecure."

"No, dear," I said to my friend with a chuckle, *"she must be a woman in love."*

My friend Brian is a good guy—but he's a guy. He didn't have a lot of experience being in long-term relationships, and the way Lori was loving him seemed strange to him, even unhealthy, because he didn't understand the first secret about who women are: *The world of women is a world of love.* To love, to be devoted, to cherish intimate relationships is our nature.

What Women Want Men to Know:

Women put love first.

When I say women put love first, I don't mean women *choose* to make love and relationships a priority—these things just *are* a priority in our awareness. We don't choose to have our heart focused on the man we love—*it just is.* We don't choose to always be thinking of ways to connect with you—*we just do.* We don't decide to put love first—*it just is first.*

The Love Pie

Here's an easy and visual way to understand the way women feel about love and relationships. I call it the "Love Pie."

Visualize two circles, like pies, one representing a man's consciousness and the other representing a woman's consciousness. Now imagine a tiny slice cut out in each circle, like a piece of the pie, perhaps one-tenth of the whole. In the man's circle, that small slice is the percentage of his awareness that he focuses on love and intimate relationships. Everything outside of that slice, the other nine-tenths of the circle, is his awareness focused on his work, his hobbies, his projects, and other activities.

In the woman's circle, however, it is exactly the opposite: The tiny slice of the pie is the focus of her awareness on work, hobbies, and projects, and all the rest of the pie is the focus of her awareness on love, family life, and relationships!

Okay, this is probably somewhat of an exaggeration, but you get my point. Whenever I draw the Love Pie for my seminar audiences, it evokes peals of laughter from both sexes. Why? Because instinctively, we all know it's true, and as we'll see, it explains so many of the issues that become problems between men and women.

Here's an important distinction to remember: The Love Pie doesn't symbolize how we divide our time, or how many hours we spend on love versus other activities. It depicts *where our awareness is focused on the inside*, no matter what we are doing on the outside. For instance, a woman may work in her own career, whether outside or inside the home, for as many hours as her husband does in his, so it's not like she's spending one-tenth of the time he does focusing on work, and nine-tenths of her time shopping for lingerie, writing love poems, or fantasizing about how much she adores him. But you can bet that while she is doing her job, she probably thinks more about him than he does about her, and from day to day she is more conscious of the emotional rhythms of the relationship, and more focused on wanting more connection and intimacy.

Sometimes when I share the Love Pie analogy with women, they don't completely relate to it until I remind them that focusing on love includes focusing on their children. Single mothers can understand this: Perhaps they aren't in an intimate relationship, *but*

their awareness is still on love the majority of the time—the love
and concern they have for their children. Even women who are
married often feel the large portion of their Love Pie is more dedicated to their everyday relationship with their kids than to the relationship with their husband. Whether this is healthy or not is a
whole other topic, but the point is the same: She is a woman whose
awareness, thoughts, and feelings are naturally focused on putting
love first.

Taking a Trip into the Mind of a Woman

I've always said that if men spent a day in the mind of a woman
in love, they'd be shocked and amazed at how much we think
about them, how aware we are of them no matter what else we are
doing. There's an exercise I sometimes give couples to help the
man understand how women put love first, and to give him an experience of our Love Pie: I ask the female partner to keep a
"Thought Diary" throughout a typical day, writing down each time
her awareness focuses on her mate and describing the situation.
Then, she shows him her list. Without exception in the couples I've
worked with, the male partner is astonished at how often during a
day the female partner thinks about him.

I wanted to give you male readers a chance to experience this,
so here's a sample from one woman's list that she kept in relation
to her boyfriend, Joseph. Melissa is an executive at a radio station
and has been involved with Joseph for almost a year. I've actually
only included half of a day's diary—a full day would go on for
pages!

Melissa's Thought Diary

6:45 AM	I wake up thinking about Joseph, excited that I am going to see him tonight. I lie in bed fantasizing about it for a while.
7:00 AM	I want to call Joseph to say good morning, but I tell myself I should wait to see if he calls me.
7:10 AM	I can't decide whether or not to wash my hair now, or wait until just before my date so it's really clean when I see Joseph.
7:15 AM	I decide to wait to wash my hair, but while in the shower I remind myself that I need to put out the new body lotion Joseph said he likes so I'll remember to use it after my shower this evening.
7:40 AM	I am eating breakfast, remembering how sweet it was last weekend when Joseph stayed over and we had breakfast together.
7:50 AM	I'm watching TV and there's a report on the news about Caribbean hideaways. Joseph and I have been talking about taking a trip there soon, and I write down the information the reporter mentions.
7:55 AM	Still no call from Joseph. I am wondering whether or not I should call him and mention the TV travel report. I decide to wait another ten minutes.
8:05 AM	I call Joseph and we talk for a few minutes. He is racing around getting ready for an important meeting at work, so he can't really concentrate, but he says he can't wait to see me later, so I am happy.

8:20 AM   While I am putting on my makeup, I think about the conversation I just had with Joseph, and replay the sweet things he said.

8:35 AM   I am in my closet, deciding what to wear for work, and start thinking about which outfit I should wear tonight when I see Joseph. I bought a new top a few days ago that I think he will like, and I try it on just to verify that I am still pleased with it.

8:50 AM   I am making the bed, and decide that I will change the sheets later before Joseph gets here. Of course, I am hoping he will spend the night.

9:20 AM   I am driving to work, listening to the radio. A song by Carlos Santana comes on that Joseph and I love, and it reminds me of a road trip we took to San Diego when we played the Santana album the whole way. I smile thinking about what a great time we had. I am tempted to call Joseph on his cell phone and tell him I am remembering San Diego, but I know he is probably on his way to a meeting and focusing on what he needs to accomplish.

10:45 AM   I am looking at Joseph's picture on my desk, and decide that I want to get a nicer frame for it.

11:30 AM   I notice the time, and wonder if Joseph's meeting is over and how it went. I am hoping he's happy with it, so that he'll be in a good mood tonight.

11:50 AM   Joseph calls for a second on his way back from the meeting. He sounds pleased. I tell him about hearing the Santana song this morning.

11:57 AM   I notice that I've been a little agitated since Joseph called, and I realize I am feeling concerned about something he said on the phone regarding his needing to go out of town next week.

12:30 PM   I am at a lunch meeting with a new client at a restaurant I've never been to before, and I'm thinking that Joseph would really like it, and that we should come here some time.

2:10 PM   I pass a grocery store, and remember that I am out of Joseph's favorite soap. I decide to stop and pick up the soap, and once inside, I walk through the produce section and notice that they have beautiful raspberries which Joseph would love, and buy some.

2:35 PM   I check my messages back at the office, and even though I just talked with Joseph a few hours ago, I feel a tiny bit of disappointment that there's no message from him. I know this is silly, but it's how I feel.

2:55 PM   I open my mail, and discover an invitation to a party celebrating a well-known writer who is doing a benefit lecture in town next month. I make a mental note to myself to ask Joseph if he will be able to come with me.

3:15 PM   I glance at the time on my computer clock, and feel a twinge of excitement that I will see Joseph in less than four hours.

————

So what's your response to Melissa's Thought Diary? When I show this list to women, they read it and say, "Oh my gosh, that's exactly what I do!" Perhaps the *content* is varied for married women or women with children, but the *frequency of thought* is very similar. Men, on the other hand, have a very different reaction to this list. Some think I'm playing a joke on them, that a list like this can't be genuine. Others make comments like: "This Melissa seems pretty neurotic," or "Sounds like she needs to get a life!" Little do these men realize that their own girlfriends or wives probably think about them as much as Melissa thinks about her boyfriend, Joseph.

For Melissa, as for many women, love is a constant theme in her awareness. It's the biggest piece of the pie of her consciousness. That doesn't mean she isn't focused on her job, or on other areas of her life—actually, she has a very busy schedule and a demanding career. *It just means that when she is in an intimate relationship, she sees the world through the lens of love.* It's as if she is wearing a special pair of glasses whose prescription is her love for Joseph, and her experience of life is perceived through those love glasses. A news story on TV isn't just a news story—it becomes something she can share with her sweetheart. A song on the radio isn't just a song—it evokes memories and special emotions that remind her of her man. Raspberries aren't just raspberries—they are the fruit that her partner loves.

Men: Please know that this process is so natural to a woman, so much a part of her nature, that she isn't even aware that it's going on. In fact, when Melissa read her own Thought Diary, she herself was surprised at how often she was thinking about Joseph. Normally, these thoughts about him just float in and out of her awareness. They're just a part of how she is when she's involved in a relationship, a reflection of how, like so many women, she puts love first.

How Men and Women Love Differently

After years of research and personal experience, I've concluded that love is experienced very differently by men and by women:

> **For most women, love is a nonstop reality,**
> **a consistent awareness that never quite disappears**
> **even when we are working or performing tasks**
> **that seem to have nothing to do with love.**
> **For most men, on the other hand,**
> **the experience of love is much more** *compartmentalized:*
> *It is an appointment men make with a part of themselves.*

Women don't have to shift into a loving awareness—they are in it most of the time, whether it's being expressed or not. On the contrary, *most men do have to consciously choose to make a shift into love mode.*

Let's go back for a minute to Brian, my friend who thought his new girlfriend must have psychological problems. This difference we've been examining between men and women explains why to Brian and probably to most men, a woman's focus on him may seem excessive. Brian can't imagine himself focusing on the relationship as much as Lori does. If he did that, he'd have to block out the rest of his life and consciously concentrate on her. To him, this would feel unbalanced, even obsessive. **So he incorrectly assumes that if this is how Lori feels about him, she must be making a huge effort to love him in this manner, and therefore, she must be unbalanced and obsessive.**

Many men make this same error in judgment—they see a woman putting love first, and have a hard time relating to it. *"If I was behaving that way or feeling that way,"* they think to themselves, *"it would mean that I didn't have a life, that I was really needy and desperate."* Then they conclude that their partner must be needy, empty, and insecure to love that much or focus on them that consistently.

Women, however, know better. Lori isn't making any effort at all. She's in love, and focusing on Brian is as natural to her as breathing. She doesn't even think about it—it just happens. It's the same with Melissa—she isn't trying to think about Joseph; she isn't thinking about him because she has a problem, or no life of her own. She is thinking about him because that's the way she loves as a woman.

T he analogy of the Love Pie illustrates how men and women *think* about their relationship. Here's a second analogy, one that illustrates how men and women *function* in relationships.

Imagine a man's consciousness and a woman's consciousness are like houses, with different rooms for the different areas our mind focuses on in our life—a "work" room; a "body" room; a "recreation" room, etc. **For most women, every room in the house of her consciousness is also a Love Room**, even when it is dedicated to other functions. It's as if all the space in the house of her consciousness is used for love. It's a Love House!

For men, however, there is only one Love Room in the house of their mind. Therefore, if the man wants to put his focus on love and the relationship, he consciously has to leave the other rooms and go to his Love Room.

This analogy of the Love Room explains a phenomenon I've experienced so often in my own relationships, one I know other women have as well:

I'm with my partner, and I reach out to relate to him in a romantic way, but he doesn't respond. I know he loves me, so I can't understand why he seems a little distant. When I ask him if something is wrong, he invariably replies, *"No, nothing's wrong."* I begin to feel frustrated and uncomfortable, because I'm trying to connect with him in an emotional way, but he is not reciprocating.

What's actually happening in this situation? *I am in my Love House, which is full of Love Rooms, and I am relating to my mate in a loving, intimate way, only he is not in his Love Room!* Maybe he's in the Work Room of his mind, and is thinking about a project he needs to complete; maybe he's in the Money Room of his mind, and is contemplating what to do about his investments; maybe he is in his Relaxing Room watching TV or surfing the Internet on his computer. Suddenly, there I am wanting to relate to him emotionally, which he translates as my wanting him to go to his Love Room, where he can be with me that way. But he doesn't want to go to his Love Room—he's busy in some other room of his consciousness.

Of course, if I don't understand this concept of the Love Room, then I don't realize that my partner is not available to me emotionally at that moment—it just feels as though he is somehow shutting me out. And here's the most unfortunate part: Since my partner is not in his Love Room, my attempt to connect emotionally can feel to him as if I'm trying to control him, or tell him what to do.

So, when I say to my mate, "What's wrong?" it probably feels as if I am actually saying: *"Why aren't you in your Love Room right now? Why can't you just drop everything and go there so we can be romantic?"* This explains the reactions women often get from men—ranging from amusement, mild annoyance, impatience, and irritation all the way up the scale to anger and shutting down—when we try to create an emotional or romantic moment out of the blue. *We're trying to love him; he feels like we're trying*

*to make him shift out of the state of awareness he is in and drag
him into his Love Room!!*

Recently my partner and I went on a brief vacation and had a
delightful and romantic time. The morning of the day we were
leaving, we felt so close, and commented on how wonderful the
trip had been. A few hours later, we left for the airport to fly home.
After we checked in for our flight, I noticed that my partner
seemed to have become a little distant. He wasn't responding to
me in the same way as earlier in the day, and felt kind of far away.

"Is something wrong, darling?" I asked.

"No," he replied. But something had changed and I couldn't
figure out what it was. I began to feel agitated and worried. What
could be going on? I continued to ask him if he was all right during
our first flight, and during our wait at the second airport for the
connecting flight, and of course the more I tried to get him to talk,
the farther and farther away he seemed to go. By the time we got
home late that evening, things just felt awful.

The next day, everything was fine again. But I was still perplexed. What had happened during our trip home to create such an
upset feeling between us?

Then, it dawned on me. When my mate and I were on vacation at the hotel, it was as if he spent the whole time in the Love
Room of his consciousness. He had no work, no obligations, and
gladly went to that part of himself where he could connect with
me emotionally and romantically. Then we left for home, and
without my realizing it, he left his Love Room and moved into
his Traveling-on-a-Journey Room, in which he was focused on
the logistics of dealing with taxis, airports, crowds, finding gates,
etc.

I, too, was paying attention to the details of our trip and went to
a more businesslike portion of my awareness. However, being a

woman, I brought the Love Room consciousness with me. So there I was snuggling up to him while we waited for the plane, talking about romantic things we'd done on our vacation, trying to continue the same mood we'd shared during those few days, totally unaware that *he had checked out of his Love Room hours before!* No wonder I felt sort of abandoned and alone—he was no longer keeping me company in the Love Room. And no wonder he felt irritated—it appeared to him that I wasn't acknowledging or approving of his choice to shift gears.

What Women Want Men to Know:

When a woman tries to connect with you emotionally, she doesn't realize you may not be in your Love Room.

What Men Can Do:

When you notice your partner looking for you in your Love Room, and you're not there at the moment, either make an attempt to meet her there, or gently let her know you are in a different mode.

When your woman comes knocking on the door of your Love Room, she is hoping to find you there. So when she discovers the room is empty, and you aren't where you were, say, the hour before or the night before, *she can become confused and hurt, and feel as if somehow, you've gone away*. When you notice her looking at you sort of bewildered, and asking "What's wrong?" remind yourself that it's likely you're not in your Love Room, but she's in one of hers. She's not trying to criticize you for where you are—

she's just trying to make a connection. (I'll talk a lot more about this later in the book.)

Then, you have two choices:

1. You can make a quick visit to your Love Room, if that works for you, shifting into Love mode for a minute to give her a hug, or say something sweet.

2. You can let her know that you're in a different room of your consciousness at the moment—thinking about work, concentrating on driving, trying to look something up on your computer, and that you'll try to meet her in your Love Room a little later.

I've suggested this remedy to many couples, and they've all reported great results. One man told me recently that he and his wife developed a kind of verbal shorthand to communicate with each other about their emotional moods. When he notices her trying to connect with him emotionally, he will say, *"Honey, are you in your Love Room right now?"* This way he can be sure of what her intention is in trying to get him to talk or be affectionate or whatever. When she answers, "Yes I am!" and he knows he's not in that same mode, he sweetly replies, *"Well, I'm not in my Love Room right now, but I appreciate you stopping by, and maybe I'll catch you later!"* That's all she needs to hear in order to know that her husband appreciates her attempt to connect, and isn't connecting the way she would like him to *not* because anything is wrong, but because he is occupied in another room of his consciousness.

In some of the chapters that follow, I'll suggest really simple and effective techniques that can help take a man to his Love Room with very little effort.

Why Women Put Love First

Are you beginning to understand how differently men and women see themselves when it comes to love? This contrast has its source in the way we each value ourselves as a human being:

> **Women define and value themselves
> by how successfully they *love and relate*.
> Men define and value themselves
> by how successfully they *achieve
> and accomplish*.**

How did men and women get to be this way? The reasons are sociological and cultural, going back thousands and thousands of years. Simply put, in more primitive times, a man's value was measured by his ability to hunt and provide his family or group with food, his ability to defend himself and those he was responsible for, and his standing in the tribe or community. His success at these tasks literally meant life or death for him and those he loved. Still today, society judges men on how much money they make, how high up the ladder of success they've climbed, how successful they are at "hunting" as demonstrated by their house, their car, their clothing, etc.

A woman in primitive times, on the other hand, was valued for very different characteristics—her ability to take care of a man and their children, her ability to emotionally and sexually satisfy him and thereby keep him interested enough to continue providing for and protecting her, her ability to get along with him, his relatives, and the other members of the community. Her success at these tasks also had life-or-death consequences, for females who did not please men and win their favor had no way to take care of themselves and ultimately would perish.

Now it's becoming clear why women put love first: **We have done it for thousands of years. Our very survival depended on it.** We have learned to maintain a continual awareness of the state of our love life, doing our best to make sure everything is okay, that there aren't any problems we're overlooking, that our partner is still happy with us. So when things are good in our relationship, we feel good about ourselves, and when they're not, we feel unsettled and insecure.

This explains a secret all women know about ourselves: No matter how smoothly things are going in our professional life, or with our projects, hobbies, and interests, *if there's a problem in our intimate relationship, we're miserable*. We could be having a fantastic day at the office, but if things are bad at home, it ends up feeling like a bad day. It doesn't even have to be a substantial problem—maybe we just had a little argument with our husband the night before—but that will be enough to make our heart ache all day long, in spite of whatever accomplishments we experience at work.

I will confess that I've experienced this time and time again in my own life. I could be having the most exciting day, doing a TV show, promoting a new book, or giving a seminar to thousands of people, but if there's some lack of harmony in my relationship with my partner, it's very difficult for me to fully feel the joy of my achievements. Why? *Because like many women, I define myself so strongly by the big part of my Love Pie—the content of my heart, and the state of love in my life*. The truth is that all the applause or book sales or attention in the world can't remove the sadness I feel when my mate and I aren't as connected as I want to be.

Most men experience the opposite of this phenomenon: If things are wonderful with their love life, but they're having a bad day at work, it is difficult for them to feel good. Why? *Because men also*

*tend to define themselves by the big part of their Love Pie—only in
the case of men, it's their achievements in their career, their accomplishments in the world, how well they think they're measuring up
to their image of who they think they should be.*

One of the hardest lessons about love I have had to learn as a
woman has to do with not misinterpreting a man's behavior just
because he doesn't respond as I do. When a man doesn't seem to
want to give us as much time, attention, and focus as we think he
should, our tendency is to assume that something is wrong. We think,
"If I was behaving that way, it would mean that I was really angry with
him, or that I didn't care, or that he wasn't that important to me."

What Women Want Men to Know:

**Women sometimes assume that your lack of focus
on the relationship means that you don't love us
or care as much as we do.
This is why we get upset or hurt when you don't put us
first—because we want to feel you are as committed
to the relationship as we are, and that you
value us as much as we value you.**

I agree that, as women, we need to remember that men are different, and that they don't always show their commitment to love
in the same way we do. But you can help us out a lot, guys, first by
understanding *why* we get so disappointed, concerned, or upset
when it looks to us like you don't care, or that you're not taking us
into account, or that you're not valuing the relationship; and second by not making us feel wrong for our emotional reactions.

How to Apply This Information to Your Relationship
and Why You Should Want To

Men, I am going to be making this point over and over again throughout the book: **Each time you refuse to understand why your mate is feeling upset about something, whether you realize it or not you end up causing or exacerbating the very behaviors and emotions you dislike in her!** In other words, she may not start out feeling insecure—she's just behaving in ways women do when they put love first—but your critical reaction to her behavior alarms her, and then she *does* begin feeling insecure.

In my years working with thousands of women, and in the research and interviews I did for the book, this information is one of the most essential things women wanted men to know.

What Women Want Men to Know:

When you don't make an effort to understand a little
bit more about why women are the way we are,
you can unwittingly contribute to
the very behaviors in your partner that
you can't stand!

Remember the story I presented earlier about the woman whose husband didn't call her from his out-of-town trip? He couldn't understand why she was so upset and accused her of being insecure for needing to speak with him. Well, the reason she was upset was simple: She was imagining herself in her husband's situation, and she knew that if she had been the one who was out of town, and didn't call home for almost twenty-four hours, it would have meant that she was deliberately avoiding him, and that something was terribly wrong. She would have never *not* checked in with him, so she concluded that his not checking in with her meant he didn't care about her feelings.

Her husband didn't understand this principle. He just knew that she was upset, and this made him feel a bunch of feelings he didn't want to feel: that he'd done something wrong; that he'd somehow upset her; that she had certain expectations of him that took away his sense of being independent and free; that suddenly there was a problem between them. *Rather than taking the time to understand why she might have been upset, or expressing his remorse for worrying her, he blamed her for being upset in the first place. It was as if he was saying: "You're upset because there is something wrong with you, and not because of anything I may have done or not done."*

His wife received this message loud and clear. What was the result? *It only made her feel worse, and actually created the very insecurity he accused her of. The more he invalidated her feelings and attributed them to her neediness rather than to her love, the more hurt and worried she became.*

Guys, this story is a perfect illustration of why I believe you should be motivated to put what you've read here into practice. Wouldn't it be great to know that, by handling conversations or situations with your mate just a little differently, you could prevent many of the upsets and stressful moments that you dread in your relationship? When you try some of what I suggest in the following section, you will be amazed to see how well the woman you love responds.

Here's a summary of what I think are the most important points to remember about everything we've been discussing. Men, this is the section where you can really get the bottom-line information that will help you understand and get along better with your part-

ner. And ladies, this is the part of the chapter you want to show to
your husband or boyfriend even if he hasn't read the rest!

#1 What Women Do When We Put Love First:
We always want to invest time and energy into our relationship.

- We want to talk to our man, be with him, work on staying connected.

- We want to make plans, to create special memories.

- We want to do whatever we can to make the relationship close,
  strong and lasting.

How Men Misinterpret This:

- You think we aren't independent enough.

- You think we are too needy.

- You think we are insecure.

- You think we want to control you by making you give us your
  time and attention.

What Women Want Men to Know:

Women think of love as our job.

**That is why we always want to work on it, because we feel
if things are not going well in our relationship, it means
that somehow we have failed to do our job properly.**

So when we are trying to talk to you about "us" or get you to make plans to spend time together, or when we seem to be too "into" you, it's NOT because we are insecure or needy; it's NOT because we are trying to control you. *It's because we are trying to create the best relationship possible. It's because we are trying to improve and develop our most valued investment. It's because we are doing what our heart tells us is our job—to put love first.*

What Women Would Like Men to Do:

- *We would love it if you expressed your appreciation for how much attention we put into wanting to create a wonderful relationship, rather than criticizing us for how focused we are on it.*

- *We would love it if you let us know you value our dedication and cherish our devotion as beautiful qualities rather than thinking we are neurotic.*

- *We would love it if, when we try to plan time with you, you remind yourself we are doing this because we love you, NOT because we're trying to control your time.*

#2 What Women Do When We Put Love First:
We always want to work on the relationship.

- We want to continually improve things, to become closer and more intimate.

- We want to know if there is a problem, and then we want to fix it.

- We persist in trying to find out how a man is feeling when we suspect he may not be happy with us.

How Men Misinterpret This:

- You think we're too obsessive and can't just relax and let things be.

- You think we are too emotional and reactive.

- You think we're criticizing you and saying you aren't good enough.

- You think we want to control you and tell you how to do things.

What Women Want Men to Know:

Women are fierce protectors of love.

Because love is so important to women, we feel a responsibility to maintain and protect it. That is why we are always evaluating our relationship to see if there are any problems lurking about, or any issues we need to deal with, so they don't blow up into major stumbling blocks. All of the time and energy a women puts into trying to work on the relationship are just reflections of her commitment to love, and her commitment to you—*she is investing in and attempting to protect her most valuable asset.*

Women have a powerful system of internal radar for de-

---

tecting emotional tension in other people, particularly our mates. It is as if we are always on guard, watching for anything that might threaten the integrity of our relationship from the outside, or from the inside. So when we ask you "What's wrong?" or suggest we talk about a problem, it's NOT because we are trying to "stir things up" or ruin your peaceful evening; it's NOT because we are nervous and paranoid, and are simply overreacting. *It's because we feel something is off between us, or something is going on inside of you, and we want to make sure that nothing goes undetected that could hurt us or come between us. It's because we care so much, and don't want to lose you.*

What Women Would Like Men to Do:

- *We would love it if you expressed your appreciation for how concerned we are about the state of our relationship, and how diligently we try to pinpoint and eliminate tension and problems before they become damaging.*

- *We would love it if you would see our desire to work on the relationship as an expression of our passion for you, rather than a sign that we are obsessed with making everything perfect and that we'll never be satisfied.*

- *We would love it if you took the initiative to notice where the relationship could improve, and expressed a desire to work on it, rather than waiting for us to always be the one to bring up issues so we look like the "troublemaker."*

How can you apply these suggestions to situations that come up in your relationship? Here's a chart for men with very specific suggestions for how to keep what you've learned in mind and respond to your partner with more compassion and less judgment. Remember: Understanding that a woman puts love first means seeing her behavior from this new point of view, rather than simply dismissing it as insecurity or neediness.

HOW MEN CAN RESPOND WHEN THEY REMEMBER THAT WOMEN PUT LOVE FIRST

INCIDENT: *Your girlfriend tries to make plans with you for an upcoming weekend.*

OLD RESPONSES	NEW RESPONSES
"Why can't you just be spontaneous?"	"You're so sweet to want to spend time with me."
"Why do you always have to plan everything?"	"Thank you for thinking about this in advance. It will be fun."

INCIDENT: *Your wife says she was worried when you didn't call when you were working very late one night.*

OLD RESPONSES	NEW RESPONSES
"Why do you get so worked up over nothing?"	"I'm sorry I didn't call— I can see how you could have been worried."

"Calm down—you always make yourself paranoid."

"It feels good to know you care so much about me."

INCIDENT: *Your girlfriend asks you what's bothering you because you've been very quiet during dinner.*

OLD RESPONSES

"Do I have to always be talkative and romantic around you, or you'll get upset? You are so needy."

"Why do you always have to watch every little thing I do? Can't I do anything without being scrutinized?"

NEW RESPONSES

"You're right—I am feeling quiet. I had a very stressful day and I guess I just need to not talk much right now."

"Thank you for noticing. I have a lot on my mind tonight concerning work. It has nothing to do with you."

INCIDENT: *Your wife gives you this book and suggests you both read it to help improve your relationship.*

OLD RESPONSES

"Here you go again, saying it's all my fault. I don't need you to fix me."

NEW RESPONSES

"You are sweet to always look for ways we can get closer. I am sure I can learn something new."

"I'm not into that kind of self-help stuff. It's for women. You read it if you want to."

"You know I have a hard time with books like this, but if you think it has some valuable information for us, then I will definitely read it, because I do want to be a great husband."*

*I couldn't resist including the last example!

Can you see how the old responses are all based on *misinterpretations* of a woman's behavior when she is putting love first—assumptions that she must be needy or insecure or trying to control her partner? The new responses, on the other hand, are all based on an understanding of the *true intention* behind her behavior and are examples of how a man can express his acknowledgment of that loving intention. Guys, please try experimenting with these suggestions, even if it feels awkward at first. I promise you will love the results!

Don't Expect Your Woman to Love You Like a Man

To the men reading this: I know that, in spite of how hard I've worked here to explain that women put love first, you may still be secretly grumbling to yourself: *"Why can't a woman's Love Pie look more like mine? Mine is much more reasonable—a little slice focused on love and the rest focused on life. This is a much more sane way to live. Why does she have to be so focused on me all the time? Why do I have to read charts about how to talk to her? Why can't it all be much simpler?"*

This complaint reminds me of an experience I had many years ago. I was in a serious relationship with a man I loved very much. We were in the middle of a difficult discussion about "us"—you know, one of those talks that make men want to flee—and I was trying to explain why I needed him to check in with me more often, plan more time with me, and not disappear for days on end when I didn't hear from him. He listened to my arguments silently, and then responded:

"Why can't you focus on your own life and not think so much about me?" he asked with annoyance. "I wish you could just do your own thing, concentrate on your work, your projects and your interests, and then, if I happen to call you, you'd say casually *'Oh hello, it's nice to hear from you. I've been very busy. Well, how are you?'* Instead," he continued, "when I call you now, you are so excited, and when I don't call, you get upset and make it a big deal. Why can't you just be more into yourself, and not so concerned with me?"

"In other words," I replied sarcastically, "you wish I were a man!"

"No, I didn't say that," he retorted. "I just wish you weren't so focused on love all the time."

"Like I said," I continued, "you wish I were a man!"

"Why do you keep repeating that? I don't want a man—I just want you to not care so much about whether I call you or we see each other, to go ahead with your own life and if I show up, I show up."

"I hear you," I responded with irritation. "You wish I were a man! I keep saying that because that's who you're describing!"

I share this story as a response to those men who, after taking in all the information in this chapter, still might be lamenting, as Professor Henry Higgins sang in the classic Broadway musical

My Fair Lady, "Why can't a woman be more like a man?" You have several choices if you really feel this way:

1. You can change your sexual preference and not have to deal with women at all. (This is probably not an option for most of you!)

2. You can find a woman who is cut off from the female part of herself and demands very little from you and from love. (This may feel comfortable for a while, but eventually, you will feel emotionally frustrated and ripped off.)

OR...

3. You can learn to understand why women are the way we are, and appreciate our nature rather than resist it.

Personally, I recommend the third option. As you'll see throughout the rest of this book, the more you value and honor the love a woman has for you, the more she will end up giving you exactly what you want and need, offering you satisfaction and contentment in ways you couldn't even have imagined.

Let me share a story with you about a man I knew who ended up breaking his own heart because he turned away from a woman who put love first, thinking it would be easier to be with a woman who didn't care as much. Jonathan was in his thirties and had been living with his girlfriend, Kristen, for two years. Kristen was a bright, warm, and energetic person who adored Jonathan and wanted to spend her life with him. Although Jonathan deeply loved Kristen, he had a difficult time with how much she loved him. She was devoted, thoughtful, consistent, and definitely a woman who put love first, and it sometimes felt overwhelming to

Jonathan, who thought of himself as very independent and unconventional.

I remember a conversation I had with Jonathan in which he confessed that he was craving his freedom and fantasizing about being in a less demanding relationship. "It just feels like it's too much," he complained.

"Jonathan," I suggested, "I don't think Kristen is doing anything but loving you. She's offered you her whole heart. What's wrong with that?"

"I don't know," he replied. "Sometimes I wish she didn't love me as much—it would make it easier to be with her."

I was sad but not surprised when, several months later, Jonathan called to tell me that he had broken up with Kristen. I listened silently as he described a new woman he was dating, Abby, and how much more comfortable he felt. "Abby's really different from Kristen," he explained. "She's not very emotional, not needy at all, and she gives me my space."

I had a sinking feeling in my stomach as Jonathan spoke about his new girlfriend. I suspected I knew the kind of woman he was talking about—a woman who had been hurt, had closed off her heart and thus demanded very little from the men in her life. My worries were corroborated when I met Abby. She was, indeed, cold and aloof. She treated Jonathan dispassionately, although he didn't seem to notice any of this. He sat there with his arm around her making conversation, oblivious to the fact that, although she was pleasant, she was hardly paying any special attention to him. When Abby went to the restroom, Jonathan told me that he'd never felt so relaxed or free in a relationship in his life. "Naturally," I thought to myself, "because you're not really in an emotional relationship." But I said nothing.

A few months later, I received a wedding invitation from Jonathan and Abby. I wanted to warn him of what I feared would be the inevitable painful outcome of his choice, but I bit my tongue and wished them the best in my heart. I couldn't help thinking about Kristen and how devastated she would be when she found out Jonathan was marrying someone else.

What happened to Jonathan? Unfortunately, just what I thought would happen. At first, he felt relieved to be in a relationship that put so few emotional demands on him. But as time passed, he began to feel neglected by Abby. She didn't seem to care what he did, where he went, or what was going on inside of him. She didn't make any efforts to spend intimate time together. She wasn't too interested in sex, and seemed content to focus on her career, hang out with her friends, and decorate their house. Basically, she just left Jonathan alone.

Slowly, Jonathan realized that he was starving for attention and affection. He began thinking about Kristen, remembering how much in love with him she'd been, and he found himself longing to feel that loved again. When he tried to talk to Abby about his needs, she showed no interest in working out their problems, insisting that she felt everything was just fine the way it was. Finally, Jonathan accepted the inevitable—he had made a terrible mistake. He had married the wrong woman.

Jonathan called me a year later to tell me he was getting a divorce. He was depressed and lonely. He'd contacted Kristen, secretly hoping that she would take him back, and was heartbroken to find she was engaged to be married to someone else. "I blew it," he confessed to me, his voice choked with tears. "What was I thinking? Why did I convince myself I would be better off with a woman who didn't know how to love?"

What's the answer? Why did Jonathan turn away from the deep love he shared with Kristen for the hands-off, dispassionate kind of relationship he had with Abby? Because it seemed easier. *Because it put no demands on him. Because it supported the illusion that, if he was free to do as he pleased without having to pay attention to a woman's needs, he would be happy.* Of course, Jonathan was wrong. He made a tragic mistake that many men make—he did not value the presence of a woman in his life who put love first.

Remember, men: A woman with an open, loving, passionate heart is offering you a profound gift. She is not trying to take anything from you, but rather give you her love, her commitment, her devotion, her joy. Not all women are capable of doing this. If you have one who is, hold tightly to her and thank your lucky stars that you found her.

Learning to Celebrate Your Ability to Love

A few days ago, I sent this chapter to a female friend of mine and asked her if she would read it and give me some feedback. As soon as she was finished, she called me. "Do you know how I felt reading this?" she asked. "I felt *normal.* It's not like I haven't heard some of this information before, or that I didn't know how important love was to me. But to have it presented in the way you did helped me become more accepting of myself, and less judgmental. The truth is that for years, I've beat myself up for doing what I thought was *loving too much.* It feels so much better to think of my loving heart as a gift, not a weakness."

I was so gratified to hear my friend's reaction to this information, for that has been one of my main intentions in writing this chapter, and the others to follow in this section—*to help women accept and love themselves more for who they are and the powerful way in which they love.*

> ## What Women Need to Know:
>
> **Having a tender, open heart is not a curse, but a
> blessing. Loving deeply and with devotion is not a
> mistake, but a gift. Putting love first is not a weakness,
> but an expression of who you are as a woman.**

It is difficult to always remember this when we spend our lives defending how we love to men, and when we are constantly told that something is wrong with us for giving so much of ourselves in a relationship. I've struggled with this dilemma myself ever since I can remember, wondering if I wouldn't somehow be better off if my heart was less open. I remember going to see a psychic once and complaining about how deeply I loved, and how much I felt. She looked at me and said, *"Barbara, you worked hard for lifetimes to learn how to love this much. Don't apologize for it. It's a reward. You've earned it."*

This wise woman's words shot through me like a bolt of lightning. I knew instinctively that what she was telling me was true. My ability to love so completely was indeed a blessing. Over the years, I've had to continually remind myself that putting love first is not a "problem" I have, or an unhealthy habit I need to get rid of—it is the way I am as a woman. When I am putting love first, I am surrendering to my most essential and joyous nature.

I believe that when we as women learn to celebrate our ability to love deeply, and to honor ourselves for our beautiful, abundant hearts, we will make it easier for the men in our lives to do the same.

———

Perhaps you're a woman reading this chapter and having a different experience from that of my friend. Perhaps you're thinking that the information doesn't completely apply to you, because your heart doesn't feel as loving as you think it should. Sometimes life's painful experiences can cause a woman to shut down her heart, to vow never to put love first again.

If you grew up in an emotionally cold family, for instance, you may have made an unconscious decision as a young girl that it wasn't safe to share your love and open yourself to intimacy. A painful childhood can put a damper on a woman's inherent tendency to love deeply. The love is there, but you just don't allow yourself to let it flow.

Sometimes it's what happens to us as an adult that drives us to turn away from loving. An emotionally damaging relationship with a man can leave a woman feeling wounded and closed off. Often women who've been hurt will consciously take their focus off of love, and put it exclusively on work and career, hoping to avoid more pain. Their Love Pie may look more like a traditional male's, with very little conscious focus on relationships. This **"love reversal" is a form of protection. It's as if we unconsciously decide to become more cold and unfeeling—like the people who've hurt us.**

Whenever I work with women who have wounded hearts, I discover that deep inside, *their longing for intimacy and connection is just as powerful as ever—it's the willingness to seek it out that has changed.* So perhaps you might say that for these women, their outer Love Pie looks more like a man's, but their "inner" Love Pie is still more traditionally female.

Perhaps you've had times in your life when you've been that wounded woman. Perhaps you're still there and are struggling to break free of those emotional chains and love again. I hope that the information I've presented will help you begin to heal your judgments about yourself, to love and accept yourself the way you are, and cherish the gift of your beautiful heart.

If you are a man who has loved or does love a wounded woman, know that what you'll learn from this book will help you to help her learn to trust her own love again. The more you let her know what a gift her love is to you, the more she will begin to value herself as a woman.

CHAPTER TWO

Women Are Creators

Why do women always want to make things better?
Why do we feel compelled to talk about the problems
in our relationship with our partner?
Why do we feel the need to help when we see the
man we love going through a hard time?
Why do we so enjoy making plans?
Why do we work so hard to ensure harmony with our lover?

In this chapter, I'm going to share with you a second secret about who women are that's the motivation for so much of how we behave in relationships. It is one of the most beautiful qualities women possess, one that is such an integral part of our psyche that we don't even think about it. And it's the answer to all of the above questions.

What Women Want Men to Know:

Women are creators.

It is a woman's nature to create. Women are life-givers. This is our mystery and our magic—*we have the power to bring forth something out of nothing.*

This ability to give birth to life is most obvious when we become mothers and bring a child into the world. But whether or not we have children, as women we are always giving birth: *always creating something where nothing existed before, if not with our bodies, then with our words, our actions, our love.* We do this when we give birth to a delicious meal for our family, or a party for a friend, or a bedtime story for our child, or a more effective way to market our company's product, or an intimate conversation with our partner, or a display of flowers in a vase.

As creators, women are also alchemists; *we change the form of things.* We transmute the ordinary into the beautiful, the empty into the meaningful, that which was struggling into that which suddenly flourishes. We rarely encounter things that we do not feel inspired or at least tempted to improve upon, whether it's the way a room is decorated or the way a friend is handling a problem in her relationship, the way we are wearing our hair or the way we have organized our jewelry in a drawer, the way our partner set the table for dinner or the way the two of us are communicating.

Women reading these words will feel a throb of recognition in their hearts. *"Yes,"* a voice within you says, *"I know this to be true."* And for most women, it is. Yet our nature to create is so much a part of us, we rarely think about it or acknowledge it for what it is. We just do it. For instance:

• When you first moved in, your empty house or apartment looked like nothing. But as you walked through the rooms, you thought, "I know just what to do to make it beautiful. I'm going to paint the walls a very pale peach; I'll put my couch over here and my chairs over here; I'll get a rug that will brighten up the floor; I'll arrange my plants in these two corners." And before long, it looked fantastic. Where there was nothing, you created a warm and inviting home. And it was the most natural thing in the world for you to do.

- Your little girl comes to you and says, "Mommy, I need a costume for school tomorrow." You have nothing ready-made, but you go through the house and gather up some colorful scarves, fabric leftovers, ribbons, old costume jewelry, and other odds and ends, and within a few hours, you've created a fabulous gypsy costume for your delighted daughter. Out of nothing, you gave birth to something.

- It's Saturday morning, and your husband is sleeping late, exhausted from a difficult week of work. He seemed depressed last night, and it frustrates you to see him so down. You sit at the kitchen table drinking your coffee, and suddenly, a plan emerges in your mind. Quickly, you begin to put it into action. You prepare his favorite breakfast; you look through the paper and find an ad for the Electronics Expo that's in town for the weekend; you make a reservation at a restaurant he loves for dinner that evening, and call his best friend and his wife, inviting them to join you. By the time he wakes up, you greet him with delicious pancakes, plans to go to the Expo, and dinner reservations with people he really enjoys. He is thrilled. You transformed what probably would have been a depressing day into a string of fun-filled events that will cheer him up and give him a chance to unwind.

All of the above scenarios sound lovely, and harmless enough, don't they? How, then, could a woman's creative expression be a problem in her relationship with a man? Read on to learn how women create, yet why it's easy for a man to misinterpret and misunderstand a woman's creative instincts.

How Women Create, and What Men Need to Know

1. Manifesting

Manifesting means creating what wasn't there before. Women love to manifest. *The very act of starting with nothing and ending up with something thrills us in a deep part of our being.*

What Women Want Men to Know:

Women like to manifest beauty, celebration,
connection, and love that did not exist before.
When we do this, we feel a deep sense
of fulfillment and purpose.

This joy we experience in manifesting expresses itself in big and small ways every day:

- We hear that a friend is coming to town and quickly create an impromptu party around her visit.

- We find ourselves with a weekend free of obligations and plan a last-minute excursion to the country for ourselves and the man we love.

- We share some of our deep feelings with our partner while walking in the park, and all at once what was just a stroll transforms into a sweet experience of intimacy.

- We buy a little table, place some pictures on it, and turn what was an empty corner of a room into an attractive area.

- We receive a necklace as a gift, and build our whole outfit around it when we get dressed for work the next day.

- We overhear our husband mention to a friend a computer game he's interested in, and when he's at work that day, we search the Internet until we find the product and order it for him as a surprise.

When women manifest, they can create a special moment, an experience for others to share, an improvement in the environment, something beautiful to look at, or something that brings another person joy.

Another way women manifest is *in creating and re-creating ourselves*. All you need to do for proof of this is to walk into any major department store and look around at the cosmetics department. There before you are dozens upon dozens of counters, each displaying hundreds of shades of eye shadow and lipstick, powder and blush, along with innumerable bottles of perfume, body lotion, and every other potion you could imagine. In front of those counters are hundreds of women trying on makeup, testing new scents, and enjoying themselves immensely. Men imagine this scene and roll their eyes, perhaps concluding that women are vain or superficial. *But what's happening in this store isn't vanity—it's creativity.* It is women creating a look, an image, using their own face as a canvas as they become the artist.

It is the same with clothing, or jewelry, or any of the other ways women adorn our bodies—these female pastimes are all means for the female creative urge to express itself. *This is why so many women love to shop, even when we don't buy anything—we are doing research for our next creative undertaking!*

These are things we and other women understand, but have a difficult time explaining to men. Why, for instance, do we need new makeup when we already own a drawerful of it? And must we really have so many different shades of lipstick? I mean, how many kinds of red are there? Women know the answers to these questions, of course: There are *many* kinds of red, and yes, they are all different, and yes, we need new makeup once in a while, just as an artist needs new paints and brushes.

Last week I decided to treat myself to a manicure and pedicure in a little beauty salon down the street from my house. I sat there in a chair watching all the other female customers and concluded that this salon was a hotbed of female creativity, a perfect example of what I've written about in this section of the book. Each woman who came in took time to carefully look over the hundreds of bottles of polish, seriously examining this one and that one before she chose the color that would be applied to her fingernails or toenails. Not just any red would do this week—it had to be a blue-red, as opposed to a fire engine red, or a coral red. Or maybe since last week it was red, this week it would be a dark chocolate color. Or for fun, icy blue! The nails had to be shaped just so, perhaps square or oval or round—each woman definitely had her preference. Any man who ever thought women were wishy-washy or indecisive should come to a beauty salon, where after witnessing the precision with which women choose their nail polish color and shape, he would change his mind forever!

What is it that a woman is actually doing in the beauty salon? She is turning her hands and feet into a work of art, decorating them for the enjoyment of herself and the man who might happen to have the good fortune to gaze upon her shimmering toenails. She is taking a few moments out of her busy day to express her creativity by choosing that hot pink polish. She is manifesting: Where there once were dull, boring toes, now there are exciting, sexy toes!

Why Women Love to Fill a Space and Make Plans

One morning while Kim and her husband are having breakfast, she decides to discuss the schedule for a weekend coming up the following month.

"Listen, Eric, I wanted to remind you that Aimee is going to be on a trip with her school on the weekend after Easter, and since we have those days all to ourselves, I thought we should plan something special."

"That's weeks away," Eric responds casually, going back to reading his paper. "Let's talk about it later."

"But darling," she replies, trying again, "it's so rare that we have time together alone, and I just felt the sooner we discussed it, the more options we would have for doing something really terrific."

"Why do we have to talk about it now? I don't even know what I'll be in the mood to do tomorrow, let alone next month. Besides, I don't see what the rush is."

"Well, I just don't like not knowing what we're going to do that weekend," Kim explains. "Can't you just focus on it for five minutes with me?"

Eric grabs his paper and gets up from the table. "I can't do this now, Kim," he says in a tense voice. "I really can't." And he leaves the room.

Kim sits staring at her calendar, feeling hurt and disappointed. The empty squares marking that weekend stare back at her.

———————

Men and women have very different reactions to this story when I share it with them at my seminars. The men make comments like:

"Boy, can I relate to this. My wife tries to get me to plan every second of my free time, and I hate it. I think she gets a kick out of locking me into a schedule."

"The woman is trying to control her husband's time, to pin him down so she can be in charge."

"Kim is obviously insecure and high strung. Why else would she need to have every little detail of her life figured out in advance?"

The women, on the other hand, make these kinds of comments:

> *"I could scream, hearing this story. I go through this with my boyfriend all the time. He refuses to make plans, so I never have anything to look forward to."*

> *"Eric is a typical man. What is their problem with planning ahead? It just sets up his wife to look like a nag when she brings it up the next time."*

> *"This is one of my biggest complaints about men—that they just seem oblivious to what's happening around them. Doesn't he realize that it takes time to plan special experiences? Kim's just trying to be a good wife, and he isn't respecting her at all."*

What do the women see in this scenario that the men are missing? They understand what Kim is doing, because it is something all women do. They know she is doing much more than trying to make plans, or get her schedule sorted out—Kim is *filling the space*.

Filling the space is what women do when we see an empty table, and think about what we could put on it to make it look better; it's what we do when there is an awkward silence in a conversation and we invent something clever to say to help break the ice; it's what we do when we see a vacation is coming up, and we start fantasizing about where we could go with our lover.

This term describes one of the ways women express their desire to create—**we like to fill up what is empty.** Women's creative force is stimulated by emptiness. **It is as if when we see something that is empty or blank, we feel the need to fill it, to manifest something in that space so that it becomes occupied with life, with beauty, with love.**

What is it about emptiness, whether in a space or a conversation or a calendar, that urges a woman's creativity into action? Is it because in the sexual act, we feel the primal urge to fill the physical space inside ourselves with a man? Or is it something in our genetic makeup as life-givers that makes an empty space too tempting? Whatever the cause, one thing is certain—women like filling space with our energy.

One of the most common ways women fill the space is by making plans. We love to plan. We love to take what was a blank space in the future and turn it into something exciting and meaningful. We don't do this, as some men conclude, out of insecurity or a need to control our partner's time. We plan because it is a way for us to honor time, as we will see in Chapter 3, and because when we plan, we give our creative power a wonderful outlet in which to express itself.

What Women Want Men to Know:

Women love making plans because it allows us to fill up an empty space in time with our love, our passion, and our creativity.

I don't think men realize the joy women take in planning, especially when it involves their intimate relationship. *That's because for most men, planning is not an emotional activity as it is for most women. When a man plans, he is doing a task, figuring out the details. He is getting something off his to-do list, and then he moves on to the next thing. When women plan, however, it is an act of love.* Whether it's a party, an evening out, a vacation, or a special dinner, the process of planning becomes a channel through which a woman's devotion can flow. It is as creative an act for her as painting a picture or composing a song. She is giving birth to an event, a happening, an opportunity for relaxation or romance or recreation. And this makes her very happy.

2. Improving

Improving is the second way a woman's creative nature expresses itself. What's the difference between manifesting and improving? Manifesting is creating from scratch: birthing something out of nothing. **Improving, on the other hand, is taking something that already exists and making it better. It is rebirthing.**

The urge to improve is so much a part of most women's character that we're not even aware of its almost omnipresent existence in our speech, behavior, and attitude toward others. We accept it in ourselves, just as we accept it in other women. It is just the way we are.

What Women Want Men to Know:

**Women see the potential in everything,
and we want to help that potential grow.
That is why we like to improve things.**

The desire to improve what is within us and around us is really the act of seeing the potential in things, the possibility hidden beneath the surface, and doing what we can to help that potential manifest. Women seem to possess this kind of vision that sees the flower waiting to erupt from the seed, and also the tendency to nurture that seed until it blossoms. Perhaps this vision of potentiality is so strong in us because we are genetically designed to be mothers, to nurture what is small so that it can grow. We exercise this part of ourselves in big and small ways every day:

- A coworker in your office shows you the new scarf her boyfriend just bought her. "Isn't this lovely?" she says. "Tom gave it to me."

  "It's gorgeous," you reply. "What a great color for you." Then, without even thinking, you add, "Here, let me just pull this part a bit tighter and tuck in these ends. Now it looks perfect. What do you think?"

  Your friend looks in the mirror, and replies, "You're right—it does look better. Thanks!" It was totally natural for you to want to improve upon the way she had tied the scarf. *You saw a way it could be better.* And she intuitively understood this, and welcomed your input.

- Your sister invites you over to see her new couch and love seat. "What do you think?" she asks as you enter the living room. You stand back and assess the room, noticing how the furniture looks where it is, and then visualizing how it might look if it were re-arranged.

  "Have you thought about trying to switch the two pieces?" you suggest. "That way, you'll have more space between the couch and the bookshelf."

  Your sister doesn't hesitate for a moment. "Let's try it and see how it looks," she replies. The two of you slide the furniture around until it is arranged in a different configuration.

  "What do you think?" you ask her, trying to catch your breath.

  "You know, I like it better!" she says enthusiastically. "It isn't so cluttered. I knew I needed your opinion. I'd lost perspective since I live here all the time."

  When you looked at your sister's living room, your eye naturally noticed a way the furniture could look better. You didn't try to scrutinize it—*you just spontaneously saw how it could be improved.*

* You and a close friend who owns her own business are having lunch, and for the third time that week she's complaining about one of her employees who's not managing his department well. "I just don't know what to do with Louis," your friend says, shaking her head. "He's a dedicated guy, but lately he's gotten so sloppy. It's starting to affect the morale in his division."

    "Have you talked to him?" you ask.

    "I've tried," your friend replies with frustration, "but I just don't seem to be getting through to him, because I've seen no visible improvement."

    You ask your friend to replay her conversations with Louis for you, and as you listen, you get a sense of what the problem might be.

    "You know, it sounds to me like you've been telling Louis what you're unhappy with, but perhaps not asking enough questions about what's going on with him. I mean, maybe he's getting a divorce; maybe he has some family problem, or health concern that you don't know about. What if you asked him what he thinks the problem might be?"

    "That's something I hadn't thought of," your friend admits. "I guess I was just hoping the problem would go away after my first warning to him, but obviously it hasn't. Thanks for the suggestion. I am going to talk to him as soon as I get back to the office."

    As you heard your friend lament over her office problem, your mind instantly began searching for a solution. *You weren't trying to tell her what to do—you simply saw a way she might handle things differently, and you wanted to help.*

———

L adies, I'll bet most of you can relate to all three of these examples. They illustrate how this tendency to improve is such an integral part of our consciousness. Notice that in the three stories, each of the women was grateful for the input she received. Why? Other women understand and accept this quality, the desire to improve, for it is who they are as well.

Now for a contrast, imagine the first two scenarios enacted by two men instead of two women:

The new item of clothing: *First of all, a guy wouldn't show off the new tie his girlfriend bought him to his male coworker. Second, the coworker wouldn't comment that the tie needed to be straightened, let alone just reach out and do it. And third, if he did, the guy with the tie would feel like his boundaries had been violated, not to mention probably make assumptions, correct or not, about his coworker's sexual preference.*

The furniture: A man wouldn't ask the opinion of his friend or relative about how his furniture was arranged, let alone care that much one way or the other himself. If he was asked, the brother would probably just look at the couch and love seat and say, "Nice," and that would be that. Finally, if he did offer to rearrange things just to see how they looked, his brother who owned the house would probably say, "I don't want to deal with it right now. Let's go watch the game on TV."

What's my point? It's that men don't have this nonstop creative urge to improve things. Not only that, they actually interpret offers of help or advice as unnecessary, unwelcome, and intrusive.

Take the last story, for instance, and this time, imagine that instead of two friends having lunch, it's a husband with the employee problem having a meal with his wife. Let's replay the conversation as it would probably unfold:

I just don't know what to do with Louis," your husband says, shaking his head. "He's a dedicated guy, but lately, he's gotten so sloppy. It's starting to affect the morale in his division."

"Have you talked to him?" you ask.

"I've tried," your husband replies with frustration. "But I just don't seem to be making any headway, because I've seen no visible improvement."

"Why don't you tell me about your conversations with Louis, and maybe I can help figure out a better way to get through to him," you suggest.

"It's no big deal. I'll figure something out," your husband answers.

"But I have some ideas about what might be happening," you explain, "and I really think we could come up with a solution if we discussed it. After all, honey, it's been bothering you all week."

"Look, I can handle it myself, okay? I don't want to get into a big discussion about it right now," he says in a tense voice. "I'm sorry you don't approve of the way I'm dealing with it. Let's just change the subject."

Ouch. This conversation certainly had a different ending than the one between the two girlfriends. What happened? *The woman's husband misinterpreted her desire to help him improve a situation he was dealing with as criticism and control, rather than seeing it as an expression of her love and concern for him.*

What Women Want Men to Know:

When a woman wants to improve something,
whether in her environment or her relationship,
it isn't because she *disapproves* of it—
it's because she sees the *potential for making it better*.

Women are natural fixers, natural healers, natural helpers. We are always on the lookout for whatever or whoever needs assistance. If we hear just a little change of tone in our baby's cry while she's in her crib, we quickly go in to check and make sure she's all right. If we see a woman in a store struggling to zip up the back of her dress, we volunteer to help. If we know a friend is going through a difficult time, we call just to see if she needs anything. If we sense our lover is having a rough day, we ask him what's wrong, and if there's anything we can do.

Again, perhaps it is because we are genetically designed to be mothers that we have such an elaborate system of built-in radar that detects need in others. Over and over again in my interviews with women for this book, they asked me to explain this to men: **When a woman is trying to help or improve something in her relationship with you, she isn't doing it out of a desire to criticize or make you feel wrong—she's doing it out of love, and with a vision of the potential for something even greater to blossom between you.**

Why Men Feel Controlled When Women's Creative Energy Flows

I believe that, at times, men love the part of a woman that is a "manifester" and "improver," but they can also fear and mistrust it. There is a force to that expression of a woman's nature that often makes men uncomfortable, like gazing upon a rushing body of water that can't be stopped as it moves forward. They know they are witnessing something intense, something powerful, and something that appears, at times, almost relentless in its mission to manifest a particular outcome. And in a way, they are right—for when a woman is in a creative mode, she is tapping into the primordial life force that reverberates deep inside of her. Whether she is conscious of this or not, she is, in that moment, a channel for what the Eastern mystics call the shakti, the life-giving principle, the creative power that is responsible for every form of manifestation.

Here's an important point I want to share with you: **The intensity of the creative life force manifesting itself in a woman's behavior or intention can mistakenly appear aggressive, domineering, and controlling to a man.**

What Women Want Men to Know:

A woman's tendency to *create or improve*
can be misinterpreted by men as a tendency to *control*.

Men, a woman could be expressing her tendency to manifest or improve by planning a trip for the two of you, redecorating the bedroom, attempting to offer her suggestions for a problem you've been having with a coworker, proposing you both go to a therapist to work on your relationship, or asking you what you'd like for dinner—it often doesn't matter what her specific behavior is—*and somehow you end up feeling as if she is trying to control you, to get you to do things her way.*

Let me share a story from my past that perfectly illustrates this point:

Many years ago when I was in one of my first serious relationships, my partner and I decided to take a trip to the Caribbean—neither of us had been there before and we agreed that we would treat ourselves and go. I asked him if he wanted to make the arrangements, and he suggested I go ahead and look into it. Our vacation was approaching in only four months, so I thought I'd better get started on the plans right away.

The next day, I went to the bookstore and bought several guidebooks for the Caribbean islands. I began researching all of the different places we could stay, called the 800 numbers to order free brochures from various hotels, and got in touch with some friends who'd taken several trips to a number of islands to ask their opinion of the best places to visit. Within days, I had pages of data about every aspect of our upcoming journey.

One evening later that week, I enthusiastically showed my partner all the information I'd discovered, explaining in detail which hotels in our budget seemed best, which islands had the most features suited to our taste, and what airlines offered the most convenient and economical flights. I sat there bursting with excitement as I shared the results of my vacation project, and couldn't wait to see my mate's reaction, for I was certain he'd be so pleased with me and the thorough job I'd done.

You can imagine my surprise, therefore, when I finished my presentation and looked at my partner, only to discover that he had a horribly cold look on his face.

"Is something wrong?" I asked him. He didn't respond; he just kept looking at me with that same uncomfortable stare.

"Didn't you like the places I showed you?" I probed.

"They were fine," he finally said in a flat voice, breaking the icy silence.

"But what's the matter?" I pleaded. "Why do you look like you're mad at me?"

"It's just the way you did all of this," he said in a sharp tone. "Why did you even bother telling me about it? I mean, it looks like you've already made up your mind about where you want to go and what you like best. Since it's your plan, there's really nothing for me to say."

My plan? What was he talking about? It was our vacation. All I did was do the research. I couldn't understand why he was so upset with me.

"But I thought you told me to go ahead and look into this," I reminded him.

"Yeah, but I didn't think you'd make it into a full-time job," he retorted sarcastically. "As usual, you're taking control and doing things your way."

Tears began to fill my eyes, and trickle down my cheeks. "I wasn't trying to take control," I insisted, my voice trembling with emotion. "I was just trying to plan a wonderful vacation. And now you've ruined it!"

I forget how the conversation ended, but I remember exactly how I felt: I was shocked, confused, and very hurt. How could he interpret my trying to create the perfect vacation as controlling? My only intention had been to make him happy, and to get information that would help us make the best decisions. What had gone wrong?

Many years have passed since this incident, but I've experienced others like it over and over again, and heard countless stories from women about similar circumstances—*she is happily in her creative mode, focused on a plan or project or purpose for herself and her partner, and he reacts with irritation, annoyance, or even anger. She ends up feeling hurt and unappreciated. He ends up feeling controlled and manipulated*.

Why do men interpret a woman's creative focus as an attempt to control them? The answer is complicated, but in part it has to do with a man's need to feel autonomous, *and his habit of rebelling when he feels he is being told what to do*. (See Chapter 8 for more on this.) For instance, in the story about my boyfriend and the Caribbean trip, my thorough and passionate presentation of the travel information unconsciously made him feel as though he had no choice, as if I was announcing, "This is what we are doing." Of course, that was not my intention at all; my theory is that **he interpreted the intensity and detail of my communication almost as a command**.

What Women Want Men to Know:

**When a woman plans or suggests something
for your relationship,
she is *not* trying to *control* you—she is trying
to *contribute*, to create more love and happiness.**

How Men Misinterpret This:

**Men often mistake a woman's creative enthusiasm
for domination,
and the intensity of her passion for a direct order.**

Remember: In most cases, a *woman's true intention really isn't to tell you what to do*. It's to share her input and offer her creative contribution, whether by planning a vacation or finding you a new doctor or suggesting she redecorate the living room, or asking that you spend some time together to talk about issues in your relationship.

Don't mistake the intensity of her creative energy for a dominant attitude. Usually, she's not being aggressive— she's just being enthusiastic. She's not being controlling— she's being caring.

What Men Can Do:

1. **When you find yourself feeling controlled by the woman in your life, ask yourself:**

"What is her true intention in doing this?"

This is a powerful question that can snap you out of the unconscious reflex of concluding that she is controlling you. If you take the time to ask this question, you'll probably discover the true answer within your own heart:

"She is doing this because she loves me."

"She wants to manifest something wonderful or make something better, or plan something delightful, but her intention is *not* to control me."

Note: I'm not saying there aren't angry, controlling women out there. But I've found that much of the time when a man who's in a pretty good relationship feels controlled, he's misinterpreting his woman's behavior in the ways you've been reading about.

2. **Practice recognizing the things she does as expressions of her creative nature, rather than reacting to them in the old critical way.**

Instead of seeing her as:	See her as:
Controlling	Caring
Aggressive	Passionate
Commanding	Enthusiastic
Relentless	Dedicated
Intrusive	Loyal
Interfering	Helpful
Pushy	Proactive

How a Woman's Creative Nature Can Backfire

The propensity to create something out of nothing is a woman's blessing, but it can also be our curse. It is a blessing when we are inspired to decorate an empty house and turn it into a home, or create a costume for our child from scratch, or manifest a romantic evening for our mate. But it is a problem when we create an emotional problem where there really wasn't any. Here are some examples I know every woman will relate to:

• *Your husband has a funny look on his face when he leaves the house, and you can't get it out of your mind. All day long, you create scenario after scenario about what might be wrong, and by the time he comes home you are sure he wants a divorce and just hasn't told you yet. Later, he tells you that he had a terrible case of indigestion.*

• *You call your boyfriend at work to check on your plans together for the evening. He sounds distant, and not very excited about seeing you. When you get off the phone, you begin to worry. Maybe he's feeling too cramped in the relationship, stifled because you're spending so much time together. Maybe he's trying to tell you that he wants to slow things down. When he comes over to pick you up for dinner, you are a nervous wreck. However, he is sweet and loving, as if everything is fine. Over your meal he tells you that he'd just come out of a very tense staff meeting when you called and had someone waiting in his office to speak with him about it.*

What Women Want Men to Know:

A woman's habit of creating can sometimes work against us as we create unnecessary worry, insecurity, or fear about our relationship.

We admit it, guys: Women know we do this, and believe me, we don't like this part of ourselves. So while we try to work on it (and that's in another book!), we'd appreciate it if you can remember that when we get *too* creative and imagine things that aren't there, you can help prevent a negative emotional spiral by telling us what's going on with you.

What Women Would Like Men to Do:

- **When you realize we look or sound upset and you have no idea why, ASK US WHAT'S WRONG. This gives us an opportunity to tell you what we *think* is happening, so if we are mistaken, you can correct it, and we can avoid being upset over nothing.**

- **If you notice in a particular moment that you aren't feeling well, or are stressed or worried, try to let us know. You don't have to go into details, but just informing us that you are anxious for some reason that has nothing to do with us, will allow us *not* to jump to the wrong conclusion and create a problem where there isn't any.**

I know that putting these suggestions into practice may feel unnatural at first, guys, but believe me, you will like the results: Your woman will be calmer, less emotionally reactive for no reason, and much more fun to be around.

CHAPTER THREE

Women Have a Sacred
Relationship with Time

To really understand the nature of a woman, you have to understand the nature of her relationship with time. Learning how a
woman experiences time, thinks about time, and makes decisions
about time will teach you the secrets of her mind and heart. This is
something you've probably never thought of before. Frankly, I
hadn't either until I began doing the research for this book. But as
I interviewed women and collected questionnaires they'd filled out
for me, a pattern began to emerge: *Over and over again, what
these women wanted men to know had something to do with time.*

The more I thought about this, the more I realized that, indeed,
issues about time are often at the very center of our love life. If you
examine the disagreements, conflicts and areas of tension in your
intimate relationship, you'll discover, perhaps to your surprise,
that many of them have to do with time. Here are some examples:

Conflicts over *giving time:*

- Disagreeing about how much time you spend together

- Disagreeing about how much intimate time is enough or too
  much

- Disagreeing about staying in touch—phone calls, checking in,
  etc.

- Wanting to spend time apart

- Not understanding the importance of sharing special time

- Promising time to someone or something else when your partner expected you to give her your time instead

Conflicts over *remembering time:*

- Forgetting to perform promised tasks, such as making a reservation or passing on a message

- Forgetting to ask how an important event in time turned out, like how her doctor's appointment went or what happened at your child's school meeting

- Forgetting to inform her of something that affects the future, such as the fact that you'll be out of town on the weekend of the big church social

Conflicts over *respecting time:*

- Being late

- Procrastinating about doing things you say you will do

- Diminishing the significance of an event a woman thinks is important

Conflicts over *planning time:*

- Waiting until the last minute to make plans

- Criticizing your partner for wanting to plan in advance

Conflicts over *celebrating time*:

• Disagreeing about how to celebrate special occasions

• Disagreeing about what constitutes a special occasion

• Forgetting birthdays, anniversaries, etc.

Are you as amazed reading this list as I was? I'd never realized how many conflicts over time couples get into. However, once I thought back over my own relationships, I could see that time issues were often indeed the source of many disagreements. Getting this feedback from women made me decide to talk about time early on in this book.

Men and women have very different ways of relating to time, and these differences create continual misunderstandings between us that are the cause of ongoing conflict in our relationship.

To women, time is not simply something that passes, or a way to measure our experience of living. *Time is something we are very intimate with, and therefore something we honor and hold sacred.*

What Women Want Men to Know:

Women have a sacred relationship with time.

Why is this true for women? It is not something we are taught, or even something we are conscious of. Like our nature to put love first and to create, having a special and sacred relationship with time is part of who we are.

This intimate relationship with time is programmed into a woman's biology. At this most fundamental level of our existence, women are intimately aware of the cycles of time in a way men are not, for our body cycles in a monthly rhythm. From the moment we begin menstruating as young girls, we become conscious of each day, each week that passes, waiting for another cycle to begin. *This is where we first learn our habit of counting, and we never stop.* The counting and watching of time continues through other cycles in different phases of our lives: when we are pregnant, as we count the months until our baby is born; when we have a child, and count the hours between feedings, and then later, the time between doctor's visits, meals, and baths.

Let's look at several ways a woman's relationship with time manifests itself in her behavior, and how men often misinterpret or misunderstand this behavior:

1. Women are natural timekeepers.

Women like to keep track of time. Ask us how long it's been since our daughter's last dental checkup, or since our dog's last bath, or since we spoke on the phone to our mother, or since we had our hair cut, or since we made love with our husband, and we will tell you. *Accurately.* Men are always astonished at our ability to do this, and often become quite annoyed with us, particularly when we correct them.

"You know, we haven't been to the movies in a long time," a woman says to her husband. "I'd love to go out Friday night if we can get a baby-sitter."

"What do you mean—we just went to the movies. Wasn't it a few weeks ago?"

"No," she replies with certainty, "it wasn't a few weeks ago; it was more like two months ago! I remember exactly when we went, because it was right after my parents were here for my cousin's wedding."

"Whatever," he grumbles. Of course, now that she explains it, he knows she is right. But he's still irritated with her for remembering so precisely!

This penchant women have for accurately chronicling time manifests itself in many ways:

- *Women keep track of tasks men don't want to be reminded of.*

  "You haven't called your mother in three weeks."

  "It's been a month since you mowed the lawn."

  "You were supposed to drop off that package for your brother five days ago."

- *Women keep track of how accurately men keep promises about time.*

  "You said we'd talk this weekend about possibly re-landscaping the front yard next spring, but it's Sunday night and we still haven't discussed it."

  "Where have you been? You told me you'd get home by six so we'd have time to eat before going to the play, and it's almost seven!"

  "You promised you'd call me when you got to your hotel, but I didn't hear from you until late last night."

- *Women keep track of romantic and intimate time.*

  "It's been months since the last time we talked about our relationship and where we're going in terms of commitment for the future."

"We haven't taken the time to really make love when it wasn't just a quickie for five weeks now."

"The only time you give me a romantic card is once a year on our anniversary."

• *Women are conscious of rhythms and patterns in time.*

I've noticed that because women pay more attention to time in general, we see rhythms and patterns that men may not recognize. We notice how certain behaviors or experiences repeat themselves over and over again. Men, on the other hand, often don't connect these events to one another within the context of time.

For instance:

It's a Friday night, and your boyfriend, Robert, is spending the evening with his old college roommate, Frank. You've been dreading this for months—actually, since the last time Robert and Frank got together—because whenever your boyfriend hangs around with Frank, the two of you end up in a fight afterward. This has happened over and over again, and you're hoping by some miracle that tonight will be different.

It's almost two in the morning when Robert arrives back at the apartment. "Hi, honey," you say as he walks into the bedroom. "You guys must have had a good time—you stayed out late, didn't you?"

"Were you watching the clock or something?" Robert responds.

Here he goes, you groan to yourself. *It's happening again.* "No, I wasn't watching the clock. I was just commenting on the time," you say in as sweet a voice as possible.

"Well, I'm a big boy and I can take care of myself," Robert snaps.

"You know, Robert, you don't have to talk to me in that tone.

Why are you picking a fight with me? Every time you go out with Frank, you come home like this—feeling mad at the world."

"I do not," Robert insists. "You're just pissed off that I stayed out late."

"No," you reply strongly, "I'm not pissed off that you stayed out late. I'm pissed off that every time you are with Frank, you are in an angry, defiant mood for days. In fact, the last four times you've been with him, we've had a fight when you got home."

"What are you, the CIA?" your boyfriend says angrily.

———————

I have heard so many versions of this kind of dynamic between a man and a woman, when she recognizes a pattern of cause and effect that repeats itself over time and he just doesn't see it:

• A man doesn't notice that he gets depressed for days every time he talks to his ex-wife on the phone. When his girlfriend tries to point this out, he blames her for being jealous.

• A father isn't aware that whenever his little boy goes to a certain friend's house to play, he comes home and behaves aggressively. When his wife tries to discuss this, he tells her "boys will be boys," and that she's just being too protective.

• A man doesn't realize that every year around the time of the anniversary of his father's death, he becomes despondent and withdrawn. When his wife suggests there may be a correlation, he insists she overanalyzes everything and is making something out of nothing.

How Men Misunderstand This

When women appear to be counting or chronicling time, men often misinterpret our intention: **You conclude that we are picky,**

finicky, neurotic, and bossy. The result is that you end up feeling controlled, commanded, scolded, and spied upon.

When men react this way to our focus on time, women feel hurt and misunderstood. *"I was only trying to be helpful,"* we think sadly. And that is the truth, guys. We're not trying to control you or act like your mother, even though it may appear that way—*we just think we're doing our job*, in the same way we keep track of when the kids last ate, or when the laundry needs to be done, or when the mortgage is due.

What Women Want Men to Know:

**Women keep track of time because we
are trying to be helpful,
not because we are trying to be controlling.**

More accurately, women keep track of time and its rhythms because that is just the way we have been designed. We don't really even think about it.

2. Women experience time differently from men.

- Your boyfriend lives in another part of the country, so you rely heavily on the phone to stay connected. Several days have passed, and you haven't heard from him. Finally, he calls.

    "Where have you been?" you ask.

    "What do you mean?" your boyfriend responds.

    "You haven't called me," you explain in an agitated voice.

    "We just talked Friday," he responds defiantly.

    "That's what I mean—it's been three whole days!"

    "I don't get it," he says. *"It's only been three days. What's the big deal?"*

- It's one o'clock on a Saturday afternoon, and your husband says he's going out to do a few errands. The hours pass, and by dinnertime he still isn't home. Finally, at seven o'clock he drives up.

  "Do you know what time it is?" you ask him. *"You were out for six hours!"*

  "Gee, I didn't realize it was that long," he says. *"I had a lot to do."*

  "But you said you were going out to do a few errands—I thought you'd be back by dark for sure."

  "I guess I lost track of time," he replies absentmindedly. *"It didn't seem like that much time had passed."*

  "That's an understatement—why didn't you at least call me?"

  "Why should I have called?" he asks in a puzzled voice. *"You knew I'd be home eventually."*

———

Both of these examples illustrate one point: *Women experience time very differently from men.* After decades of observation and personal experience, my theory is that **women experience each increment of time as lasting much longer than men experience that same increment of time**. It's similar to "dog years" versus "people years," and according to veterinary science, a dog year is seven times longer than a people year. In the same way, I am certain that "female time" is much longer than "male time"! One of my girlfriends and I decided, unscientifically of course, that one male hour was the equivalent of ten female hours, one male day the equivalent of ten female days, and so on.

Doesn't this explain a phenomenon we've all experienced over and over again in our relationships—that in so many instances, *men think almost no time has passed, and women feel so much time has passed.* I believe this is because:

Time shrinks for men and stretches for women!

The previous stories are perfect examples—the woman feels as if the three days without talking to her boyfriend were an eternity, and he feels as if it's *only* been three days since they spoke—hardly any time at all. For her, the time was stretched; for him, it was shrunk. It's the same with the husband who went out for errands and came back six hours later: To his wife that six hours felt really long, probably because she had expected him back earlier, but for the husband, it seemed as if he'd only been gone for a little while.

I've come up with some examples of words men use that illustrate *the shrunken male version of time*:

Just can mean anything from in the last few minutes to the last few years, as in:

"Didn't we *just* get new carpet?" (five years ago)
"Wasn't your mother *just* here for a visit?" (three months ago)
"I thought we *just* discussed that." (six weeks ago)
"Didn't we *just* have some intimate time?" (three weeks ago)

A lot can be used to describe amounts that range from noticeable to minuscule, as in:

"I think we've spent *a lot* of time talking and working on our relationship lately." (one counseling session and one long talk in the past three months)

"I feel I've been *a lot* better about complimenting you, haven't I?" (two compliments in two weeks)

"Why are you complaining? I call you *a lot* when I'm out of town." (once a day if she's lucky)

Why do men and women experience time so differently? It seems to me that men tend to plant themselves more completely in the present moment when it comes to relationships and deal with the next moment when it arrives. Women, on the other hand, tend to extend themselves through time into the future.

Men's relationship to love and time is more immediate.
Women's relationship to love and time is more extended.

This principle doesn't apply to all parts of our lives. Men obviously have extended vision when it comes to running their business or designing their career. But somehow, when it comes to love, intimacy, and related topics, the above descriptions do seem accurate.

The result of these very different approaches to and experiences of time is a lot of misunderstandings and hurt feelings in our relationships.

What Women Want Men to Know:

When you don't seem to be aware of how much time
has passed since you spoke to us or saw us,
or spent special time with us,
or when you forget important events in time,
we end up feeling like you don't care.

It's easy for women to interpret men's casual, and sometimes even oblivious, attitude toward time as a lack of caring or commitment. The following are comments women made to me while I researched this book:

"How could he not call me for three days unless he just doesn't love me?"

"Why didn't he remember to let me know he arrived at the hotel when he knew I'd be worrying, unless he just wasn't thinking of me at all?"

"It's been weeks since we've spent any special romantic time together, but he says it's too soon to plan another evening, that we just did it—maybe he doesn't want to be close ~~with~~ me."

"I always want to be with my boyfriend whenever possible, but he goes about his business for days and seems unaware of how much time has passed. It makes me feel like I am not very special to him."

Guys, please understand that I am *not* saying you don't care, because I know you do. You just may not be aware of how your more casual relationship to time feels to us as women. **Remember the 10-to-1 Rule:** If you don't call for a day, it feels like it's been ten days to us; if we haven't spent special time alone without kids or distractions for two weeks, it feels like twenty weeks. Of course, this rule also works another way: If you've been dating a woman for one month, she may act like you've been dating for ten months, making you wonder why she is so serious so quickly!

I don't believe that men and women will ever change their experience of time. However, men, if you really want to please the woman you love, consider experimenting with the following suggestions:

What Women Would Like Men to Do:

1. We would love you to remember that whatever increment of time you are experiencing, it feels much longer to us.

2. Keeping this in mind, we would love you to consider adjusting your behavior once in a while by *doing things sooner than you normally would:*

- Call us *more frequently* than you think is necessary.

- Do or plan something special *before* you think the effect of the last time has worn off.

- Tell us you love us or compliment us *more times* in a day than feels normal to you.

- Be willing to spend *more intimate moments* with us than you normally would.

- One easy way to put this into practice with the woman you care about is to *do everything that is an expression of love twice as much.* That means DOUBLE the amount of calls, special dates, compliments, intimate moments, and so on. If you would usually call your girlfriend once a day, try calling twice a day. If you would normally agree to one romantic activity a month with your wife, try planning two a month.

  It is safe to assume that she will be happy with more, and I think you will be pleasantly surprised at how this small investment of extra time and effort

> **pays off in the gratitude, the sweetness, and the contentment you will see radiating from your partner.**

3. Women honor the cycles of time by celebrating special occasions.

Ever since I can remember, my mother has kept a little book containing a list of special occasions: the birthdays and anniversaries of friends and family members. Not a week goes by when she doesn't send a card to someone. Often these cards go to a person my mother hasn't seen or spoken to in a long time, yet she still remembers her birthday or anniversary and finds joy in celebrating the cycle of time through the expression of her love.

I am sure many of you have mothers like this, or are women like this. I know I definitely take after my mother and have boxes of cards that I keep on hand for the many special occasions I like to celebrate. But ask yourself: How many of your fathers had special occasion books? How many men reading this keep a list of everyone's birthdays and anniversaries, and remember to honor them in some way?

Remember, women are always counting time, so we are usually much more aware of cycles than men are. Ways that women express our sacred relationship with time is by *honoring these cycles of experience and marking the passage of time with celebration.* Women delight in doing this, but even the most sensitive men often don't understand why we are so into celebrating special occasions.

Take, for instance, Julia and Adam. They met at a yoga class and knew at once it was love at first sight. Julia was ecstatic—she was sure Adam was her soul mate, and secretly hoped one day they would be married. One month passed, and on that night when Adam came over to pick Julia up for dinner, she handed him a card.

"What's this?" Adam asked with a smile.

"You'll see," Julia replied, squeezing his arm.

Adam opened the envelope to find a card that said, *"Happy Anniversary."* At first he looked a little puzzled, but then Julia piped in: "It's our one-month anniversary—one month ago tonight, March twelfth, we met at the yoga class!"

"You are such a romantic." Adam laughed, giving Julia a kiss.

The months passed, and Adam and Julia grew closer and closer. On the twelfth of every month, Julia would wish Adam a happy anniversary, and give him a card or note or small gift. Soon, they marked one year together, and celebrated by going away for the weekend to the seaside.

Four weeks later, Adam and Julia were lying in bed, and Julia pulled out a card from under the covers and placed it on Adam's chest with a giggle. Sure enough, it was a Happy Anniversary card. "Thank you, sweetheart," Adam said, "But didn't we just have our one-year anniversary last month?"

"Yes, Adam," Julia replied, "but we still can celebrate our one-month anniversaries too."

Adam looked confused and almost disappointed: "I guess I thought once we passed a year, we wouldn't have to do the one-months anymore."

———

When I share this story with people, men and women have different reactions. The women all understand Julia perfectly. "I think she is being sweet remembering the day they met each month," they agree. "It was kind of insensitive of Adam to say he thought he wouldn't have to celebrate them anymore, as if it was some kind of burden." Men do not see it this way at all. "Adam's right," they exclaim. "One anniversary a year is enough."

One special occasion a year is enough? What a foreign thought this is to most women! We see opportunities for celebrating the passage of time everywhere we look:

"It's the six-week anniversary of when we first said 'I love you.'"

"It's the three-month anniversary of when we first made love."

"It's our one-month anniversary of being married."

I remember the shocked look on a boyfriend's face once when I said: "Guess what today is? It's the tenth anniversary of the day I lost my virginity."

"You remember the date?" he asked with incredulity.

"Of course I do," I answered. "It was an important occasion."

"Tell me, how does one celebrate an anniversary like this?"

I smiled. "You figure it out."

I confess this personal vignette to make the point that I, like so many woman, keep track of the love and happiness in my life by remembering special moments.

What Women Want Men to Know:

Celebrating cycles and special occasions is a woman's way of counting the joy and marking the growth of the love.

When I stop and become aware of the time that has passed since meeting a special person, or falling in love, or starting on a spiritual path, or giving up an unhealthy habit, I am not only honoring the cycles of time—I am honoring myself and how I have grown. When Julia celebrates the monthly anniversary of meeting her boyfriend, she is marking the growth of their love. When a wife wants to do something special for her wedding anniversary with her husband, she is saying, "I want to honor how hard we have worked to stay together. I want to honor the love."

• • •

How do men misinterpret a woman's love for celebrating time? When I interviewed women about this, they made these comments:

"My boyfriend thinks I am silly for caring so much about special occasions. He said it makes me appear like a little girl to him when I get excited about birthdays, holidays, and anniversaries, and that really hurt my feelings."

"I think my husband tolerates my enjoyment of special occasions. He is a good guy, and he does it because he knows it means something to me, but the whole time I know he is counting the seconds until it is over. I wish he would understand how important they are in reestablishing the bond of love."

"My husband thinks I make a big deal about nothing on special days. I've tried to explain that when we celebrate our anniversary, it is like renewing our commitment to each other, and that is a big deal."

"Whenever my partner forgets an occasion, it makes me feel like I don't matter. He puts things in his memory bank that are important, so if a special evening or celebration isn't in there, it must be because it's just not important to him."

Here's what women are trying to say to men: The way we count anniversaries or remember special occasions isn't any different from the way a man checks his stock portfolio to see if the value has increased, or the way a dad has his son stand against the wall as he makes a mark measuring how much taller he's gotten, or the way a guy saves ticket stubs from all the playoff games he's attended over the years. **These are all ways men count and measure what is valuable to them. Women count and measure love and intimacy, because that is what is valuable to us.**

What Women Would Like Men to Do:

- Instead of feeling special occasions are silly and frivolous, we would love it if you would be grateful that you are with a woman who cares enough about the relationship to celebrate it, and who values you enough as a partner to honor your presence in her life.

- Try being the one who remembers the special occasion and suggests making plans to celebrate it. Allow yourself to be creative in the planning, and you may be surprised to find you are feeling more in love just by focusing on honoring the love—a secret, by the way, that women have always known about. She will be thrilled that you took the lead, and you will definitely get points for that!

4. Women honor the sanctity of time by celebrating daily cycles.

Recently I called a friend of mine who's in her seventies and has been married for over fifty years. When she picked up the phone and I heard her voice, I knew something was wrong.

"Lois, you sound terrible. What happened?" I asked.

"It's Herbert," she answered.

"Oh my God, is he sick?"

"No, he's not sick," she replied in an exasperated voice.

"Well, then what's wrong?"

"He left the house to do errands and didn't even bother to say good-bye!"

As I listened compassionately to Lois vent her feelings about this for a while, one thought kept going through my head: *It doesn't matter what age we are, the issues women have with men are the same!* I knew just how Lois felt. I'd had the same experience hundreds of times myself, as most women have, whether it was a man not saying hello or good-bye properly, or not wishing us a sweet good morning or a loving good night. **It was the feeling that he was taking me and the relationship for granted.**

Men, I want you to know that this topic was one of the most commented upon in the questionnaires I received from women. In almost every response, women wrote about how much it meant to them when men paid attention to these daily cycles, and how much it hurt and disappointed them when men treated these moments as unimportant.

Remember the story earlier in this book describing the woman whose husband was out of town and didn't call her to say good night or good morning? I've shared that story with men, and almost all of them respond with statements like:

"I don't see what the big deal was. He called her eventually, right?"

"Sounds like that guy has a ball and chain wrapped around his leg."

"What difference does it make if he called her first thing in the morning or later that afternoon? I don't understand."

Women who have read that story begged me to make sure I explained, because it illustrates something fundamental about women that we really want men to understand.

What Women Want Men to Know:

**Women are in tune with the sanctity of each day
and like to honor its transitions and cycles.
This is why hellos and good-byes are so important to us.**

As timekeepers, and as the celebrators of cycles, women are highly conscious of the transitions and shifts that occur during each day. This is why we make such a big deal out of hellos and good-byes and good mornings and good nights. **When we focus on these moments, it is not about wanting affection or needing reassurance—it is about honoring the day we began together with our man, and honoring our presence in each other's lives.**

What Women Would Like Men to Do:
Say Good Morning

When you say good morning in bed, embrace your wife and give her a sweet kiss. Don't rush through the process— instead, enjoy the moment. This is as if you are saying, "We are starting this new day together. I am acknowledging that you are here with me, I am grateful to find you in my bed, I am grateful to have you in my life." It is a recommitment to the relationship. It makes the day sacred with your love.

How it feels to a woman: We feel our day is already happy because you are loving us. We feel we can handle anything the day brings because we had this special moment.

Say Good-bye

When you say good-bye, even if it is a brief moment before you walk out the door, stop for at least ten seconds, give your partner a hug or kiss (not a distracted peck on the cheek), and say something like "Have a good day, darling." This is a way of blessing her, of sending her off on her day with your love, and of taking a token of her love with you as you step out into the world.

How it feels to a woman: We feel like you are glad we will be there when you come home. We feel as if you have protected us with a shield of love

Say Good Night

When you reach over to say good night, wish her a sweet sleep, and tell her you love her. Take a moment to look into her eyes and smile so that she knows you are happy that you are ending the day together. Then whatever she went through during the day will have been worth it.

How it feels to a woman: A sweet good night means so many things to a woman—we hear *"I love you," "I am so glad to be sleeping next to you," "I am here, watching over you."* Your words make us feel safe and happy.

Each day of life is truly a gift, and the time we spend with the people we love is precious. If you allow her to, a woman will help you experience the joy and sweetness of that gift of time as she creates special moments of celebration that turn the everyday into the magical.

The Three Secret Needs Every Woman Has

Here's a letter I recently received from a man about his relationship with his wife:

Dear Barbara,

My wife has read all of your books and tries to explain her needs to me, but I feel like the list just goes on and on, and I end up feeling overwhelmed, and that she's impossible to please. She insists that this isn't the case, and says she's not complicated at all, and that it wouldn't take much for me to be a better partner. She suggested that I write and ask you for your opinion.

I have to be honest—I'm not much for complicated instructions about relationships. If you could tell me three things that sum up what she needs, it would simplify it all for me, and maybe I could remember them.

Sincerely,
Steven T.

I laughed when I read this letter, not because I thought it was funny, but because it was so honest. Steven wasn't trying to be humorous by asking me to sum women up with three key points that he could memorize—he was sincere in his desire to understand his wife, and had turned to me for an overview of women that would be easy for him to remember and apply. His letter challenged me to contemplate seriously the topic of what it is that women need. Was there a way, as he requested, to summarize the many needs women have in relationships, and therefore make them simpler for us and the men in our lives to understand?

After working with the information collected from thousands

of seminars, interviews, conversations, and letters, I've concluded that the answer is "yes." If we listen to what women share about their needs in love and relationships, it adds up to three basic things.

The Three Secret Needs Every Woman Has:

1. Women need to feel safe.
2. Women need to feel connected.
3. Women need to feel valued.

The next three chapters are about these three secret needs. I call them secret not because they are so mysterious, but because often we as women aren't even aware that we have these needs, and therefore men certainly can't be expected to know about them either.

If you are a woman, and you take the time to truly understand these needs, you will know much more about yourself, and why you feel and react as you do. If you are a man, learning about these three needs will help you understand and love the woman in your life as you never have before.

CHAPTER FOUR

Women Need to Feel Safe

*Why do women seem to need more reassurance
in their relationships than men do?*

*Why do women always try to make plans for the
future with their partner?*

*Why do women constantly want to know what their
partner is feeling or thinking?*

*Why do women become so unsettled and worried
when a man won't share what's bothering him?*

The answer to all of these questions is the same: **Because one of our most basic needs as women in an intimate relationship is the need to feel safe.** I'm not talking about physical safety, but rather the feeling of *emotional safety*. It is the deep sense that the relationship is solid, that our partner's affections are serious and committed, that we can trust the love we feel, and thus allow ourselves to open fully to give and receive it.

This emotional safety is the key that unlocks a woman's heart and soul. When we feel safe, we are able to open up. When we feel safe, we are able to risk. When we feel safe, we are able to relax. When we feel safe, we are able to shine.

Why is this need for a feeling of safety so important to a woman? *I believe that it's because, in some place deep inside of us, all women feel unsafe.* This may be politically incorrect to say, but I feel that it is true. No matter how much we consider ourselves liberated, independent, and self-reliant, this is a woman's secret—a part of our psyche that we continually battle against, negotiate with, criticize ourselves for, but somehow never completely eliminate.

Where does this sense of not being safe come from? To begin, it is the result of living in what is still essentially a man's world in so many ways, in a society that only in the past few decades has begun to value and respect women and offer us some of what men have been entitled to since the beginning of recorded history. Still today in many parts of this planet, male life is considered so much more valuable than female life and female babies are killed, thought to be worthless or burdensome to the family who wants sons and heirs. We may hear about this and say, "Yes, but that kind of thing happens in undeveloped countries." Yet in the most developed of nations, the United States, women get paid substantially less than men when they perform the same job. This may not appear to be as dramatic as the sacrifice of female infants, but isn't the message the same—*that a man's life and contribution are worth more than a woman's?*

We learn this silent lesson about our value as women from the time we are born. Until recently, in the majority of families, children are given their father's last name and not their mother's. Most of us never think about the impact this has on us, but again it sends a message to women about being less important, and when we feel we are seen as less important, we unconsciously feel less safe.

Even on the physical level, women experience an inherent sense of extreme vulnerability, which contributes to a feeling of lack of safety: Our bodies can be penetrated by a man; we can be raped and entered against our will. Most of us are not as physically strong as men. Even though we may not consciously think about these realities, they constantly affect our feeling of physical and psychic safety as we go through our lives each day.

But to really understand why as women we may feel unsafe, we need to go back in time to the beginnings of civilization and pay a visit to our female ancestors. These women were totally dependent on men for their survival. Men were the hunters, and therefore the ones who could provide food; they were also the warriors, the ones who were strong enough and skilled enough to fight off animal or human threats, and thus protect us and our children from death. As for the women, most of us had only one goal in mind: to find a man to take care of us and the many offspring we would inevitably have as soon as we were of the age to bear children.

Imagine knowing that, without a man, you literally could not stay alive. Imagine knowing that if your mate became displeased with you, he could kick you and your babies out of his cave or dwelling, and you would freeze or starve or be devoured by wild beasts. How could you ever truly feel secure? How could you ever truly feel safe?

Even as humanity evolved over several thousand years, women remained physically, financially, and socially dependent on men. We could not support ourselves. We had none of the opportunities or freedoms men had, and thus our sense of personal power was limited at best. Remember—it was only in the last century when it finally became widely acceptable and possible for women to work and thus have the choice to survive independent from a man if we wanted to, as well as to choose, with the advent of birth control, whether or not we would like to have children.

These are the historical roots that all women come from. Whether you're a woman of eighteen or eighty, whether you consider yourself totally empowered or are still struggling to get there, we all share this legacy. I believe that we have a certain genetic memory that keeps the past alive in us. It speaks to our hearts in almost inaudible whispers, saying things like, *"You can't live without him." "You'll die if he leaves." "You can't do or achieve that—only men can become that powerful." "You'd better find someone to take care of you, because you'll never be able to do it yourself."* Embedded in these messages, the bottom line: *"You're not safe."*

If you're a man reading this, please know that I offer these thoughts not as a complaint or judgment against men, but simply as an explanation for why women often feel a deep sense of insecurity whose source we can't pinpoint and a need for reassurance that appears to go beyond what should be required. Most men never really consider women from this perspective, because as men, you have a very different history as a species and thus an understandably very different way of operating in the world. You may be thinking, *"But I'm not that sexist caveman you're writing about. I don't care if my girlfriend uses my last name when we get married. I love her. I don't want to limit her in any way."* To that I say: Your girlfriend is lucky to be with such a great guy. But to really know her heart, you need to know the psychology she may have inherited from generations of women who came before her.

Why Women Want Men's Approval and Become Insecure When We Don't Receive It

Have you ever wondered why, as a woman, you often find yourself desperately wanting a man's approval more than you think you should, sometimes even a man you may not totally respect? Perhaps this explains it: **If historically women have been taught that our survival depends on men, then our "job" is to attract**

a man and to keep his interest so we don't lose him. How we look, how good we are in bed, how we express ourselves, how we take care of our home, how much we edit the expression of our feelings so he won't be uncomfortable—all of these habits, decisions, and behaviors have at their basis one thought: *"Will this make him happy?"* Our unconscious reasoning tells us that if we keep a man happy, he will stay with us; and if he stays with us, then we will be safe.

This is why women often constantly look to our men for cues to tell us how we are doing. *"Is he pleased with me?"* we ask ourselves. *"Does he seem content in this relationship?"* When we see signs that indicate the answer is "yes," we breathe a sigh of relief and allow ourselves to relax into a certain level of safety. However, if we think we perceive signs that a man is unhappy with us in some way, our sense of safety diminishes radically.

I know that for myself, and for most women I've worked with, this pattern of seeking approval in order to feel safe is not a conscious process. It's more a primal reaction that surfaces in a relationship with a man, one that often surprises us with its intensity. *"Why do I care so much what he thinks?"* we ask ourselves. *"Why do I get so insecure when just one little thing goes wrong?"* **The answer, I believe, is that a man's apparent disapproval of or displeasure with us can trigger a woman's unconscious survival mechanism, creating the feeling that she is somehow in danger and therefore is not safe.**

Let's look at a typical scenario that illustrates this: Cathy and Juan have been living together for two years, and they recently became engaged. One Sunday afternoon, Cathy notices that Juan seems withdrawn and irritable with her, but when she asks him if anything is wrong, he responds, "No—nothing's wrong." Cathy tries to get Juan to talk about what's going on, telling him that he's acting like he's mad at her about something, and that it's worrying her. Juan becomes more and more silent. Finally, Cathy starts to cry and asks Juan if he is having second thoughts about the engagement. Juan becomes angry, saying, "I don't know what your problem is, but I can't deal with this," and goes into the next room to watch TV.

What is Cathy feeling? She is anxious, worried, and has a knot of dread in the pit of her stomach. "Something is wrong!" her instincts scream. Juan's apparent displeasure with her triggered her survival mechanism. It's as if she sniffs trouble, and warning bells go off in her psyche indicating "DANGER, DANGER!" All of this happens so automatically that she isn't even aware of it.

What's Juan feeling? He is annoyed, irritated, and confused. He can't understand why Cathy was so upset today, or why she got so dramatic and scared. Nothing was going on except that he had a headache and just wanted to spend some time alone watching TV.

So who's responsible for this couple's being upset? They both are. Cathy needs to become more aware of how her survival mechanism gets triggered when she doesn't feel safe, and learn to moderate her reactions. And Juan needs to become more aware of what he does that triggers Cathy's unease—in this case, not giving her any information about what was going on with him, thus allowing her to jump to her own scary conclusions. Both of them will benefit from understanding this information about a woman's need to feel safe.

———

I remember vividly one of the first times I gave a lecture about this particular topic to a group of men and women. The women sat nodding their heads, many with tears in their eyes as they acknowledged a deep wound they all shared; a hidden and hurt place inside that many had never fully understood before. And the men? They listened sincerely and respectfully, their brows furrowed, their eyes pensive, attempting to understand a way of being that was very foreign to them.

One man approached me after the seminar, holding tightly his wife's hand, and his comment summed up what I think most men were feeling: "I've never thought about women this way," he said. "Everything you explained makes so much sense, but *it's like being told the woman you love has this invisible part of her you didn't know anything about. I thought I was a sensitive guy, but I had no idea....*"

I could see that this man was a sensitive guy. But even the most sensitive men in the world do not feel the same need for safety as women do, because they are not the product of thousands of years of programming! As his voice trailed off, the man's wife put her arms around him and gave him a tender kiss on his cheek. Her kiss said everything. For the first time, her husband understood what was indeed an invisible part of her that even she hadn't been able to explain to him, let alone articulate to herself. What was the result? **Just knowing he cared enough to understand created the very safety in her that we'd been talking about.**

What Women Want Men to Know:

A woman needs to feel safe in order to be relaxed and confident in her intimate relationship.

This is a simple but powerful truth: **When women feel safe, we are at our best**. We are more relaxed and less tense, more confident and less insecure, more independent and less needy—in other words, more of all the good stuff men like about us, and less of all the stuff that drives men crazy. And here's something else that's important to remember: Women instinctively know that when we feel safe, we are more of who we want to be, as well as who men want us to be. Therefore we try, consciously or unconsciously, to get our man to do those things that will make us feel safe.

What Women Want Men to Know:

So many of the things women ask men for,
or secretly wish men would do in a relationship,
are really our way of asking for that which will
make us feel safe.

Men, why do we want you to tell us you love us, or share how you're feeling, or express your appreciation for all we do, or make time for us, or any of the other things on the list your woman has of how she wishes you'd act? It's NOT to control you or have power over you or get our own way. **It's because we know these things will make us feel safe. And when we feel safe, we will be a better partner for you, and happier with ourselves.**

How Women Respond When We Don't Feel Safe and What Men Can Do to Help

If we women are at our best when we feel emotionally safe, *then we are at our worst when we don't feel safe*. The sense of being unsafe makes us fearful, and when we are afraid, we resort to behaviors that neither we nor the men in our lives find appealing:

What Women Want Men to Know:

Many of the behaviors you can't stand in women occur
because we aren't feeling safe.

---

1. We may become more needy, clingy, or possessive.

The more unsafe a woman feels, the more she may crave demonstrations of what will make her feel safe again. *She wants more affection, more attention, more reassurance.* To a man, it can seem as though his mate has suddenly fallen apart, and that she's become too weak and needy. To her, it seems as if she's reverting to behaviors that reflect her most insecure self.

What Men Do That Doesn't Work:

Typically, most men do not have a positive reaction to a woman's neediness or insecurity. Even though these are the times when a woman needs the most reassurance from her partner, *often a man's response is to withdraw and actually give her less reassurance than normal, which of course only makes things worse.*

This begins an unhealthy, vicious cycle that most couples are all too familiar with: The woman feels unsafe and becomes a little needy; the man reacts negatively to her neediness by pulling away; the more he pulls away, the more unsafe she feels, and the needier she gets; then he pulls away even further, and the whole situation spirals downward.

———

Every woman has dozens of stories about this phenomenon from her own relationship, times when her mate did or said something that stirred up unsafe feelings, and she instinctively responded by becoming more needy, only to have him react negatively to her insecurity. I remember one incident in my own life years ago that perfectly illustrates this pattern. At the time I was in a committed relationship with a man I loved very much. One day he announced that his former girlfriend was visiting from out of town, and that he was meeting her for lunch. Instantly, I became anxious and tense. My stomach tied itself in knots, my heart started to beat faster, and

my mind filled with fearful thoughts. This reaction wasn't totally un-
called for—my boyfriend had always told me he suspected his former lover still had the hots for him. So when I knew he was going to
see her, it definitely stirred up unsafe feelings for me.

"Does Cindy know about us?" I asked him in a strained voice.

"I'm sure she does," he answered defensively. "My friends
must have told her by now."

"You mean you didn't talk about me when she called?" I responded, becoming even more agitated.

"We only spoke for a few minutes," he retorted. "Why are you
getting all bent out of shape over this?"

"Why do you think? I know Cindy wants you back, and I don't
like the idea of you going to lunch with her, as if you're available
and interested."

"Don't be ridiculous, Barbara!" he said angrily. "I can't believe
how insecure you are. Stop acting like my mother and telling me
what to do. I can have lunch with whoever I want to."

If I'd been feeling a little insecure and unsafe when this conversation began, now I was feeling twenty times worse. *Instead of realizing that the situation naturally stirred up unsafe feelings in me,
my boyfriend only saw that I had turned into an insecure, needy,
paranoid woman, which obviously turned him off and made him
withdraw even more.*

How could this drama have been prevented? Well, he could
have refused to see his on-the-prowl former girlfriend, but that's a
different discussion. More important, if he'd understood the information in this chapter, he could have realized that, rightly or
wrongly, I wasn't feeling safe, and he could have done something
to reassure me. For instance, if he'd taken me in his arms and said,
"Sweetheart, you don't have to worry about her. I love you. I plan
to tell her all about how happy we are together," I still wouldn't

have been thrilled about the lunch, but my safety level would have instantly gone way up.

Men may read this and think, "It can't be that easy," but I disagree. It often doesn't take much to dissipate unsafe feelings in a woman. You'd be surprised how rapidly we can shift out of our anxiety when you give us some reassurance.

What Women Want Men to Know:

Most women recover very quickly from feeling unsafe when men offer us some love, caring, and reassurance. Just a little bit of effort from a man at these times can go a long way, and will definitely be worth it since it will prevent the situation from getting even worse.

Guys, I can't emphasize this point enough: Most women have a very quick recovery time from being upset if you just do something to make us feel safe again. I know you don't like to feel you "have" to behave a certain way, just because a woman wants you to. But I assure you that you'll be saving yourself so much trouble, time, and energy if you give this a try.

What Women Would Like Men to Do:

If you sense we suddenly have become more needy and for some reason are exhibiting symptoms of not feeling emotionally safe:

- *Don't criticize us for our neediness and make us feel even more unsafe.*

> • *Don't pull away or avoid us and make us feel even more unsafe.*
>
> Instead, we would love it if you would accept that we're feeling unsafe, whether it makes sense to you or not, and offer us some reassurance, some affection, and some tenderness.

2. We may become more irritable, cold, or sexually indifferent.

Some women deal with unsafe feelings not by becoming more vulnerable, but by becoming less vulnerable. When something triggers a lack of emotional safety in us, we shut off our feelings and barricade the doors to our heart, hoping to protect ourselves from getting hurt. Women like this may suddenly turn cold toward their partner, get critical and irritable, and even feel sexually turned off.

The problem with this kind of reaction is that most of the time men have no idea that we're actually hurting or afraid—we just look pissed off. So it's much more difficult for them to think, *"Gee, my sweetheart must be feeling unsafe right now. I think I'll reassure her."* Instead, they withdraw even more, hoping to shield themselves from our anger or rejection.

> ### What Women Need to Know:
>
> **If you have a tendency to put up your emotional walls when you're feeling unsafe,**

> **please consider the fact that your partner probably
> won't realize that you are hurting,
> and therefore won't be able to give you the love
> and reassurance you're actually needing.**

If we're going to ask men to try to understand our needs, we have a responsibility not to make them have to work like a detective to figure out what is going on with us. *Don't play games. Don't conclude that he'll get the hint and figure out what you want if you are cold, because he won't.* Be honest and try to explain how you're feeling. This will give you a much better chance of getting through to him, and hopefully, he'll respond by offering you the reassurance you are asking for. Of course, this advice applies to men as well, but we'll talk more about that later in the book.

> ## What Men Need to Know:
>
> **When your woman suddenly appears to be
> cold or angry, don't automatically assume
> that's how she's really feeling.
> Remember:** *She may not be angry—she may just
> be afraid*. **Ask yourself if there's any reason she
> might not be feeling safe and try to offer her
> some affection and reassurance. Better yet, ask her
> to talk about how she's feeling, and be sure to listen.**

I'm not suggesting that it's acceptable for women to shut down emotionally when we're feeling unsafe. But if you are a man, and are with a woman you suspect does this, you may be able to help her heal this pattern by remembering the information in this chapter, *and reaching out with love even when it appears that she's pushing you away.*

I gave this advice to a male friend recently, and he was amazed at how well it worked. His girlfriend had a habit of freezing up whenever she got scared in the relationship, only she never told him this was what was happening, so he concluded she had serious doubts about him. I knew from what he shared with me that this woman had been really hurt before, and I sensed that what she really wanted was not to withdraw, but to be reassured.

"What should I do when she gets like this?" Andrew asked me.

"Do the opposite of what it appears she's asking for—reach out and put your arms around her, and tell her you're sorry she's been so hurt in the past, and that you never want to hurt her, but just want to love her."

"You've got to be kidding," Andrew responded with skepticism. "If I try that, I feel like she'll push me away."

"Just do it," I coaxed him. "What do you have to lose? This pattern is driving you crazy."

Several days later, Andrew called me, sounding elated. "You won't believe what happened!" he exclaimed. "Last night Patty and I were together, and we were discussing some trips I have to take for work. Suddenly, she just froze up, and at first I thought, 'Here we go again.' Then I remembered your advice, so I moved over to the couch, sat next to her, took her hands in mine and told her that I didn't like the idea of traveling and being away from her, and that she didn't have to worry—I'd be faithful and committed to our relationship, because I really loved her.

"To my surprise, Patty burst into tears and clung to me like a little girl. It was as if that whole cold front shattered, and her real feelings came out. She confessed that her last boyfriend had always cheated on her when he was on the road, and that she didn't want to lose me. You were right—she wasn't feeling safe, but she didn't know how to tell me that until I reached out to her."

Guys, I can't promise you that all women will open up as quickly as Patty did, but I do know that **many times that mask of coldness or indifference you see is really a mask of fear.** At those times, all it may take is a little reassuring effort on your part for the shut-down woman before you to transform back into the loving woman you want to be with.

What Makes a Woman Feel Safe

Perhaps by now the men reading this are thinking, *"All right, I get it. I need to make my partner feel safe. But exactly how do I do that?"*

What is it that makes a woman feel safe? Here are a few of the most common things that create a deep sense of emotional safety in a woman.

1. Women feel safe when we spend time with our partners.

The presence of the man we love and who loves us creates a primal feeling of safety for a woman. His absence, particularly too much of it, creates the opposite—a lack of safety. Of course, I'm not saying that when a man goes to work during the day his wife suddenly feels unsafe, or that we always feel safe and loved when we're physically together. Generally, however, spending time together with her man creates a feeling of safety in a woman because, in a very primal way, it sends a message to her brain that she is not alone, that she is cared for. Remember Chapter 3 and what you learned about how women value time, and you can see why spending time with the man we love is one of the most powerful ways for us to feel safe.

Here are some comments about this from women who participated in my survey:

> *"I feel safe when he wants to spend his free time with me, because I know where he is and that he wants to be there with me."*

> *"When my boyfriend shows me that he wants to make time for me in his schedule, I feel like he doesn't want to lose me, like he is showing me how committed he is to our relationship, and that I am a priority."*

> *"One of the most reassuring things my husband can do in our marriage is to tell me that he misses me, and suggest that we spend special time together. It doesn't matter what else he's done to upset me—when he shows me he wants to be with me, I just melt."*

For every woman, there is an internal barometer of how much time together or apart creates a level of emotional safety we are comfortable with. But one thing is always true: **Spending special time with the man we love is one of the most reassuring things for us in our intimate relationship, and not spending enough special time together inevitably can cause our safety level to drop.**

2. Women feel safe when a man allows us entry into his inner world.

One of the most difficult things for many men to do is to open up and let a woman into the world of their hearts. Men have been trained since the beginning of time that showing emotions, particularly vulnerable ones, is a sign of weakness, and therefore dangerous to do. (More about this can be found in my book *Secrets About Men Every Woman Should Know*.) Instinctively, men don't often allow others entry into their inner world. Yet the irony is that this is precisely one of the things that makes a woman feel the most safe with and loved by her man—when he opens up and shares his deepest self.

I know this is easier said than done, guys, and we'll be talking more about it later. For now, just know that if you really want to know the secrets for making a woman feel safe, opening up to her is definitely one of them. Here's what some women said in my survey:

"If I am going to be open and vulnerable, I need to see that he is also willing to be open and vulnerable. Otherwise, I am left sitting there with my heart hanging out, and he hasn't risked a thing."

"Nothing makes me feel closer to my husband than when he tells me what's bothering him, or shares his dreams or fears. I know how hard this is for him, but even if he does it a little bit, it makes me feel like he really loves me and trusts me, like I'm his best friend."

"A guaranteed way a man can make me feel insecure in a relationship is to let me share all about myself and my feelings, but never really share his. I feel like I'm naked and exposed, and he's dressed, and doesn't care enough about me to confide in me."

What are some ways a man can allow a woman entry into his world?

- **Communicate about what's going on with you and your life.**
- **Involve her in your decisions.**
- **Let her know your needs.**
- **Tell her when you're going through a difficult time.**
- **Ask her advice or opinion.**

3. Women feel safe when a man reassures us of his love.

Recently a friend told me about a couple we knew who'd just divorced. Both partners were in their fifties. My friend said, "I feel sorry for Gwen. Tom will probably go out and have his pick of any woman he wants, but it's going to be a lot harder for Gwen—the men her age will be looking for thirty-year-olds." When I heard this comment, I thought to myself that this was precisely one of the reasons women don't feel emotionally safe in the society we live in. Men are given the message that at any age there will be an abundance of women available to them. As women, we know this, and *no matter how good we feel about ourselves, I believe we always live with a certain deep insecurity that men will never fully understand, an insecurity born of the reality of how easy women are to leave and to replace.*

Again, this lack of safety goes back to our ancient roots when to keep a man meant to survive. Today, thousands of years later, women are still keenly tuned in to this need, and highly sensitive to anything that appears to threaten the existence of our intimate relationship from within or without. For this reason, **I believe most women need more emotional reassurance from our partners than men could ever imagine.**

What Women Want Men to Know:

Reassuring a woman of your love and commitment is one of the most effective ways of making us feel emotionally safe.

Here are a few of the ways a man can reassure the woman he loves:

- *Express your love and appreciation for her with words.*

- *Tell her you need her in your life and explain why.*

- *Be physically affectionate, not just before sex, but at other times.*

- *When she lets you know she's insecure in the relationship, tell her what she needs to hear to stop worrying—not just once, but several times.*

- *Check in with her frequently so she knows you're thinking of her (see Chapter 3).*

Each woman has her own list of what makes her feel safe or unsafe in a relationship. Here's a brief summary of what women have told me as I gathered information for this book.

What makes us feel safe	*What makes us feel unsafe*
Fidelity......................................	Flirting
Compliments...........................	Criticism

What makes us feel safe	What makes us feel unsafe
Consistency	Inconsistency
Reliability	Irresponsibility
Inclusion	Exclusion
Compassion	Judgment
Reaching out	Withdrawal
Communication	Silence
Confronting issues	Denial
Scheduling time and plans	Vagueness and ambiguity
Reassurance	Lack of commitment

We'll talk a lot more about many of these behaviors throughout the rest of the book, and I'll offer you suggestions for how to integrate them into your relationship.

If you're a woman, I suggest you take some time and make your own list of what makes you feel safe and what erodes your feeling of safety. Share it with your partner if you can. And men, if your lover offers to show you her list, please think carefully about what it says. She is giving you an important key to understanding her heart.

CHAPTER FIVE

Women Need to Feel Connected

Q. Men, what do all of the following female behaviors have in common?

- Reaching out and taking your hand when we're walking together

- Asking you if something is wrong because you've been so quiet

- Pointing out something beautiful that we noticed as we're taking a drive

- Asking if you like how we rearranged the plants in the living room

- Bugging you late at night to talk about our relationship

- Telling you in detail about our conversation with your sister

- Wanting to know all about your day at work

- Giving you a quick kiss as we pass in the hallway

- Showing you the new pair of shoes we bought on sale

A. They are all ways your woman is trying to *connect* with you.

Some of the items on the list are probably things men love about women, and some are the things that drive men crazy, but they all qualify as a woman's attempt to create a sense of connection in your relationship.

What does it mean to want to "connect"? I have to confess—
I've never thought that word needed an explanation until a conversation I had recently with a man I know. I told him that I was
writing a book called *What Women Want Men to Know*, and he
asked me to give him some examples of the information I would be
presenting. I happened to choose this section about the three most
important needs every woman has, and listed them: "A woman
needs to feel safe, to feel connected, and to feel valued," I said. Immediately I noticed that he had a puzzled look on his face. "Is
something wrong?" I asked.

"Can you explain something to me that I've never understood?"
he inquired.

"Sure, what is it?"

"What does that term actually mean—'connect'? My girlfriend
uses it all the time: 'We haven't connected all week,' or 'I had such
an immediate connection with my new assistant at work,' or 'I
need you to connect with me more when we make love.' To tell you
the truth, I have no clue what the heck she's trying to say."

I listened to this man, whom I really like and respect, and realized that he wasn't teasing me—he was being totally honest. Could
it be possible that other men felt this way too, and that a term that
was so much a part of most women's vocabularies and the experience it defines was something that men didn't really understand?

I suspect that the answer to this question is "yes." I suspect that
men often feel they are "connecting" with women when we feel
they aren't even close. I suspect that men severely underestimate
how important the experience of connecting is to a woman, and
how frequently we want to experience it. And I suspect that most
men dread hearing their woman say, "Honey, I don't feel like
we've connected enough lately," because they aren't sure exactly
what they're supposed to do about it.

> **Connecting is about creating an experience
> of intimacy, bridging the gap between oneself
> and someone or something else.**

So much of what we do as women is about connecting, building intimate moments in both small and significant ways. It is our nature to connect—we do it without even thinking.

Have you ever watched women shop in a department store? We don't just walk through and look at the items. We touch the merchandise as we pass by, feeling the fabric of a sweater, stroking the silk of a scarf, picking up a purse and turning it over in our hands. What are we doing? *We are connecting.* And we don't stop at connecting with the objects being sold. We make conversation with the salespeople, even with other female customers, admiring their purchases, offering advice on the fit of a dress, expressing our approval of the look of a shoe. In other words, *we don't just shop— we have relationships!*

None of this may seem unusual until you watch men in a store and observe the difference. Most men, if they *must* be in a store to begin with (unless it's an electronics store), move through it as though they're maneuvering their way through a minefield in battle—they try to avoid touching anything, even when they're considering buying it. If they could purchase an item without any contact at all, they probably would. "I'll take *that*," they'd say, pointing at the shirt or jacket as if it's a foreign object. Unlike women, the men are trying to avoid much connection of any kind.

Of course, when women take men shopping, that's another story. I often watch this happen with great amusement—the woman floats confidently down the aisles, greeting the merchandise with friendly touches while the man walks reluctantly behind, looking as though he's about to have dental surgery. "Should I get that salesperson to come over and help us?" she asks her partner cheerfully. "No!" he answers with dread, since he wants to avoid any contact with anyone if possible. Then all at once, she seizes an article of clothing such as a sweater or coat, thrusts it toward her mate and says, "Here, honey, *feel* this material." Yep—she wants him to *touch* it! And the guy usually grits his teeth, reaches out two fingers, barely grazing the garment, and then, as quickly as possible, snaps his hand away (hoping no other guy saw him, of course).

All right—so maybe I'm exaggerating a little bit to amuse you. But here's the point: To most women, connecting is as natural as breathing. **It is the way we relate to the world around us. Men, on the other hand, are much more hesitant to connect. Their nature is to be more autonomous.**

Last summer I decided to have a small gathering of people at my house, almost none of whom knew each other. It was a warm afternoon when everyone arrived, and we made our way out to the patio, which offers a beautiful view of the hills and, in the distance, the ocean. Several moments had passed when I suddenly noticed the most amazing thing: All of the women, about six of us, had spontaneously congregated, and we were standing very close together in a small circle facing each other. However, when I looked over at the men, also a group of five or six, they were lined up in a row, almost military style, all facing outward away from each other and looking at the scenery! The way the two sexes had unconsciously configured themselves was so stereotypical that I began to laugh. **The women had positioned our bodies so that we would have the maximum opportunity for *connection*, and the men had positioned themselves so they didn't even have to look at each other.**

This is not a comment about right or wrong, but simply an observation about the way women are—*we seek out connection even when we aren't aware that we're doing it.*

Ladies, watch yourself for a day, paying particular attention to all of the ways you create moments of connection:

- *You're the first one to reach out to touch or kiss your children or husband.*

- *You call a friend to offer your encouragement because you know she has an important interview that day.*

- *You stop your car for a moment on your way to work to speak to a neighbor and inquire about her child who has been ill.*

- *You wave a thank-you in your rearview mirror to the driver of the car that let you cut into his lane.*

- *You compliment your coworker on how nice she looks that morning.*

- *You e-mail a thank-you note to a client who did a favor for you last week.*

- *You strike up a conversation with the woman behind you while waiting in line to buy coffee at Starbucks.*

- *You call your husband in the afternoon just to tell him you love him.*

Why is connecting so important to women? Perhaps it is because we give birth to children, and thus have been genetically programmed to connect as a way to ensure that we will be good and nurturing mothers. Perhaps it is because, as we discussed in Chapter 1, women put love first, and connection is the way love expresses itself. Women understand that connection creates intimacy and intimacy feeds our heart. And perhaps it, too, goes way back thousands of years to the genesis of our socialization as women, when *our value to a male or a community was in our ability to connect, to harmonize, to create bonds of cooperation.* **Our success with a mate or within a tribe or group—indeed our very survival—was dependent on our ability to connect.**

For all of these reasons, **when a woman feels connected, she feels safe.** She is aligned, she is supported, she is not alone. And the reverse is true as well—**the sense of disconnection creates a feeling of fear and loss.**

In her excellent book *Loving Him Without Losing You*, Beverly Engel includes a quote from Jean Baher Miller:

> *Women's sense of self becomes very much organized around being able to maintain affiliations and relationships. Eventually for many women the threat of disruption of connection is perceived not just as a loss of relationship but as something close to a total loss of self.*

I think men know and accept this secret about how women like to create connection with other women—with our girlfriends, our sisters, our mothers, our daughters. What men often don't realize is how essential it is for us to create this same kind of intimate connection with them. I remember hearing a comment once from a very traditional man who was married to an acquaintance of mine: *"My wife always talks about wanting more intimacy in her life. I tell her that's what her female friends are for, right?"* Wrong.

What Women Want Men to Know:

Women crave emotional connection with the man we love. It allows our minds to relax and our hearts to open.

When we feel connected to the man we love, it's as if our hearts have been joined by an emotional pipe or cable, and love and support flow back and forth between the two, making us feel like a unit, a team. Instead of walls or barriers, we experience doorways and openings that invite the other person in. We feel welcomed into the deepest part of our lover, and this is what creates the powerful experience of intimacy.

This kind of intimacy born of connection allows a woman to mentally relax, to give wholeheartedly, to feel safe. In fact, connection is one of the most effective ways to create the kind of emotional safety we talked about at the beginning of the chapter.

What Women Want Men to Know:

Often when women aren't feeling safe, we reach out and try to connect with our partner in some way.

To feel disconnected in a relationship is to feel cut off from the man we love, to feel that the cord between our hearts has been severed, or at least, is temporarily out of order. Women crave connection because we understand that the price of disconnection is too high and we dread paying it. When women sense this, we often reach out, attempting to reconnect with affection or conversation or time spent together—anything that will restore the harmonious feeling between ourselves and our mate. **Remember: Since women put love first, we in some sense consider ourselves the guardian of our relationship, responsible for maintaining the emotional connection. Therefore, connecting with our mate becomes the way we manifest our commitment to keeping the love alive.**

Do You Know the Difference Between
Bonding and Intimacy?

Here's a true story told to me by a girlfriend of mine:

Joan and her husband, Benjamin, decided to go on a four-day canoe trip with another couple who were close friends. All of them
were into wilderness sports, and they were excited about exploring a
river they'd heard a lot about. The plan was that they'd travel together
for the first day, and on the second day, the couples would split up—
Joan and Abby would go off on their own ladies' retreat, and Benjamin and Craig would have their own men's retreat. Then they
would all meet up together for the fourth and final day of the trip.

The second day of their adventure arrived. Joan and Abby said
good-bye to their husbands and paddled away, setting up camp
later that evening on a beautiful spot near the riverbank. They ate
dinner, watched the stars come out, and talked for hours and hours
until they finally fell asleep. The next day went as smoothly as the
one before, and by the time they met Benjamin and Craig on the
morning of the fourth day, they felt as close as sisters.

The couples finished their final day together, packed up their
equipment, and shared affectionate farewells before they got into
their separate vehicles to drive back home. Joan and Benjamin
spent the first hour of the trip home comparing notes on the sights
they'd seen and sharing the highlights of their experience. Then
Joan asked her husband, "How did you get along with Craig?"

"Oh, we got along just fine," Benjamin said. "He's a terrific
person, and we got pretty close."

"I'm so glad to hear that," Joan responded happily, knowing
Benjamin didn't have many male friends he could open up with.
"What did you guys talk about?"

"Talk about? I don't know . . . lots of stuff."

"Well, like what?" Joan asked curiously.

"Hmm, let me think. Well, we talked a lot about ecology. Craig studied it when he went to college. And we had some really good discussions about camping equipment. There are some new manufacturers coming out with breakthrough products that sound really exciting. Oh yeah, we also spent a lot of time talking about the stock market. Craig's brother is a broker, and he had some very revolutionary ideas about how to divide up a portfolio that I think could be helpful to me."

As Joan listened to her husband report on his conversations of two days with his friend, she could hardly believe her ears. This was what they'd shared that made him feel close to Craig? This was all they'd discussed after spending forty-eight hours alone together with nothing else to do? Surely he was leaving something out. She tried again:

"Honey, did Craig mention anything about his relationship with Abby?"

"No, why do you ask?"

"What about his father, did he talk about him at all?" Joan probed.

"His father—why would he bring something like that up?" Benjamin answered in a puzzled voice.

"Benjamin, this is just baffling to me. Didn't Craig tell you that Abby is thinking of leaving him, that they'd been talking about it for a few months already? Or that his father has Alzheimer's and Craig just had to put him in a nursing home last week right before the trip? And what about their daughter's heart condition—didn't he at least mention that?"

"How do you know all of this?" Benjamin asked his wife suspiciously.

"What do you mean, how do I know? Abby told me," Joan responded.

"When?"

"When? Honey, on our trip, when do you think? I can't believe Craig didn't share any of this with you. Abby told me this stuff the first hour after we left you guys! She poured her heart out to me, and I ended up sharing so much about myself with her, and by the time we met up with you again, we felt so connected, like we'd known each other all of our lives. I don't understand how Craig could spend two days with you and not talk about anything that was really going on with him."

"Well, I didn't know any of this," Benjamin answered a little defensively. "But I'm telling you, we had a good time and got really close."

———

I love this story. It's such a great example of an important point that I want to share with you: **the difference between bonding and intimacy.** Joan had a profound experience of *intimacy* with her friend Abby. *They shared their deepest secrets and feelings— they connected from the heart.* This is what made them feel so close. But when Joan heard the content of Benjamin and Craig's conversations, she couldn't understand how they could possibly feel any kind of closeness, for they hadn't shared emotions or inner truths with each other. What she didn't realize was that Benjamin and Craig did indeed feel close, not because they'd been intimate, but because they'd *bonded*.

Bonding requires physical proximity, and occurs when we share an important experience with another person. We belong to the same fraternity in college or play on the same team; we work together on the same committee to elect a political candidate or plan a project at work; we get trapped in the same elevator or sit next to each other on the same plane that is delayed for hours; we both have children on the same soccer team and watch the games together; we go through the same training seminar or travel on a canoe trip together.

Most of the time when men think about connecting, they mean bonding. Bonding is the most common way men feel close to one another—they share in a communal activity. They meet for a set of racquetball, or watch a football game on TV, or show each other new tricks they've learned on their computer, or go to a bar for a drink. Benjamin and Craig bonded on their canoe trip because they shared two days of adventuring together.

On the other hand, **when women say they've connected with each other, we usually mean we've experienced intimacy.** What's the difference between bonding and intimacy?

- **Bonding is a shared experience of connection that *includes physical closeness or proximity*.**

- **Intimacy is a shared experience of connection that *includes emotional closeness and mutual vulnerability*.**

Abby and Joan experienced intimacy *because they shared emotional content with each other.* They connected not just by being physically close and enjoying a mutual activity but by being emotionally close and mutually vulnerable. You could say they bonded and also experienced intimacy.

How does this difference between bonding and intimacy affect men and women in our intimate relationships? In every possible way!

For many men, *bonding passes as intimacy*. When they want to feel close to someone, they think of ways they can bond.

> **Men hear that women want to connect, to be intimate,
> and often they think we are saying we want to bond.
> But when women say we want to connect, we mean
> we want to experience *emotional closeness*.**

This distinction between bonding and intimacy was a revelation to me when I figured it out. All my life, I'd never understood why men thought they were being intimate when, in my opinion, they weren't at all. In my own relationships, I can recall so many moments of confusion or being upset about this. Maybe I'd be on vacation with a partner, and after a few days I'd find myself depressed. Even though I was having a good time, I wasn't feeling we were really connecting. However, when I tried to explain this to him, he didn't seem to get what I was saying. "We're doing lots of fun things!" he'd explain. "What more do you want?"

Or maybe I'd find myself feeling dissatisfied with a phone call from a man with whom I was in a long-distance relationship. Nothing bad happened on the call—I just didn't feel we'd really connected. When I'd bring this up on the next phone call, he'd become irritated with me. "What do you want me to say?" he'd ask. "We talked for a whole hour. Isn't that enough for you?"

Looking back, I can now see what the problem was. *We were bonding, but not connecting intimately*. To the men, this seemed perfectly acceptable, and they didn't feel the need for anything more. But like many women, I needed a more intimate kind of connection.

I remember counseling a couple once where the wife was feeling neglected and wanted more connection and the husband listened as if he had no idea what she was talking about. "But we do connect!" he protested. "We spent all of last weekend together cleaning out the garage. We were together the whole time. How can you say we don't spend enough time connecting?"

The wife would look at me with pleading eyes that said, "Do you see what I mean? HELP!" And I'd think to myself, "Does this man really believe that cleaning out the garage together constitutes intimacy?" Now I realize that he was describing *bonding*. He sincerely felt that he and his wife had connected because they'd shared a bonding activity.

Where do men learn to bond rather than to be intimate? They learn it from their own fathers, and from the way society encourages boys to be together, as opposed to how girls get to interact with one another. *Traditionally, boys are taught from a very early age that their value is in doing things, whereas girls are taught that their value is not just in doing, but also in relating.*

Imagine two small boys playing harmoniously together with trucks on the floor. Their parents will notice this and say, "Very good, kids. You're playing nicely." Now imagine two small girls sitting side by side, giggling and telling secrets for hours. Their parents notice this and say, "Very good, girls." Now, imagine two small boys sitting side by side, giggling and telling secrets for hours. Something about it is unsettling, isn't it? Why? Because we are used to seeing little girls connect by being intimate with one another, but we aren't used to seeing little boys connect with intimacy. These are the roots of how Abby and Joan connected on their canoe trip, and how Benjamin and Craig connected, and why there was such a difference.

What Women Want Men to Know:

True connection doesn't just mean coexistence or bonding. It involves much more than just being

> **with the person. Connection requires more than
> proximity. It requires *intimacy*.**

Once I heard a definition of intimacy that expresses the essence of what intimacy is: **INTO-ME-SEE.** Intimacy means allowing someone to see into you, and conversely, seeing into him or her. It means not simply coexisting together on the outside, but *sharing who you are and what you feel on the inside*. As we'll see in Part Two of this book, intimacy is one of the most important ingredients for creating successful relationships.

NOTE: Please understand that I'm not saying there is anything wrong with bonding. Bonding is an essential part of a relationship between two people, and it is an important way a couple connects with each other. But for the love affair to really thrive, it also needs a strong component of intimacy.

As I've been preparing the material for this book, I've incorporated it into the lectures and seminars I give in different cities around the country. Recently I was in New York City sharing some of this material with an audience. Afterward, a couple asked if they could speak to me for a moment. "You just saved our marriage," the woman began. "We've been together for seven years, and have always loved each other very much, but ever since our son was born, things haven't been good between us. I've tried to tell my husband that I wasn't happy, but I couldn't really explain what the problem was."

"I felt like she was just nagging and complaining," the man piped up. "And when I would ask her what was wrong, she'd say, 'I just don't feel connected to you like I used to.' When I'd hear this, it was as if she was kicking me in the stomach. I was trying to be a good father, to work hard and take care of my family, but it seemed like nothing was going to be good enough for her."

"But tonight, we got it!" the woman said excitedly. "It was what you said about connecting—*we were bonding, but we weren't being intimate*. That's what was missing. And when my husband heard it put that way, he understood what I've been trying to say, and I understood why he felt he wasn't being appreciated for the things he was doing."

The man nodded as he heard his wife explain their break-through. "I realize we have a long way to go," he said in a soft voice, "but I feel like now we know what we need to work on, and I really want to try."

I embraced this couple, and as I watched them walk away, my eyes filled with tears. I felt so gratified to have been able to share information that clarified their problem and pointed them in the right direction. It had taken me years to be able to articulate this understanding to myself, and so to see it making a difference in their lives made all of my own personal challenges worthwhile. Since that time, I've received the same kind of feedback from hundreds of couples as they learn about the distinction between bonding and intimacy. Perhaps as you read this, you, too, are having a breakthrough in understanding about your present or past relationship. If so, I hope this book will help you to discover new ways of loving that will bring you the fulfillment you've been longing for.

What Makes a Woman Feel Connected and Intimate

Many of the same things we discussed in the previous chapter that make a woman feel safe also make her feel connected: spending time together with her partner; verbal reassurance; entry into his inner world. In fact, most of the information throughout this book, whether it's about sex, communication, or other topics, includes ways a man can connect and be intimate with his mate, and I'll discuss this in much more detail in Part Two on "What Women Want Men to Know About Love, Intimacy, and Communication." For now, here are some great ways to create connection and intimacy.

1. Women feel connected and intimate when a man communicates with us.

For women, connection is very much about communication. Most women are traditionally more verbal than most men, *so one of the fastest and most effective ways to connect with a woman is with words.*

What Women Want Men to Know:

Words build a bridge between a man's inner world and the heart of the woman he loves. They create instant intimacy.

What do women want men to communicate about? Of course, you already know the answer: EVERYTHING! We want to know about your work and your worries, your dreams and your fears, your ups and your downs. Remember: *Emotional connection is created when you share what's inside of you with your partner, and communication is the only way to do that.*

I'm well aware that men have many issues about opening up and revealing themselves. We'll talk more about these in our communication section. The point here is just to remind men of how powerful communication is in helping your woman feel connected to you. *"When my boyfriend shares things with me he doesn't share with anyone else,"* one woman told me, *"it makes me feel special and loved. I know he wouldn't open up to me like that if he didn't really cherish me."*

If communicating with a woman makes her feel connected, not communicating with her about important things definitely creates a feeling of being disconnected. Here's what women expressed about this:

> *"When a man keeps things from me, and doesn't share something important that is going on with him, I feel disconnected and discounted, like we're in two different worlds, and he's put a wall between us."*

> *"Withholding information is the biggest turnoff to me. I don't understand how my husband expects me to want to have sex when I know he hasn't been sharing much about himself. If he wants me to open up, I need him to open up."*

What Women Want Men to Know:

Withholding feelings or information from your partner is not a harmless act. It creates a sense of disconnection between you and eventually destroys the intimacy.

---

2. Women feel connected and intimate when a man includes us in the process of his life.

Remember my analogy in Chapter 1 of the Love Room? I talked about how men tend to compartmentalize their intimate relationship from the rest of their life, checking in when they are

ready for love, sex, or companionship. One of the negative consequences of this compartmentalization is that men often don't include their partners in the other "rooms"—work, recreation,
health, etc. They either figure that we're not interested or, out of
habit, don't make the effort to share what's going on. The result is
that as women, we feel excluded from so much of what makes up
our mate's world, and thus feel very disconnected.

One of the most powerful ways to create an intimate connection with your partner and make her feel truly loved and cared for
is to include her in the process of your life.

Including your partner in your life means:

• **Share the details of your daily experiences.**

When you share with your mate about what goes on during
your day, it allows her to harmonize more with you and feel
closer since she understands what you've experienced. **Talking
about your everyday experiences invites her more deeply into
your life, and that creates a powerful sense of connection, as if
your two separate worlds are linked together as one.**

• **Inform her about problems or difficulties you're facing.**

Conventional wisdom plus thousands of years of conditioning tells a man to shield the woman he loves from his problems—that if he appears to be weak or not know the answer, he
will lose her affection. Nothing could be farther from the truth.
**An emotionally healthy woman will feel even closer to you
when you share your difficulties, because she will realize you
are opening your heart to her.** One wife said:

*"When my husband tells me he's feeling down or sad or in-
secure about something, my heart just opens up even wider
to him. It makes me feel like he really trusts me. To tell you
the truth, it's one of the most intimate things he can do."*

Remember: Shared vulnerability creates intimacy. Besides, hiding problems never works—she will feel it anyway, and the act of not reaching out to her will make her feel you don't value her. More about this later.

- *Involve her in decisions you need to make that affect her.*

So many women mentioned this point in the surveys and interviews I did for this book. **When a man internalizes his thinking or decision-making process, and doesn't discuss it with his partner, it makes her feel very left out and disconnected.** I know many men don't do this on purpose, nor do they want their mate to feel shut out. But this is, indeed, the effect it has.

> *"I feel so disconnected from my husband when he disengages and acts in isolation,"* one woman told me. *"He makes decisions alone without asking for my opinion, as if I don't exist. He just goes ahead on his own and shuts me out of the process, like that part of his life has nothing to do with me."*

3. Women feel connected and intimate when men do any of the things that make us feel safe.

As described in Chapter 4, letting a woman into your world, reassuring her, spending special time with her—these behaviors not only make a woman feel safe but also help her feel emotionally connected. In fact, they also make her feel valued—the third of a woman's three secret needs. So, guys, when you make the effort to do any of these, you get three results for the price of one!

———

E very woman has her own list of what makes us feel particularly connected or disconnected from our partner. Here are just a few examples. Of course, you'll notice that many of them are repeats of what makes a woman feel safe from the chart in Chapter 4.

What makes us feel connected	What makes us feel disconnected
Physical affection	Coldness
Communication	Lack of communication
Sharing information	Withholding information
Harmony	Dissension
Inclusion	Exclusion
Reaching out	Withdrawal
Compliments	Criticism
Reassurance	Ambiguity
Scheduling time and plans	Procrastination

Ladies, don't forget to share with your partner what makes you feel particularly connected or disconnected. You may be surprised at some of the items on your list, and so will he. And men, I promise that with a little practice, you will not only learn to enjoy "connecting," but you'll discover another secret: *The more you connect with your woman emotionally, the more she'll be willing to connect with you sexually* . . . but you'll have to wait until later in the book for that chapter!

CHAPTER SIX

Women Need to Feel Valued

Just last week one of my best girlfriends called me up to complain about her boyfriend of three years. "It happened again," she began in an irritated tone. "Danny had lunch with our friend Suzie, and apparently went on and on to her about how much he loves me, how terrific I am, and how happy he is in this relationship."

"Well, that sounds wonderful," I replied. "But I don't understand why you're so angry."

"I'll tell you why," she exclaimed. "Because Danny never says those things to me in person!"

Sadly enough, I don't think my friend is alone. In my many years of working with couples, I've come to the conclusion that most men highly underestimate one of women's most essential needs—*our need to feel valued*—and become lazy about expressing how important their partner is to them. Over and over again, I've met women who complain that they don't feel their mate really appreciates or values them, only to discover when I talk to the male partner that, on the contrary, he really does value her—*he just doesn't let her know this through his speech and his behavior.*

Why is feeling valued one of a woman's most important secret needs? It is related to the other two needs we discussed: a woman's need to feel safe and to feel connected. Let's go back again to our ancient ancestors and recall how essential it was for a woman to feel safe, and how her sense of safety was tied to her very survival.

What could really ensure a woman's safety with her mate? *If he valued her, she would feel safe, because then he would be more likely to stay with her.* And so she did all she could to increase her value in his eyes—she tried to be a caring mother and a good cook and sew the hides well and make him happy in every way. And when her mate expressed his satisfaction with her, acknowledging her value in his life, she felt safe.

Throughout history, women have been seen for their value— the value of their father's property, the value of their dowry, the value of their family ties and influence, the value of their youth and beauty and thus their ability to bear healthy children. Yes, times have changed for many of us women in modern societies; we are no longer bartered for land or married off for financial reasons. What has remained, however, is the feeling deep within a woman that she wants and needs her man to value her.

Like so many women who consider ourselves strong and independent, I too have struggled throughout my life with this need to feel valued by a man. *"It shouldn't matter what he thinks of you!"* one part of me insists. And deep in my soul, I know that ultimately, it doesn't. But as it affects the day-to-day experience of my relationship, I cannot pretend that I do not need the validation and approval my partner's love gives me, nor can I hide the fact that, when I don't feel valued by the man I love, it brings out my worst fears and insecurities.

I've spoken to many very successful, high-powered women about this secret need we have to know our man sees and appreciates our value. You'd think that a woman who is a well-known actress or a renowned physician or a multimillionaire would have so much self-confidence from having accomplished great things in her life that everyday gestures of appreciation and respect from her partner wouldn't make much of a difference to her—but they do. As a famous female singer once told me:

"This may be hard to believe, but none of the accolades I receive mean as much to me as when my husband thanks me for the special dinner I cooked, or says that I'm a good mother to our kids, or asks my advice about one of his business concerns, and tells me afterward how smart I am. I could win ten Grammy Awards and have dozens of number one hits, but it's his opinion of me that really matters."

What Women Want Men to Know:

**Women need to feel valued
and to hear that we make a difference in your life.**

To a woman, being valued means that a man values her presence in his life, that she makes a difference in the quality of his existence, and that without her, something would be missing. *"I feel valued when my husband makes it clear that he'd be unhappy if he couldn't be with me, that he wouldn't be as happy without me,"* one woman wrote in my survey. What she describes is the need women have to believe that our man knows we are making a unique contribution to his life, and that he doesn't want to lose us.

I truly believe that most men have no idea how much women need to feel valued; how much we want to feel that we make a positive difference in your lives in both small and significant ways. This is especially true when men see their woman as competent or strong. *They wrongly assume that this confidence means we already feel so good about ourselves that we don't need them to tell us how wonderful we are.* But, of course, we do.

What Happens to Women Who Don't Feel Valued

Over the years, I've received thousands of letters from readers and fans. Some people write to thank me; others write asking if I'll answer a question, or offer them some advice on a particular situation they find themselves in. But by far, some of the saddest letters I receive are from men who write to tell me that their heart is broken because they've lost the woman they loved, and to confess that it is their own fault.

These men usually share a similar story. They describe falling in love with a wonderful woman who sounds like the ideal girlfriend or wife—loving, loyal, attentive, patient, and forgiving. At first, everything is smooth in the relationship. But at one point, the woman begins to express to her partner that she needs more from him in some area, whether it's time or help around the house or communication or simply attention. *And in each case, the man doesn't listen.* He dismisses her needs, or becomes angry, or shuts down and pulls away. Invariably his partner continues to try to reach him, to tell him how unhappy she is, but he is too stubborn or proud or oblivious to respond.

The ending to these stories is also always the same. In tragic terms, the writer describes a moment when, to his great shock and surprise, his partner tells him she's had enough, and leaves. Suddenly, the man will say in his letter, he saw the light—**he never really valued or appreciated his lover. He took her for granted.** But now, it's too late. She's gone, and he is alone and devastated, realizing what he had and what he's lost.

Here is the last paragraph of one of these letters from a young man living in Virginia, who wrote to tell me about the breakup of his four-year marriage to his college sweetheart :

As I write this, it is late and I am sitting alone in my small, gloomy apartment like I do every night, remembering Teresa, wanting her, missing her, and knowing I can never have her again. God gave me the chance to care for something precious, and I blew it, and so He took her away. And the part that tortures me, Dr. De Angelis, is that I know how much she loved me. She really did love me, and all she wanted in return was to know that I loved her that much too. *And what's really killing me is that I knew that's what she needed, but I was too stubborn and proud and selfish to give it to her. I chased her away with my indifference.* She was my angel, and she's gone and she took all the light in my life with her.

I won't ask you what I can do to get my wife back, because I know there is no hope of that. But please share my story with other men who come to your lectures or shows or read your books. Tell them not to make the same mistake I did. Tell them to cherish their woman and hold on to her real tight. Because if they don't, they will end up in the same hell I'm in now without my Teresa, and that's something I wouldn't wish on any living soul.

I cried when I first read this letter, and I am crying now as I share it with you. My tears are for this man and every man who learns too late that the true love of a woman's heart is a precious gift, and when you don't value that gift, eventually you will lose it. My tears are also for every woman, including myself, who has ever had to leave a man she deeply loved because her presence in his life was not valued and appreciated, and her love was taken for granted.

Four Secrets for Making a Woman Feel Valued

One of my male friends who's been following my progress in writing this book happened to call me this morning. He's taken it upon himself to offer his advice on whatever it is that I'm discussing in each section. And I've learned a lot by bouncing ideas off of him to see if I'm expressing myself clearly enough so that a very traditional man like him can understand what I'm trying to say.

"What's the topic of the chapter you're working on now?" he asked.

"Women need to feel valued, and men often don't show us how much they value and appreciate us," I explained. "Since you called, let me ask you a question: How do you show Melanie [his wife] that you value her?"

"How do I show her I value her?" he asked in a quizzical voice. "I married her!"

After I finished laughing and we got off the phone, I thought about what my friend had said. *Like many men, he assumed that just his mere presence in the relationship was enough to assure his wife that he loved and valued her.* It's like the old joke where the wife says to her husband: "George, do you love me?" and George answers, "I'm here, aren't I?" As amusing as this may be, it's unfortunately one of the misunderstandings men have about women—that once they've made a commitment to be in a steady relationship or live with us or get married, we should know from that moment on how much they appreciate us, and not bother them anymore!

What Women Want Men to Know:

**A woman needs more than just your participation
and presence in the relationship to feel you value her.
We need you to *demonstrate* your appreciation of
our value through actions, and *express* your appreciation through words.**

Sorry, guys, but just showing up isn't enough, unless you want to turn your woman into a needy, insecure basket case! (More about that in Chapter 8.)

Here are the Four Secrets for making the woman you love feel valued:

1. **Show her that her happiness is a priority for you.**
2. **Show interest in her life.**
3. **Show her you need her and value her input.**
4. **Show her that you don't take her for granted.**

---

1. Show her that her happiness is a priority for you.

A few years ago, I made up a joke for my women's seminars that goes like this:

Q: What do men and women have in common?
A: They both spend their time thinking about how to make the man happy.

Okay, guys, before you get reactive, let me explain myself. Most women are so used to putting love first and trying to please that we are always thinking about what will make our man happy. And, to be blunt, a lot of men are also thinking about how to make themselves happy, not having been trained to focus on their partner in the same way women have. Remember our Thought Diary from Chapter 1, where the woman is thinking about her partner dozens of times a day? We all know that the majority of men aren't like that. *The result is that men often have a habit of being more self-absorbed than they want to be or even realize they are.*

What Women Want Men to Know:

When a man shows his partner that she is a priority,
and that he values her happiness,
she feels valued as a person.

It's not that women don't think our men want to make us happy.
It's just that we often feel this falls very low on his list of priorities.
He'll get around to focusing on it after he handles his work and his
recreational activities, or when we finally make such a fuss that he
decides he'd better pay attention.

So guys, how can you show your mate that her happiness is a
priority to you? It's really not that complicated. Here are some of
the suggestions women gave me to pass on to you:

**Know what's important to your woman and go out of
your way to do those things.*
For instance, if you know your wife tends to get stressed out
putting the kids to bed at night, offer to help *before* she asks you. If
you know your partner loves chocolate chip cookies from a particular store, surprise her with them every once in a while. If your
girlfriend enjoys a particular TV show, offer to watch it with her
(at least once in a while!). If your wife mentions that she heard a
new movie is good, surprise her with tickets. If you know it makes
your girlfriend happy when you talk to her first thing in the morning, call her for a minute to say hi. If your wife mentioned a while
ago that she would like to start planning a romantic weekend get-
away for the two of you, be the one to bring up the topic again,
rather than waiting for her to do it.

Women are always giving you cues, if not specific requests, for how to make us feel happy and appreciated. Pay attention, and try what we suggest. These things usually take a very small amount of time and effort, but the result will be significant in the eyes of the woman you love.

Ask her what she would like to do or what would make her happy.

Women are usually the ones who say to our mates, "Honey, what would you like to do tonight?" or "Where would you like to eat?" or "How would you like to handle the kids' schedule this weekend?" *We can be experts at accommodation, checking out what our partner wants before we reveal our own preferences.* So when a man takes this role with us, we are ecstatic! "He asked **ME** what **I** wanted to do tonight?" we think to ourselves in wonder. "I feel so pampered, so taken care of." I'm not exaggerating about this, guys. As one woman wrote to me:

> *"When my boyfriend knows what's important to me, and goes out of his way to do it, I feel so loved because he's showing me he really cares about what I think and feel."*

To score a big jackpot and make your woman feel really valued, try simply sitting down with her sometime and asking, *"Darling, is there anything I can to do make you happier?"* Before you roll your eyes in disbelief, think about the question—if you really love your partner, don't you *want* to know what would make her happier? So why not ask her instead of trying to figure it out for yourself?

Give her your time.

Remember all of the information in Chapter 3 about women and time? *When you plan time with your partner, she feels you've made her a priority, and that therefore her happiness is valuable to you.* Don't make her beg for it—go out of your way to share your time, even if it's in small doses. More than any present, it will make her feel special and treasured.

2. Show interest in her life.

The following is a true story:

A woman visits her gynecologist for her regular checkup, and the doctor discovers something suspicious on one of the woman's ovaries. She asks the woman to come back on Thursday, and schedules her for some tests to determine whether or not there is a serious problem. That night, the woman tells her husband about her appointment, and shares how worried she is that the tests on Thursday will discover something awful like cancer. "Let's just wait until you get the results before we freak out," he responds.

Thursday morning arrives, and as he leaves for work, the woman's husband kisses her good-bye while she's still half asleep. Nervously, she dresses and a few hours later, drives to the doctor's office for her tests. She goes through the procedures, and is so relieved when the doctor informs her that all her tests turned out normal and there is nothing to worry about.

That evening, she prepares dinner, and waits for her husband to come home. He arrives looking tired and stressed as usual after he's had a particularly long day, and sits down at the table to eat. "Hey, do you mind if we turn on the TV?" he asks between mouthfuls of salad. "There's a game on I really want to see."

The woman feels her heart pounding in her chest as her husband turns on the TV, and tears fill her eyes. "He didn't even ask me about my appointment or the results of the tests! He forgot that I even went to the doctor," she thinks to herself in disbelief. She waits for a while, hoping that perhaps he'll remember when he's had a while to calm down, but as they finish dinner, and he settles in to watch another program, she realizes that he isn't going to mention the doctor, and that he probably hasn't thought about it all day. Angry and hurt, she goes upstairs alone and calls a girlfriend, crying as she explains the situation. "I feel like he doesn't even care about what happens to me," she sobs into the phone. "If he loved me, he would have remembered my appointment."

———

How do I know this is a true story? *Because once many years ago, it happened to me.* Would you be surprised if I also told you that I've personally heard dozens of different versions of this same story from friends or women I've met about similar experiences they had?

What is my point in sharing all of this? It's not to put men down or make them look bad. The person in my story was a good man, and he really had no idea that he'd forgotten my appointment or upset me so much until I let him know how I felt later that evening. But sadly for me, he was not very good at making me feel valued—he used up all his energy focusing on his own life and challenges, and didn't seem to have any left over for me.

Guys, I hate to say this, but sometimes men can really be unbelievably self-absorbed and self-centered. (Of course women can be too, but remember, that's not what this book is about.) I know men don't mean to be that way, and they're usually very surprised when it's pointed out to them because they do have good intentions. **But most men are not trained to be focused on caring for the needs of others like women are, and thus they can easily fall into the selfishness trap without knowing it.**

It's for this reason that I even have to remind men to show interest in their women's lives, that women need this to feel valued. Because sometimes, you guys simply forget. Here are some suggestions:

*Pay attention to what's going on with her.

Do you know that if a woman went on a TV game show with her husband and one of her best girlfriends, her friend might win the prize if the test was about which one of them knew the woman better? That's because her friend probably pays much closer attention to the details of what's going on in the woman's life than her husband does. Believe me, all of my girlfriends knew about my test with the gynecologist, and they remembered the date, too!

Paying attention to those we love is genetically engineered into women. For instance, this week alone, I know that on Tuesday my dear friend Robyn is going to Las Vegas for a TV convention, that she has been looking for a new purse, and that she's waiting for a contractor to repair the ceiling in her bedroom; and I also know that on Monday, my friend Julia will get the results of a blood test to see if she has low levels of iron, that she has a big presentation to give at work next week, and that she and her husband are going to a charity benefit dance this Saturday.

These important dates and events are entered into the calendar in my brain along with my own appointments. It's very possible, however, that Robyn's fiancé and Julia's husband may not even be as aware of all this information as I am, or if they are, that they neglect to check in with their partner and show interest in finding out how things are going.

So guys, please pay attention to what's important to your partner. As one woman wrote me:

> *"When my husband asks about specific things happening in my life and becomes involved, it's as if he is saying, 'If something is important to you, it's important to me, and I want to know all about it.' "*

Ask her questions about the activities that are important to her.

Ask her for updates on the events of her life.

Check back with her on how things went after the event is over.

Bring up topics you know she's been wanting to talk about with you.

A little effort on your part will make her feel as if you care about what she cares about, and that you value her.

Ask her what she is thinking and feeling.

One of the ways a woman often tries to enter a man's inner world is by asking him *"What are you thinking about?"* or *"How do you feel about that?"* For the record, let me just say I am well aware that most men **hate** these questions—they put men on the spot to come up with an instant answer, they seem vague and confusing, and they probe into areas many men don't want to have to discuss. But as women, our intention in asking is simply to let our mate know that we care about what's going on inside of him.

What Women Want Men to Know:

When you ask your partner, *"What are you feeling?"* or *"What are you thinking about?"* you send her the message that her thoughts and emotions are important to you, that you value them and therefore value her.

Asking your woman these questions is one of the easiest ways to show your interest in her life. She will truly appreciate your effort, and you will probably find out a lot more about her that you didn't know!

3. Show her you need her and value her input.

If a man asked me to choose one thing he could do to make his partner feel loved and valued, I would suggest he find ways to tell and show her how much he needs her. Do you know that most women have no idea how much their man truly needs them in his life? Time and time again in my work with couples, a woman will tell me how much she is hurting because her husband doesn't love her as much as she loves him, or that he doesn't seem to need her at all, and would probably not even miss her if she were gone. But when I talk with her husband, I am surprised to hear him profess his deep love for his wife, and confess how much he does need her and values everything she contributes to his life.

If men do need us so much, why don't women know it? Perhaps, guys, it's because you don't show us or tell us! **Men are interested in appearing self-sufficient and independent, and the idea that they need their partner can be unsettling, even frightening.** The result is that often you unconsciously try to prove to yourself that you really don't need your sweetheart as much as you do:

- **You don't ask for her help or support.**
- **You discount her input or advice.**
- **You leave her out of the decision-making process.**
- **You cover up your insecurities regarding how she feels about you.**

How do these behaviors make a woman feel? *Like you don't need, respect, or value us at all.* And this really hurts.

What Women Want Men to Know:

**When you find ways to show a woman how much
you need us in your life,
it makes us feel treasured and valued.**

Here are some specific suggestions for putting this secret into practice:

- *Tell her that you need her.*

    One of the most precious memories I have in my own love life is of a time when the man I loved really showed me that he needed me. My partner and I lived in different parts of the country, and took turns traveling back and forth visiting each other. When we were together, it was heaven, but when we were apart, it was difficult, and I missed him terribly.

    Late one night, a few days after he'd left following a wonderful visit, I was lying in bed feeling very lonely and thinking about how it seemed more like months since he'd gone. Just then, the phone rang.

    "Hi, darling," my sweetheart said in a very tender voice. "Are you awake?"

    "Yes, I'm just lying here thinking of you," I answered.

    "I know it's late," he continued softly, "but I just called for a second. I couldn't sleep because I miss you so much."

    My heart melted as I heard these words. I was usually the romantic one in the relationship, and my partner was a very independent and confident man. So to hear him tell me how much he missed me filled my heart with happiness.

    "I miss you, too," I said with tears in my eyes. After we said good night and got off the phone, I lay in the dark and noticed that a deep sense of peace had come over me. I knew what was at the source of that peace: *I felt needed.*

Find opportunities to tell the woman you love that you need her, whether it's letting her know you miss her when you aren't together, or sharing that you can't imagine your life without her, or anything else you feel will let her know how special she is to you.

- *Let her contribute to you and your life.*

    Men often have a difficult time receiving from women, even from the woman they love. There are many reasons for this—the need to feel autonomous, a fear of being controlled, the unconscious desire to protect themselves from loss or rejection. But in the end, the result is the same: The woman feels shut out, as if what she has to offer isn't valuable.

What Women Want Men to Know:

When you allow a woman to contribute to you and your life, she feels like she's made a difference, like she matters.

What are some ways you can open up to receiving a woman's contribution to your life?

Ask her opinion—on politics, on what she thinks about an item in the news, on how you can best handle a situation, on anything and everything. This shows her that you value what she thinks, and that you're interested in her views.

Allow your mate to be your teacher. Be willing to learn from her in the areas in which she's more masterful than you are. Perhaps she's great at organizing, or playing tennis or meditating.

Honor these talents and abilities by asking her to share her skills or expertise with you. And don't forget to tell her how much she's contributing to your life.

- *Ask for help and advice, or at least don't refuse it when she offers.*

    Men can be so proud and stubborn. I'm sorry to say it so bluntly, but guys, you know it's true. Somewhere in the last several thousand years, the male brain was programmed to believe *that if you received help in doing something, the accomplishment wouldn't "count" as much, or you wouldn't get the same credit, and therefore, getting through crises alone, doing things alone, and figuring things out alone was more admirable, and made you a bigger and better man.* The result of this erroneous way of thinking is that it's very difficult for most men to ask for help, for guidance, or for support—especially from the woman they love.

    This is one of the biggest complaints I hear from women about their men—when you don't allow us to be there for you, we feel left out of your process, and the painful message we get is that there's nothing valuable you think we could offer you.

What Women Want Men to Know:

When a woman knows her partner is going through a difficult time or facing some challenges in a particular area of his life and he does not come to her for support or advice, she feels devalued, as if he doesn't have enough faith in her to believe that she could possibly contribute something valuable to him.

I know that every primal fear cell in a man's body screams, *"Don't tell a woman how freaked out you are—she'll eventually use it against you!"* Maybe some disturbed women will, but most of us won't. Most of us, if you give us a chance, will simply do our best to be supportive, to be smart where we feel our ideas may be helpful, and to be caring and compassionate. Perhaps in the end what we say won't make a difference or help you find an easy solution to your problem, but I promise that the hug and kiss we give you *will* make you feel just a little bit better. And we'll feel like we were able to contribute something to you during a hard time, even if it's just our love.

- *Treat her as an equal.*

  I know most men would never admit to believing that the woman should have less rights in the relationship than the man. (Come to think of it, there are guys out there who maintain the idea of male supremacy in marriage, but I'm certain that they are not reading this book, so it's safe for me to continue!) Even the most sincere, liberated, and well-meaning man can easily fall into the trap of becoming a governing body of one, and forgetting to include his partner in the process of making the decisions that affect the relationship. We discussed this topic of inclusion briefly in Chapter 5 when we talked about what makes a woman feel connected. But it deserves another reminder here.

  I know some very old-fashioned guys who play the role of protector in their marriage, "shielding" their wife from problems or decisions. While there may be some women who enjoy this dynamic of a father caring for his child, most women, unless they inform you otherwise, would prefer to be treated more like a competent adult. Simply put, **a woman will not feel valued if you don't treat her as an equal.**

  It's not that hard to figure out how to do this. It means learning to work together as a team in the relationship and discussing things before making decisions, whether they're about finances, purchases, employment changes, children, or dealing with elderly parents.

4. Show her that you don't take her for granted.

"How can he treat me like this if he loves me?" Have you ever found yourself pondering this question about your partner? I know I have, and so have most women at one time or another. Over the years, through my profession and in my own relationships, I've learned an amazing fact about men that answers this question:

> **Men don't always see the connection between how they behave toward women and how we end up feeling in the relationship.**

As strange as this may sound, I do believe that it is true. Perhaps this explains why men with perfectly good hearts often appear to be clueless about why their mate is upset with them.

"How can she think I don't appreciate her, that I take her for granted?" a man will ask me when we're discussing his wife's unhappiness. "I am crazy about her!" As I talk more with him, I discover that, indeed, he truly adores his wife. Then she recites a list of things he does that make her feel taken for granted—he ignores her constant requests for more help with the children; he doesn't offer to help prepare meals even though they both work full-time; he's skimpy with praise or romantic expressions—and I can see her point. When I confront her mate on these issues, he usually agrees. "You're right, I know I'm not great at those things," he'll admit. "But I don't see what that has to do with her feeling like I don't love or appreciate her." And he's not kidding, either—he really doesn't see it.

What's going on here? It relates to how men compartmentalize their life, as we discussed in Chapter 1. This husband really does not understand the cause-and-effect relationship between the ways he doesn't respect his wife's time and energy, and any possible feeling it might bring up in her of being taken for granted. Why not? **Because he doesn't experience a connection between how he feels about her and how he treats her**. To men, their feelings about their partner are often in one "room" of their consciousness, and their behavioral habits and everyday decisions are in other rooms. In other words, as bizarre as it sounds:

> *How a man treats a woman may or may not always
> have something to do with how he feels about us!*

I tried to explain this concept to one of my male friends just last week. He's been dating a woman for about seven months in a fairly serious relationship, and when I asked how things were, he said they were fine, but he hadn't talked to her in five days because he'd been very busy at work.

"Elliot," I said in a scolding tone, "you haven't called Denise in five days? I'm sure she's been terribly worried and upset."

"Do you think so?" he asked innocently.

"Of course I think so! She's used to talking with you just about every day, and suddenly you vanish with no explanation. I'm sure she feels afraid that you're breaking up with her."

"Well," Elliot confessed, "she's left me a few messages on my machine asking if I was okay, and she sounded kind of emotional."

"You see! I'm telling you, she's probably a mess."

"But I don't understand why," he insisted in a perplexed voice. "The last time we were together we had a great time, and she knows I care deeply for her."

"Oh really? Do you think she feels you care deeply for her

when you don't call her for five days and don't respond to her messages?"

"Well," he said, "I guess I thought she'd figure I was busy, and I'd call when I had time."

"How is she supposed to know that? Is she a mind reader? All she knows is that you usually call and lately you haven't called, even when you know she wants to talk to you."

"But that has nothing to do with how I feel about her!" he exclaimed.

I felt like screaming in frustration when I heard Elliot's comment. This is one of the reasons women end up feeling a man takes us for granted—because he doesn't think that his everyday behavior matters and takes for granted that we know he loves us. *But guys, everything you do does matter.*

Here are some suggestions for how to show the woman you love that you don't take her for granted:

- *Respect her time and energy.*

    Do you know what women really hate in a relationship? *When their partner behaves as if his time or energy is more valuable than hers.* I hear this complaint frequently, from wives who are also mothers, from women who work full-time and yet still have the majority of the responsibility to care for the home, from women whose partner thinks his job is more "important" than hers because of its prestige or salary. Here are some of these women's comments:

    "Sometimes my husband just sits there while I am sweating to death running after the kids. It's as if he doesn't even notice that I need his help. Other times I'll come home late from my job and he's been home for hours already and

hasn't even started dinner. It makes me feel he just doesn't care about my time at all."

"My boyfriend and I live together, and we both work, only he feels because he's an attorney, and I'm 'just' an office manager, that somehow he is more tired than I am and therefore deserves special privileges. Whenever I ask him to help with dinner, or with cleaning, he looks at me as if I'm crazy, and then gives me a lecture on how demanding his job is. It's like he doesn't have any respect for my energy or the way I spend my time."

"I think my lover believes that his time is more valuable than my time, that it's worth more, or something. He's a TV producer, and his whole life is about scheduling things and delivering a product. But when it comes to me, he figures I can wait and don't need attending to. If I want to know whether he can come with me to a friend's party in a few weeks, he tells me he can't deal with deciding right now. However, if someone called him about a professional meeting, he'd schedule it in two seconds. And often he says he'll call me back, and doesn't call for hours, but I know he wouldn't do that to his clients. I end up feeling totally taken for granted."

What Women Want Men to Know:

When you don't respect a woman's time or energy, we feel as if you don't respect us and that you take us for granted.

What men can do:

• *Ask her if she needs help with the children or the house.*
Don't wait for your wife to show signs of collapse. Offer your help even when she doesn't ask for it or seem to need it. Just because we seem to be handling everything doesn't mean we are happy about it! We will be so appreciative that you want to contribute.

• *Respect her time and schedule by communicating responsibly.*
If you know your partner is waiting for you to call or to finalize some plans, don't just ignore her without communicating in some way. Telephone to say you can't really talk until you finish a project; let her know you want to plan a weekend away but can't discuss it for a few more days. Tell her when you are aware you're going to be late.

• *Don't push her limits, even if she doesn't push back.*
"I'm not a very good boyfriend." This is how a good-looking man in his thirties began as he stood up during the question-and-answer portion of one of my seminars. The women in the audience laughed nervously, and the man continued: "I've been dating my girlfriend for almost two years. I think I really love her, but . . . I don't know how to put this . . . she's *too* nice. She pretty much lets me do whatever I want, and never gets mad at me for anything."

"And why do you think that's a problem?" I asked.

"The problem is that I take advantage of it," the man explained. "I wait to make plans to see her until the last minute; I don't call her even when I know she's waiting to hear from me. I pretty much take her for granted. I was wondering, Dr. De Angelis, which of your books you'd recommend that I could buy her. See, I think she lacks self-confidence, and if she was stronger, then I wouldn't get away with so much."

"You make it sound like the reason you behave badly with her is that she tempts you into it by being such a nice girl," I responded, "that this is her problem. Sure, it sounds like your girlfriend needs to learn to set some boundaries, but that's not the issue here. *The real problem is that you keep pushing her limits and taking her for granted.* I don't care if she doesn't push back. That's no excuse for treating her the way you do."

I was hard on this guy because he was doing what's called "blaming the victim," claiming that his poor behavior wasn't his fault, but was instigated by the woman's lack of power. It was as if he was saying, "If she'd keep me in line, I'd treat her better, but since she's such a doormat, I can't help myself—I just become a jerk." This *"you made me do it"* defense has always made me angry, whether it is used in a therapist's office or in a courtroom.

The message behind my sharing of this story is: **Guys, don't take your partner for granted, even if she allows you to. Don't push her or test her, even if she allows you to. Don't see what you can get away with and become lazy or disrespectful in the relationship, even if she allows you to get away with it.**

As women, we're fighting hard every day against our own conditioning that advises us not to stand up for ourselves, or not to scare a man off with too many expectations. We need to work on healing old emotional wounds from mistreatment in the past. But men, you can help by treating us with respect even during those times when we'd settle for less. Remember—*there is no victory in getting away with giving less than you should in love.*

Here's a summary of some of the points we've discussed regarding what makes women feel valued:

What makes us feel valued	What makes us not feel valued
Paying attention to what's going on with us	Being self-absorbed
Verbal appreciation	Lack of acknowledgment
Acting like a team	Acting like a loner
Showing us you need us	Hiding your needs
Asking us for input	Excluding us
Making us a priority	Ignoring our needs
Respecting our time and concerns	Not checking in with us
Showing interest in our lives	Not paying attention to us

A Final Word on the Three Secret Needs Every Woman Has

The last three chapters have dealt with the three secret needs every woman has: *the need to feel safe, the need to feel connected, and the need to feel valued*. We covered a lot of material, and I know it's not easy to remember all of it, especially when you are in the middle of a difficult moment in your relationship. I thought I'd leave you with some simple questions you can ask yourself in emotionally stressful times:

What Men Can Do:

When you notice that your partner is exhibiting symptoms of being unhappy or unfulfilled, ask yourself these questions:

1. **What can I do to make her feel *safe* right now?**
2. **What can I do to make her feel *connected* right now?**
3. **What can I do to make her feel *valued* right now?**

Then, try one of the suggestions you've read about in these chapters.

For instance, let's say your wife is acting irritable one evening, and you have no idea why. Instead of simply ignoring it, or assuming she'll tell you about it if she wants to, *ask her what's wrong, and if there's anything you can do to make her feel better*. Perhaps if she's read this book, she'll let you know very specifically what she needs from you. If not, don't worry. **Just do *something* you've read about that will make her feel more safe or more connected to you or more valued by you.** It doesn't matter if it's not the perfect solution for her specific issue. Any way you reach out to her will show her that you care, and want her to feel loved.

Remember: The amount of effort it will take to do or say something that will help her make an emotional shift is nothing compared to the amount of energy you'll have to expend dealing with her continuing to be upset. *Addressing one of her three secret needs is a small investment with a big payoff!*

What Women Can Do:

Sometimes in our love life, we discover that we're feeling awful, and we aren't sure why. **When you suddenly find yourself suffering in your relationship, it may very well be because one or more of your three basic needs isn't being met. In some way you aren't feeling safe or connected or valued.**

Ask yourself:

1. *What do I need to feel safe right now?*
2. *What do I need to feel connected right now?*
3. *What do I need to feel valued right now?*

For instance, let's say that one day you notice you're feeling sad and down, but you can't pinpoint the cause. You ask yourself these three questions, and realize that you and your husband have both been very busy lately, and you need to feel more connected with him instead of distant and detached.

What can you do? You can reach out to him and express how you're feeling; you can plan something special for the two of you; you can initiate physical intimacy. At least now you know what the problem is and you can work toward creating a solution.

There are also times you might be feeling uneasy, and it has nothing to do with your intimate relationship. Remember: *Those three secret needs don't just apply to what you need from men—they are needs women have in general.* Perhaps you realize you aren't feeling valued. What can you do about it? Ask yourself if you've been giving yourself enough credit for all the goals you've accomplished lately.

Maybe you need to make a list of all the things you value about yourself. Or perhaps you haven't been sharing your accomplishments with enough of your friends, and aren't getting the positive feedback you deserve. Call a friend and talk about how much progress you've made, and you'll notice you start feeling better right away.

The more familiar you become with your three secret needs, the more you will be able to honor them, and create the kind of life you deserve.

CHAPTER SEVEN

Seven Myths Men Believe About Women
and Why They Are Absolutely Wrong

"All men want is one thing—sex."

"Men are jerks—they don't care who they hurt."

"Men are shut down and can't express their feelings."

"Men are selfish and insensitive."

"You can't trust men—they'll all break your heart."

"Men are just big babies who fall apart with the slightest pressure."

Before you get upset with me or think I've turned into a man-hater, let me explain what you just read: These are a few of the myths some women believe about men; stereotypes that are often used to describe men in less than favorable terms. I'm sure that if you're a guy reading this list, you'll react with irritation, even anger. "I'm not like that," you think defiantly. "Maybe there are some men out there who fit these descriptions, but it's not fair to say that all men do."

Of course, you're right. Myths are not fair. They are misperceptions that generalize characteristics or behavior, usually negatively, about a particular group—in this case, men. And when a man meets a woman who consciously or unconsciously believes one of these myths, he finds himself in a constant struggle to defend himself against a stereotype that may have nothing to do with him.

Well guys, as much as you don't like to be unfairly stereotyped, neither do women. *To really understand and love women means to see us as we really are, not as we've been portrayed to be.* And no matter how hard you may try not to be influenced by generalizations about the opposite sex, some of what you've heard or been exposed to is bound to have an effect on how you interpret or misinterpret a woman's behavior—even the woman you love dearly.

This chapter uncovers seven of the most common myths men have about women, and explains the reality beneath each of them. I hope as women read about these myths, you will come to a deeper comprehension of why you are the way you are, so you can criticize yourself less and honor yourself more. And guys, I hope my explanations make it easier for you to break down your stereotypes, and truly understand and appreciate the woman you love.

The Seven Myths Men Believe About Women

1. Women are never satisfied.

2. Women are high maintenance.

3. Women want to control men.

4. Women are jealous and possessive.

5. Women are too emotional.

6. Women who appear to be strong and competent don't need to be taken care of.

7. Women want to rob men of their freedom.

Myth #1: Women Are Never Satisfied

"Women are impossible to please, so why even try?"

"First she wants this, then she wants something else— there's never an end to it."

"Women just like to complain. They get a kick out of nagging us."

"I can't win with her. It will never be good enough."

Whether men say these statements out loud, or just think them as they're listening to their partners express their latest needs or attempt a conversation about improving the relationship, the point is the same: Women are never satisfied in a relationship, no matter what a man does. It stereotypes women as chronic complainers, bent on driving men crazy by criticizing everything they do or say. And since she's not going to be satisfied anyway, men consciously or unconsciously conclude, why even try?

Why is this a myth? **Because it misinterprets a woman's tendency to want to improve things as proof that she is just chronically dissatisfied. The fact is, women aren't impossible to please—it's just our nature to want to make things better.**

MYTH: **Women are never satisfied.**
TRUTH: **Women are always interested in making things better.**

Guys, you may read this and say to yourself, "Wait a minute— what's the difference between these two statements? Don't they amount to the same thing, that no matter what men do, it isn't good enough?" My answer is NO, these statements do not have the same meaning. **Wanting to make things better is not the same as never being satisfied with anything.**

If you ask your employee to redo a report, it doesn't mean you are never satisfied with anyone's work, does it? If you buy a new component for your stereo system to upgrade the quality, it doesn't mean that you will never be satisfied with anything you purchase. If you decide to trade in your car for a newer model, it doesn't mean you will never be happy with a car you drive. All of these actions are simply expressions of your desire to improve upon what you have.

It's the same with women—just because we want something improved doesn't mean we are impossible to satisfy. Now, I have to admit, I do know a few women who fit this description; the crack-the-whip types who treat their men as if they're in reform school instead of in a marriage. If you've been with a woman like this, you have my condolences. But trust me—most of us aren't this way.

It is true, of course, that often women aren't satisfied as easily as men are when it comes to their intimate relationships. I believe this is because our emotional standards are higher. Remember: Women put love first, and we are run by that urge to create. **So we feel as if it's our job to improve things and make our intimate relationship as good as it can be.**

What Woman Want Men to Know:

When a woman suggests a way to change or improve things in your relationship, she's *not* complaining or criticizing you—she's expressing her commitment to making the relationship the best it can be.

What are some of the problems that occur when men believe Myth #1, that women are never satisfied?

Men use this myth as an excuse to discount a woman's needs.

After working up her courage for a week, Janette sits down with her husband one night and confesses that she's been feeling distant from him. She explains that she really needs him to spend more time with her in the evenings and weekends, rather than doing work at home, so they can recapture the closeness they used to have. Daryl listens to her nervously, and responds: *"Nothing I do is good enough for you, is it? You're the one who encouraged me to take this new job, and now you're complaining that I'm working too hard. You'll never be happy with anything."*

Daryl has convinced himself that he doesn't have to deal with his wife's feelings or needs, because she's just a woman who is chronically dissatisfied. Therefore, the content of what she's saying is inconsequential. He uses Myth #1 as a way to hide from his own fears of inadequacy and of letting her down.

Men use this myth as an excuse to invalidate our feedback and avoid looking at themselves.

I've known a lot of men who use the excuse that women are just impossible to satisfy in order to avoid dealing with our feedback. **They immediately invalidate the legitimacy of their partner's request or communication, telling themselves, and sometimes her, that nothing will satisfy her, so they may as well not even try**. These exchanges go something like this:

HER: Honey, I wanted to talk about how we've been sharing the job of putting the kids to bed. It seems like you always claim to be tired, or to have extra work from the office, and more often than not, I end up doing it, even though we agreed we would each take every other night.

HIM: Here you go again, with your "He's a bad father" routine. It's never perfect enough for you, is it?

This tactic forces the woman suddenly to be on the defensive. I call this "bait and switch": The man baits the woman with a negative stereotype and thus switches the conversation from the topic of how he shares the duties of taking care of the children to the topic of what is wrong with her. *Instead of being willing to look at himself and his behavior, he portrays himself as the victim, a poor innocent husband persecuted by his wife's unreasonable rules and regulations.*

Men use this myth as a way to create a false sense of power.

Some men have an unreasonable belief that if a woman makes a request and he fulfills it, he will end up being a slave to every little thing she wants. *"If I give in on one thing,"* he thinks, *"it will just be the beginning—soon, I will give in on everything, and I'll totally lose my power in the relationship."* And so the moment a woman expresses a need, he overreacts. Instead of listening to what she is actually saying, he responds dramatically as if she is asking him to give up all of his personal rights. It's his way of drawing a line he believes he needs to draw.

Of course he is wrong. Most probably, his mate is not in a power struggle with him for ultimate control in the relationship—she is just expressing a need or concern. And his fear that if he gives in a little he will end up losing everything is totally unfounded. It would be as if your car needed a little tune-up, but you refuse to take it in to the mechanic because you are certain if you give up your power and agree to an oil change, he will end up telling you that you have to replace the whole engine!

Men use this myth as a way to cover up their feelings of having failed to satisfy their partner.

Here's a story I heard from a woman in one of my seminars:

"My husband and I are newlyweds," she began, "and he really is a sweet guy. It seems he decided on his own that if he took upon himself the job of taking out the trash, it would make me happy. So that's what he did, and I noticed he was always emptying all the wastebaskets into the big can and cheerfully carrying it downstairs to the bins.

"One day soon after we'd moved into our new apartment, I asked him if he'd mind helping me with the dishes. To my surprise, he became completely exasperated. 'You're never satisfied with how much I do!' he complained. 'It's never enough.' To be honest, I had no clue why he was so upset, until we talked things through. Eventually, it came out that he had his own agenda of what he thought would satisfy me in terms of sharing chores, and when it didn't, he felt he'd somehow failed to make me happy. Rather than telling me this, he just concluded that I couldn't be satisfied."

I know this scenario sounds painfully familiar to many of you, whether it's the man who buys us a gift he thinks we said we wanted, only to discover he totally misunderstood us, or the husband who proudly shows us the new system he rigged up for storing pots and pans, only to find out that we liked things the way they were, or the boyfriend who surprises us with tickets to a wrestling match because we once asked him a question about the sport, only to realize that we can't stand wrestling. *Sometimes even the most well-intentioned men do something they think will make their partner happy*—only they forget to actually ask her if this is what she wants or if it's important to her—*and when they discover that they've made the wrong assumption, they cover up their sense of failure or embarrassment by becoming angry at her for not being satisfied.*

The Truth About Myth #1

Men, I swear that this is the truth: *Women, at least most of us, are easy to satisfy!* Don't think I can't hear you laughing, because I can, but I stand by this belief. In fact, that's what this entire book is about—discussing how simple it actually is to make a woman happy when you understand what she really needs from you. If you don't believe me, I dare you to try an experiment in your relationship: Each day, give your partner three compliments, one extra phone call, five minutes of cuddling or intimacy, and one moment when you ask, "Is there anything I can do for you right now?"—and watch her melt into a satisfied puddle at your feet!

Myth #2: Women Are High Maintenance

"Women are so much work—it's exhausting."

"Women are too intense and demanding."

"Women never make relationships easy."

I think every woman has had Myth #2 thrown in her face at some point in her dating or relationship life. "This is too hard," our partner will say. "It's way too much work to be with you. I'm just not up for it." Crushed, we think to ourselves, "Is it true? Am I that difficult and demanding to be with?"

Before we answer that question, let's take a look at what men actually mean when they say a woman is high maintenance:

- **We want men to be intimate with us.**
- **We want men to communicate with us.**
- **We want men to spend time with us.**
- **We want men to confront rather than avoid problems.**
- **We want men to participate in working on the relationship.**

A man might read this list and say, "See—this is just what I mean. Look at how demanding women are. It's just too much trouble." But I disagree. These are not unusual demands from a high maintenance woman—**they are the basic requirements for any healthy, intimate relationship between two people.**

This is where men get thrown off track. They react to the natural demands of the relationship as if they're unreasonable demands from their partner.

MYTH: **Women are high maintenance.**
TRUTH: **Intimate relationships are high maintenance.**

It's not women who are high maintenance—it's relationships, at least the kind that reflect true intimacy, friendship, and growth. Successful relationships aren't easy. They *are* demanding. They *are* intense. They *do* take work. But they are worth it.

If you think about it, *everything truly valuable in life is high maintenance*, from your dream home to your children to your body to your career or business. All of these require a lot of time, attention, and effort to maintain. I don't think any man would argue with this. He understands that what is valuable needs to be taken care of.

Guys, imagine for a moment that you own a beautiful sports car, one you've wanted for a long time. Would you ever complain: *"This car is so much work—it needs gas every few days, and I have to check the oil and the tires frequently, and if I don't wash it, it looks awful. Why did I ever buy it? It's demanding too much from me."* Of course you wouldn't say these things, because you have the understanding that a quality vehicle needs quality care in order to run properly.

Well, it's the same with relationships. They need attention and work and maintenance in order to run properly. Women intuitively know this, and that's why we are always encouraging you, asking you, and yes, sometimes bugging you to connect, communicate, be intimate, and all the rest. **We know relationships are high maintenance, and we need you to help us work on the one we share with you so it can be its best.**

What Women Want Men to Know:

**Women have high standards for our intimate relationships *not* because we are being difficult,
but because we are passionately committed to love,
and we want the relationship to work.**

---

*Men use this myth as an excuse not to work on the relationship.

When a man dismisses a woman as high maintenance, he's giving us the message that he's dismissing the relationship and all that's required to make it last. It's as if by saying his partner is too high maintenance, he excuses himself from having to listen to her feedback or put any time or effort into creating and maintaining intimacy. Guys, I know it's not always fun or easy to do what it takes to make a relationship work, but as I will repeat over and over again throughout these chapters, the payoff will be worth it.

The Truth About Myth #2

A high maintenance woman is a woman committed to love. Men, if you want an outrageous relationship with a woman committed to love, you're going to have to invest time and energy into maintaining the connection with your partner. Of course, to be blunt, there are some women out there who don't care much about intimacy or the quality of the relationship; they just want a caretaker or someone to play a role. If you choose to be with a woman like this, you could probably get away with not doing much at all, as long as you paid the bills or showed up when they needed you to. But the truth is, you wouldn't be getting away with anything—in fact, you'd be ripping yourself off of the passion, the joy, and the magic that true love can be.

Myth #3: Women Want to Control Men

"Women just want to control men until we follow them around like little puppy dogs."

"Women can't just leave a situation alone—they have to pick at it until we do what they want us to do."

"Women always have to have things their way, or they get upset."

"Women want to make men into wimps."

This is one of men's favorite complaints about women, and one that women hate the most—that we are controlling and manipulative, and all our efforts to work on the relationship or communicate our needs are thinly veiled attempts to control the man in our life. We've actually already talked a lot about this in Chapter 2, but I want to mention it again, since this myth about women is one of the more difficult to dispel.

Here's what happens: *Men see women trying to contribute or get organized or plan or problem-solve, and misinterpret it as our attempt to control them.*

MYTH: **Women want to control men.**
TRUTH: **Women want to contribute, improve, and be included.**

Remember—a woman's intention is usually not to control. Rather, it's to offer whatever she can, out of love, to you or to the relationship, whether it's in the form of organization, ideas, suggestions, alternatives, or something else. **When a man dismisses her offering as an attempt to dominate or control him, he's pushing away her love in one of its most fundamental expressions.**

What do men get out of believing Myth #3, that women want to control men?

Men get to hide the truth of how they're feeling or how they're doing.

Jack is having a difficult time in his new job. It's a much more pressured environment than at his previous company, and even after a few weeks, he still doesn't feel as if he fits in. Each night, he arrives home from work exhausted and depressed, but when his wife, Ellen, asks him what's wrong, he doesn't really give her details or share what's happening. Instead, he just mumbles something about having had a hard day at the office.

Ellen has known Jack since they were teenagers, so she's completely aware of how stressed he is since he began working in his new position. As the weeks pass, she waits for Jack to open up and tell her more about his situation, but her inquiries are only met with silence. Finally, she can't take it anymore, and one night after dinner, she broaches the subject:

"Jack, I know you're having a hard time with the new job, and I've been thinking of some things that might help. My cousin Bill works in a big company with a similar corporate structure, and I remember when he first started it was hell for him. Maybe if you called and spoke to Bill you'd feel supported and calmer about the way things have been going. I was also thinking that if I took over driving the boys to soccer practice on the weekends, you'd have more time to work at home."

Ellen's heart is hurting for her husband, and all she wants to do is help make things better, so she is surprised at his response:

"Jeez, Ellen, can't you just leave things alone?" Jack says angrily. *"Do you have to be in charge of everything, including how I do my job? You want to control my every move, don't you?"*

What's happening here? **Jack is misinterpreting Ellen's desire to contribute something valuable to his situation and to be included in his process as an attempt to control him.**

Men get to feel like they're accomplishing things on their own.

One of the most common complaints I receive from women about men is that too often they leave their partner out of the decision-making process. *"When he makes a decision and doesn't mention it until it's done, I feel discounted, like I'm the camper, and he's the counselor,"* one woman said to me. Since women hate feeling this way, we make an effort to include ourselves in what's going on with the man we love—we ask questions, we offer advice. The problem occurs when a man misinterprets our interest and input as an attempt to interfere or control him.

Women want to feel like a team with their partner. You're going to read this over and over again throughout the book, because it's one of our biggest needs and issues. **So when we inquire about what's going on with our mate, or offer our input, it's *not* because we want to control him, but because we want to be involved**. We don't need to make the final decision all the time, but we would like to be in the loop.

Unfortunately, a woman's need to be included directly clashes with the need some men have to "do it alone." It's as if men believe that receiving help or advice makes them less powerful. So men conveniently dismiss their partner's offer of help by blaming her for being controlling, *and then they get to do it alone and feel autonomous.*

The Truth About Myth #3

Guys, please know that most of us women have love *at the top of our agenda, not control.* If we see you hurting, we want to make it better. If we see you struggling with a problem, we want to help you find a solution. If we see you not taking care of yourself, we want to offer our compassion and caring. If we see you feeling overwhelmed with worry, we want to be included so you know you're not alone. Why do we do all of this? Not because we want to control you, but because we love you!

Myth #4: Women Are Jealous and Possessive

"Women are so possessive—it's like they want to own men."

"Every woman I know is paranoid that their man's about to be stolen away from them."

"Guys can't even talk to another woman without their partner becoming unreasonably jealous."

"Women would be happy if they could lock men up so we'd never be able to look at another woman."

The following stories are true:

Candace is talking on the phone to her sister about her husband, Jake. "I'm so upset," she begins. "There's this woman at Jake's office that I know is after him. We were at a company function the other day, and I couldn't believe how she was acting. She kept putting her arm around him, making silly jokes, and complimenting him—all in front of me!"

"What does she look like?" Candace's sister asks.

"She's attractive, and she's single. Honestly, I felt sick watching it."

"Well, what does Jake have to say about it?"

"That's the problem. When I brought it up, he got really defensive and told me I was just being jealous and imagining things. But I'm not—I saw it with my own eyes."

Tyra's boyfriend, James, just received an invitation to a bachelor party for a friend. "Where's the party?" Tyra asks.

"Oh, at some club downtown," James replies evasively.

"What do you mean, some club? Don't tell me it's a strip club!"

"Well, I guess you could call it that."

"You aren't going, are you?" Tyra says in a tense voice.

"Of course I'm going. Phil and I went to college together. I can't miss it."

"This really upsets me, James. I hate the idea of you at some club like that, and I know what goes on at those parties."

"Don't be ridiculous," James retorts. "You're just getting possessive for no reason."

"No reason? I think having naked girls climbing all over you is a good reason!"

"Grow up, Tyra. You are so insecure!" James says angrily. "You wish you could dictate my every move, don't you? Well, I'm going to the party, and I don't want to hear any more about it."

It's nine o'clock in the evening, and Meg passes by her husband Alan's office and notices that he's on the computer. "Checking your e-mail?" she asks.

"Yes. I'll be off shortly," Alan answers.

Later as Alan comes to bed, Meg says, "You were on line for a long time. Did you get anything interesting in the mail?"

Alan pauses for a moment, and then responds, "I had a long letter from my friend Charlotte."

"Charlotte—isn't she the one you used to date?"

"Oh, that was ages ago," Alan replies. "Long before you and I even met."

"Well, what's she up to now?" Meg asks.

"She lives in Florida, and manages a health club company."

"Is she married?"

"No," Alan says with a bit of hesitation in his voice. "She's recently divorced."

"Well, do you two write often?" Meg inquires.

"What is this, *Court TV*?" Alan answers impatiently. "I feel like you're interrogating me."

"All I asked is if you wrote often."

"I don't know. I guess we write a couple of times a week."

As the conversation progresses, Meg is getting a tight knot in her stomach. He's writing this woman he used to date a couple of times a week? Taking a breath, she says, "Honey, don't you think it's kind of inappropriate for her to be writing a married man that much?"

"For God's sake, Meg," Alan says in a raised voice, "why are you making such a big deal of this? She's my friend. I can't believe how jealous and insecure you are."

Men, you're probably thinking that I've just presented three examples to illustrate that women are indeed jealous and possessive. Well, I'm sorry to disappoint you, but that's not actually what I had in mind when I shared these stories. All three of the women in these scenarios had one thing in common—**they were being protective of their intimate relationship with the man they loved. In each case, the woman felt some kind of** *possible threat or challenge to the special bond of intimacy she shared with her partner,* **and thus reacted protectively. And in each case, her man** *misinterpreted her protective instinct as jealousy.*

MYTH:	**Women are jealous and possessive.**
TRUTH:	**Women are protective of our intimate relationships.**

I have tried for years to get this point across to men. Women are instinctively protective of those we cherish and tuned in to any possible threat or danger that could come to our loved ones. You see this with mothers who are always on the lookout for a toy their child might trip over, or for a room that might be too drafty for their child to sleep in, or who are concerned about a friend with a cold who might infect their child.

This same protectiveness manifests itself in our relationship with men. Women are always tuned in to anything that might threaten our intimate connection with our beloved, and frankly one of the biggest threats is other women. I say this not as a value judgment about what goes on between people, but as an observation of the way the world is. So when a man asks his wife, "Don't you trust me?" the answer she wants to give is, "It's not a question of trusting you. *I don't trust other women.*"

When Meg became upset that her husband, Alan, was frequently e-mailing a former and newly single girlfriend, she wasn't being jealous—she was being protective. When Tyra was unhappy that James was going to a strip club where women are paid to arouse men, she wasn't being jealous, she was being protective. And when Candace told her sister she was worried about the woman at her husband's office who was falling all over him, she wasn't being jealous, she was being protective. In each case, these women's antennae went up as if their inner warning system said:

ATTENTION! ATTENTION! POSSIBLE INCOMING INAPPROPRIATE SEXUAL ENERGY DIRECTED TOWARD YOUR MAN! BE ON THE ALERT!

I have to interject here that in all the years of my own intimate relationships, I have NEVER been wrong in my suspicions that a woman was interested in my partner, or that he was flirting with her. Sometimes I didn't find out until years later that I was right, only because it took that long for the guy to admit that yes, he was attracted to that woman, or yes, he supposes she was coming on to him. But I was never just imagining it. And I feel this is true for most women—*we can smell impropriety coming from a mile away*. To be sure, there are women who have serious emotional problems and get jealous if their boyfriend so much as goes to the grocery store, but I'm not referring to that extreme kind of dysfunction. Instead, I'm focusing on the **everyday protectiveness that men mislabel as jealousy**.

What we're really talking about here is **boundaries,** *the boundaries of honoring and respecting the intimate energy shared by the two members of a committed couple; energy that shouldn't be shared with anyone else.* Women tend to be very sensitive to boundaries and anything that might threaten to break through them. Tyra had a boundary that she should be the only naked woman who sits on her boyfriend's lap, and if he went to the strip club, she was certain that boundary would be violated. Candace had a boundary that she should be the only woman to flirt with and put her arms around her husband in an intimate way, and the woman at the office violated that boundary. And Meg had a boundary that she should be the only woman with whom her husband spends hours a week communicating his thoughts and feelings, and his former girlfriend violated that boundary.

Is it possible that in each of these cases, the women were completely overreacting, and there were only the purest intentions coming from the coworker or the former lover or the lap dancer? Well, except in the case of the lap dancer, perhaps. But I have to tell you, I tend to believe that, more often than not, *women pick up on inappropriate sexual energy much earlier than do men.* Besides, even if these women were wrong in these particular instances, their intentions were still coming from a protective and not a jealous place.

What problems occur when men believe Myth #4?

*Men feel women are accusing them of being untrustworthy.

When men interpret protective behavior as possessive behavior, they often mistakenly conclude that their mate doesn't trust them and become offended and angry. But the woman's reaction usually has nothing to do with trusting him or not trusting him. It has to do with pointing out a potentially unpleasant or harmful situation.

Imagine that you are about to take a trip to a remote region of a foreign country. A friend hears about your journey, and says to you, "Listen, I was told there are poisonous spiders in this particular jungle near where you'll be, so if I were you, I'd avoid going there, just to be safe." How would you react? Would you say, *"Don't you trust me? Don't you think I can protect myself?"* Of course not. You'd thank your friend for being so thoughtful and for caring about your welfare.

Now imagine, guys, that your girlfriend detects a situation in which you might be exposed to energies that aren't particularly supportive to your intimate relationship: another woman who is interested in you, either overtly or covertly; an environment or friend that encourages temptation or infidelity. When she points this out to you, she is doing the same thing just described. **She isn't saying she doesn't trust you. She isn't saying she thinks you will cheat on her or betray her. She is merely trying to protect you from being exposed to what she considers potentially dangerous or problematic.**

What Women Want Men to Know:

Men often totally discount their woman's protective concerns because they feel insulted or unfairly accused, thus blinding themselves to a situation to which they really should pay attention.

I knew a man once who made this error and paid for it dearly. His wife had expressed concerns about a female friend of his, worrying that this woman seemed interested in being more than friends. She had no hard evidence to prove this—it was just the way the woman looked at her husband, the excuses she always found to call him about something, even her body language when she was near him. Her husband, who was a very sweet and gentle guy, felt offended that his wife would think these unkind thoughts about his female friend, and even more upset that his wife assumed he wouldn't notice something like this if it was happening, which in his opinion, it wasn't at all. His response was to totally ignore his wife's admonitions, and to rebelliously spend even more time with this other woman, just to prove to himself and his wife that there was nothing at all to worry about.

Well, you can guess what happened. One night when his wife was out of town on business, the "friend" called the husband to say she was very upset about something, and needed him to come over to her place and talk. His wife's words were ringing in his ears as he drove over to the woman's house, but the rebel in him refused to feel controlled by what he considered to be his wife's jealousy, and he put it out of his mind. As he sat on the couch with this woman, he noticed that she was wearing very revealing clothing, and even though warning bells went off in his head, he still insisted to himself that his wife was wrong and he was right. Within minutes, however, the warning bells turned to loud sirens when in a swift move, his friend pulled off her shirt, grabbed his hands and placed them on her naked breasts, and told him how much she wanted him!

In case you're wondering, no—he didn't sleep with her, or even kiss her. He awkwardly rebuffed her advances, and left. But the damage was done. *By invalidating his wife's concerns as ridiculous jealousy and overreaction, and not paying attention to the potential danger she suspected, he'd put himself in a situation where he'd ended up touching another woman's naked breasts and compromising his own sense of fidelity.* Now he had to deal with his guilt, what to tell his wife, and the knowledge that every time they saw this other woman in social settings, the sordid scene would replay itself in his mind.

You get the message, guys. **Don't let your pride and ego interfere with your better judgment. Don't lie to yourself about a situation out of stubbornness.** Protect yourself and your relationship by paying attention to the smoke, so it doesn't become a fire!

**Men get reactive and feel we're trying to curtail their freedom.*

"Stop trying to control who I decide to have in my life."

"If I want to be friends with that woman, I will be."

These are the kinds of comments women often hear when we attempt to protect our relationship by pointing out a potential problem with another woman. **Men misinterpret our protectiveness as an attempt to control them, to rob them of their freedom** (see Myth #7). Many times, *men, you can't even hear the information a woman is attempting to give you because you react to the fact that she's giving you feedback to begin with!* So you end up ignoring her concerns and rebelling, just to prove that you are free to do whatever you want. This is exactly what happened to the husband in the previous story, and he ended up with his hands full of trouble, so to speak!

The Truth About Myth #4

Women are instinctively protective about what is valuable to us. And guys, we value you. You are our treasure, and our

> releationship with you is precious. We never want anything
> to harm it, never want anything to threaten it. So we are al-
> ways on the lookout for danger—not because we don't trust
> you, but because we love you and don't want to lose you.

Myth #5: Women Are Too Emotional

*"Women are way too sensitive—you say one thing to them
and they fall apart."*

*"Everything is about feelings to women. Instead of thinking,
they just react."*

"Living with a woman is one big emotional melodrama."

This is one of the myths about women that really bugs me, because it negatively characterizes one of the most beautiful qualities
women possess—the ability to feel deeply and to express those
feelings—as a *character flaw rather than a gift*. This characteriza-
tion is based on a value judgment that says to show emotions is
somehow a less desirable state than to cover up emotions. Of
course, this is one of the messages most men received from the
time they were little boys: to hold back tears is more courageous
than to cry; to be tough is more desirable than to be afraid; to be independent is stronger than to need.

In my opinion, men spend their entire lives recovering from
this social conditioning that robs them of their ability to honor and
show emotion. But one of the many unfortunate consequences of
this kind of thinking is that men often project the standards that
have been imposed upon them onto women, and according to those

standards, we fail miserably. What's the result? **Men often misin-terpret women's natural sensitivity as weakness, our ability to feel deeply as dramatic indulgence, and our expression of emo-tion as an indication that we are a mess.**

MYTH: Women are too emotional.
TRUTH: Women are in touch with our feelings.

Once again, let me offer a disclaimer: There are women, just as there are men, who are emotionally unbalanced and out of control. But here we're talking about the average woman who feels deeply and readily expresses those feelings. The mistake men make is characterizing a woman as too emotional simply because she is in touch with her emotions.

What do men mean by "too emotional"? **I think they mean "too emotional" for how they think a man should be.** It's as if men have an invisible barometer that measures feelings, and the mea-surement has to fall below a certain point for them to feel they are normal. They can be sad, but not too sad, and crying is definitely over the top. They can be scared, but not too scared, and feeling out of control is absolutely unacceptable. Anger is okay, because it's a more macho emotion to many men, as opposed to a "weak" emo-tion. Need and loneliness, on the other hand, are more vulnerable emotions, and must be kept in check. Of course, I'm generalizing, but you get the point: **Men judge women's emotionality by their own standards regarding what is acceptable or unacceptable for a man. That's why women appear to be too emotional.**

There's another reason men misinterpret a woman's expression of emotion as a sign of weakness or instability—*women don't compartmentalize emotions like men do, and so it appears that we are not in control of our feelings.* Remember Chapter 1, in which we talked about how women put love first, and rather than having a Love Room, the whole house of our consciousness is dedicated to love? Well, for a woman, if something is not right in one room of the house, it's not right in the whole house. We are always a wife or girlfriend or lover first, no matter what else we are doing. Men, on the other hand, can walk out of the Love Room, where there may be a problem, flip a switch in their brain, and suddenly they are an accountant or a dentist or a computer programmer. *Because men are able to compartmentalize like this, it is easier for them to block off feelings, whereas it is much more difficult for most women to shut off our emotions and go about our business as if nothing is the matter.*

What Women Want Men to Know:

Just because women can't shut off feelings as easily as men can doesn't mean we are feeling too much.

As we discussed in previous chapters, women are highly tuned in to people and to the world around us. We are, for the most part, more sensitive than men, physically, emotionally, and psychically. But sensitivity is not the same as weakness. Indeed, it is a gift.

I believe one of the reasons the Higher Power that manifested the universe we live in chose to create two sexes with very different temperaments was because there is a lot we are supposed to teach each other. From men, women have the opportunity to learn about the power of focus, how to exist in the world from a position of strength, and so much more. And one of the most important lessons men get to learn from women is how to live more from the heart and honor their feelings.

When men believe Myth #5, several problems develop.

Men use this myth as an excuse to discount a woman's emotions.

Meredith and her husband, Tom, decide to meet after work for dinner at a neighborhood restaurant. Tom has been working on a difficult project and hasn't had much time to relax lately. After the waiter takes their order, they begin discussing how the day went for both of them.

"So what's going on with the project?" Meredith asks.

"It's just a mess," Tom replies. "I don't know if I can take this stress."

"Tell me what the problem is, honey. Maybe I can help you think it through."

"Oh sure," Tom retorts sarcastically, "you're going to fix it for me!"

"Tom, I'm just trying to help."

"No, you're trying to interfere."

Meredith feels her heart begin to ache, and tears fill her eyes. "Tom, you don't need to speak to me that way. It really hurts my feelings."

"Oh geez, you're so damn sensitive," Tom responds in a loud voice. "I can't even have a simple conversation with you."

What's happening here? Tom, who's usually a kind and sweet guy, is not being very polite or respectful to his wife. Yes, it's probably because he's so stressed out from work, but that's no reason for him to take it out on Meredith, and he knows it. So when Tom sees Meredith start to cry, and realizes he hurt her feelings, he feels awful. But because he's proud and doesn't like to feel he's done something wrong, it's hard for him to admit to himself or to her that he's behaving badly. What does he do instead? He turns the responsibility around and blames Meredith for being too sensitive. If she weren't so vulnerable, he tells himself, she wouldn't have reacted as strongly to what he said.

What Women Want Men to Know:

Men often blame women for being too sensitive or emotional in order to avoid taking responsibility for their own insensitive words or deeds.

This pattern of interaction I'm describing is so common that I'm sure women reading about it will think, "That's happened to me hundreds of times!" Men, if you're honest with yourself, you'll admit that you've been guilty of behaving this way with the woman you love. *You suddenly realize you've said or done something to hurt her feelings, and rather than copping to it and apologizing, you blame her for overreacting.* You use this myth as an excuse to discount her feelings and avoid dealing with your own sense of guilt or regret.

Men use this myth as a way to cover up their feelings of powerlessness.

Linda is lying in bed with her husband, Howard, confiding her fears and worries about her mother, whom she may have to put in a nursing home. Tears pour down Linda's cheeks as she describes her phone call with her mother earlier in the day. "She begged me not to put her in a home," Linda cries, holding tightly to Howard. "I tried to explain that she needs full-time care, and that she can't get it unless she's in a supervised facility, but she just went on and on about how terrified she was. I feel so guilty."

Howard listens to his wife pour her heart out and doesn't know what to say. He wants to console her, but he doesn't seem to have a solution to her problem. "Look, Linda, you just have to get a grip on things," he begins. "You can't let yourself fall apart like this."

"I can't help it," Linda sobs. "It's killing me to see Mom so sad."

"Don't make this into a bigger drama than it is," Howard says. "You're getting too emotional over this."

"Too emotional? How can you say something so cold? I'm talking about putting my mother in a nursing home for the rest of her life until she dies!" Linda replies in a shocked voice as she gets out of bed and retreats to the bathroom to cry by herself.

What's going on in this scenario? Howard is feeling powerless to do anything to help his wife with her terrible dilemma. He doesn't know what to say, and as he lies there listening to her tears, he feels as if he's letting her down because he can't make things better for her. Frustrated, he tries to get her to stop feeling how she's feeling and ends up blaming her for overreacting in order to cover up his own sense of inadequacy.

Society teaches men that their value is defined by what they do and accomplish. This makes most men *solution oriented*—they want to solve problems and fix whatever isn't working. But in the world of feelings, that's not always possible:

What Women Want Men to Know:

Often when men are faced with someone they love who is hurting, they feel powerless to do anything to take the hurt away and thus feel they've failed.

> **To cover up this feeling of failure, men may blame the women they love for having the emotions that are causing them to feel so powerless.**

Whenever I explain this pattern to men, they are genuinely surprised, and even relieved—they haven't understood why they react the way they do when their mate is upset; why sometimes they shut down, or become frustrated, irritated, or angry at their partner when she cries or is frightened. "I watch myself become more and more annoyed whenever my wife gets really vulnerable or emotional," one man confessed to me, "and I feel terrible reacting that way, but I can't seem to help it. You're right—*it's because I love her and I can't stand to see her hurting, and I don't know what to do to make it better.*"

In our chapter on communication, I'll share some suggestions for how men can talk to a woman when she's upset so that she feels loved, without having to have any solutions for her problem.

The Truth About Myth #5

Most women are not *too* emotional—we are emotional. And guess what? So are men, only you have a harder time showing it. The truth is, what you love about women is our sensitivity and our ability to feel, because that's what allows us to adore you and make you feel so good!

Myth #6: Women Who Appear to Be Strong and Competent Don't Need to Be Taken Care Of

"Women who are powerful and successful don't really want men in their lives—they'd rather be alone."

"She's so strong, she can handle anything."

"Women who are independent don't need men for anything."

Recently I was attending a meditation retreat, and I met up with a female acquaintance I've known informally for some time. Julianne is a very successful attorney and a truly radiant woman. She exudes poise and self-confidence, and regularly speaks in front of large groups. When she asked me what I was working on, I told her about this book. Instantly, her eyes lit up, and she grabbed my arm. "Listen, Barbara," Julianne said. "Here's the most important thing you need to tell men—*just because a woman is strong and independent in her career doesn't mean she has no needs. We still need nurturing; we still need to be taken care of, even if it doesn't always look like it.*"

I thanked Julianne, and as I turned to leave, she called out, "Barbara—one more thing. Call me and tell me as soon as the book comes out. I need to give a copy to my husband. He thinks I'm superwoman."

Over and over again in researching this chapter, I heard statements like Julianne's from women that all illustrate Myth #6:

"My partner doesn't understand that despite the fact that I'm very independent and strong, I often need reassurance and tenderness. At times I probably appear to be so tough that I can take anything—but sometimes I'd love a little more sympathy, empathy, and caretaking."

"When my husband says 'You're strong, I know you can handle it,' I feel like he is dismissing my needs. Yes, I'm strong, but I still like to be taken care of."

"Just because I am competent doesn't mean I don't like to be babied and pampered sometimes. When a man goes out of his way to take care of me like that, it really makes me feel loved, and very feminine."

"Even though I'm financially independent and take my career seriously, that doesn't mean I am not tender or that I don't have needs, because I do. When I come home to my husband at the end of the day, I don't want to have to be the tough, aggressive person I am from nine to five. I want to let my defenses down and be loved and reassured."

I've found that many men have erroneously determined that there are two types of women in the world: the kind that are vulnerable and dependent, and need to be protected and taken care of; and the kind that are strong, together, and capable, and therefore don't need to be taken care of. So when a man has a partner who, for instance, has a high-powered job, or is very dynamic and organized, he often mistakes her competence and confidence as an indication that she doesn't need or want to be taken care of, that she's not "the kind of woman" he needs to worry about.

MYTH: Women who appear competent and strong don't need to be taken care of.

> TRUTH: **Just because women are strong and capable doesn't mean we don't want and need to be nurtured and taken care of.**

The mistake men make is *that they misinterpret strength and competence for self-sufficiency*. Just because a woman is highly competent and confident doesn't mean she has no needs. It doesn't mean we don't need someone else to be the strong one once in a while. And it doesn't mean it isn't hard for us to do all we do without sometimes feeling tired, frightened, or as though we've run out of steam. Part of the problem stems from the fact that women are so good at handling a multitude of tasks. Men see and admire this ability, and conclude that we don't ever need their help—but we do.

> ## What Women Want Men to Know:
>
> **Just because a woman feels competent and not in need of any help in one instance doesn't mean she feels that way all the time.**

A friend of mine told me a story that perfectly illustrates this point. She and her boyfriend recently moved in together. They live in an apartment on the third floor, and every time she goes grocery shopping, she has to carry the bags up three flights of stairs. My friend is athletic, so it's not impossible for her to make several trips up and down, but it's not her favorite thing in the world to do.

One day, after having done an unusually large amount of food shopping, she walked into the apartment, her arms bursting with heavy bags, to find her boyfriend lying on the couch watching television. "Hi, honey," she puffed, trying to catch her breath. "Do you think you could help me with the rest of the groceries?"

Her boyfriend looked up with a smile and replied, "Aw, I know how strong you are. I've seen you do it for months now. You're just being lazy, sweetie."

"I'm serious, could you just help me with the last batch? The trunk is still full of stuff."

"What's gotten into you?" he replied distractedly, not taking his eyes off of the TV screen. "You always carry all the groceries."

My friend was furious at her boyfriend for assuming that just because she *could* carry the bags by herself, she *should* always carry the bags, and therefore, he was exempt from having to help. It's not that he was trying to be selfish or even insensitive—he was just falling prey to Myth #6.

Being a strong, independent, and capable woman myself, I've been on the receiving end of this myth in my own life. Because I can do so much so well, the man in my life has often assumed that I must not need his help in anything. I remember one time when I was feeling particularly overwhelmed and collapsed in tears in front of my mate, listing all the things I was worried about. This man in question actually laughed at me. "Barbara," he said, "how can you expect me to take you seriously? I mean, you're Miss Accomplishment. You can do anything."

"But I feel so vulnerable right now, and I just need your support," I answered tearfully.

"Oh come on, I've seen you conquer bigger problems than these. These are nothing. Don't let them get to you!"

How did his attitude make me feel? Like it makes most women feel—that we are being penalized for being competent, that we've given up the right to ask for support or help just because we don't need it a lot of the time, that we only have the right to reach out to our partner under the most serious conditions, or when we have turned into a basket case.

What Women Want Men to Know:

Guys, sometimes women want you to help us do something *even if we can do it ourselves*. Sometimes we just like feeling your strength, your support, your protection. Sometimes we like hearing you ask *"What can I do for you?"* because it gives us the opportunity to feel safe and valued. *And sometimes we wish you would notice that we need help even before we do, and not wait for us to have to ask.*

As one woman wrote in her survey:

"Please tell men that sometimes I need to be taken care of and sometimes I don't. If you're not sure, just ask me. But don't assume because I was fine last week, I will be this week."

What do men get out of believing Myth #6?

*Men use this myth as an excuse not to feel responsible for taking care of us emotionally.

When Ellie met Gary, an optometrist, he was just finalizing his divorce from his first wife, Claire. Gary was enthralled by Ellie and was particularly impressed that she owned her own highly successful home-decorating business and supervised a staff of six employees. "Ellie and Claire couldn't be more different," he admitted to me as he and Ellie sat before me for a consultation. "Claire never worked except for odd jobs here and there selling cosmetics, and she always seemed very fragile and vulnerable. When we were married, she'd call me ten times a day to ask me the simplest questions: What day should she tell the plumber to come and fix the sink? What should she do with the box the new microwave came in? Did I think she should make pasta for dinner, or would I rather have Chinese food? It was like she couldn't make any decisions without me."

"So how did you feel when you starting dating Ellie?" I asked.

"Relieved!" Gary exclaimed. "I felt like I was finally with a grown-up, someone I didn't have to worry about and take care of all the time."

"That's just it," Ellie piped in. "He never worries about me or feels I need him for anything, even when I ask."

"Oh come on, honey," Gary replied. "You are the most together woman I know! There's nothing you can't do or figure out—I've seen it."

"Yes, I'm strong, but that doesn't preclude me from wanting your support and protection sometimes."

"But I know you'll be fine, with or without my input, so why do I need to worry about you?"

"Because I'm your wife!" Ellie said as tears filled her eyes. *"Because I don't want to always be compared to Claire and have you think that since I'm so much more functional than she was, I don't 'qualify' to be taken care of! Because I don't want to have to be a mess to deserve a little nurturing!"*

I've seen this pattern in relationships time and time again. A man who played the role of caretaker and rescuer in a previous relationship meets a woman who seems so capable and together that he tells himself she doesn't need any nurturing. Like Gary, **he is so relieved not to have to always feel responsible for his mate this time around that he overlooks his new partner's needs, con-**

cluding that she is strong and therefore exempt from requiring
that he take care of her in any way.

Sometimes, a man has so much built-up resentment from the
years he spent acting more like a father than a husband that he even
takes this anger out on his new mate, reacting negatively when she
shows the slightest neediness or vulnerability. It's as if unconsciously he finally feels safe to express all of those bottled-up feelings because he knows it won't totally crush his new love as it
would have crushed his old love. Well, perhaps it won't crush her,
but it does hurt her. One woman complained in an interview:

*"For years when they were married, my husband ran around
catering to every little need and mood his ex-wife had. But now in
our relationship, when I ask him for the simplest thing, or tell him
I'm feeling insecure or need some support, he blows up. It's not
fair—how come she got to be taken care of all the time, but I don't
even get to feel a little needy once in a while?!"*

The Truth About Myth #6

Don't let strong, competent women fool you, men. We
are still women, and no matter how independent or capable
we seem, we do have a primal need to feel you taking care
of us sometimes in both big and small ways. There is a part
of us that melts and softens when we feel you there to support us, to believe in us, and to be our shoulder to lean on,
no matter how strong our own shoulders may be. And here
is a secret for you to remember: Guess which women need
to really feel taken care of? The ones who are so good at
taking care of others...

Myth #7: Women Want to Rob Men of Their Freedom

"Once you marry a woman, it's the ball and chain for you!"

"All women want is to tell men what to do until they have no mind of their own left."

"When you make a commitment to a woman, forget about your freedom—it's history."

Here we have one of the most notorious of the seven myths about women, the one men grumble about when they're together, the one they intone as the reason they're not in a committed relationship, the one they use to explain their resistance to going along with what their partner wants. Women just want to enslave men, this myth says. Slowly, bit by bit, women will try to take away a man's freedom until he is groveling at her feet. Naturally, this horrible fate must be avoided at all costs. How? **By not giving in to her and her requests.**

You can hear the echoes of this myth in the kinds of statements men say to each other in commenting on their relationships with women:

"She has you wrapped around her finger, buddy."

"Brother, you are whipped. That woman has her way with you."

"He can't agree to go with us until he gets permission from his 'boss,' I mean his wife, isn't that right?"

All of these remarks send one message to men: *If you aren't careful, your woman will take away your freedom and you will end up weak and powerless.*

How do men feel women try to rob them of their freedom? We want men to spend time with us. We want them to talk about their feelings. We want them to let us know they need us. We want them to communicate with us about their schedule and their plans. We want them to show us they love us. We want them to include us in their important decisions. We want them to receive our support and input. We want them to work on staying close and connected.

What do all of these requests add up to? Are they tactics women use to manipulate the man we love? Are they secret methods for emasculating him? Are they sinister techniques for making him our slave? NO! **They are simply the ways women want men to help us create a committed, intimate relationship.**

MYTH: **Women want to rob men of their freedom.**
TRUTH: **Women want to create a committed, intimate relationship.**

Here's the problem: **Men often misinterpret a woman's normal—and I believe reasonable—requests for participation in the relationship as her attempt to rob him of his freedom.** They feel that in giving in to their mate on just about anything, even if it's something as simple as agreeing to call her when he arrives at a destination, or talking about a topic she brings up, or implementing an idea she has, he will somehow be losing his independence. This fear of relinquishing his freedom and his consequential reactivity to her efforts sets up an adversarial and unhealthy dynamic in the relationship:

What Women Want Men to Know:

When a man has a big issue with proving to himself that he is free, every interaction with his mate

---

> **becomes a power struggle in which he feels he must come out on top.**

It's Sunday morning, and Patty and her husband, Matt, are lying in bed. "What do you want to do today, honey?" Patty asks.

"I don't know, let's see how the day unfolds," Matt answers.

"But it's already ten o'clock, Matt, and we agreed that this weekend we'd look for paint colors for the bathroom and check out the sale at the electronics store to see if we can pick up a new fax machine."

"I know how it works," Matt replies sarcastically. "It starts with a few errands, and before I know it, you're dragging me into a dozen stores and my day is shot."

"Gee, Matt, all I wanted was to do a few things together, and you make it sound like I'm kidnapping you or something," Patty says in a hurt voice.

"Well, that's how it feels, like I'm a hostage in my own car, like I'm trapped into a day I didn't choose."

The conversation ends, and Patty is frustrated and confused. She can't understand why it's so difficult for her husband to agree to a simple plan, and why he becomes so resistant to any little request she makes. And how is Matt feeling? He feels successful that he "won," that he didn't give in to Patty. Ironically, he actually did want to buy paint and check out the fax machine, **but a part of him couldn't say "yes" to his wife without feeling he would lose something in the process—his sense of freedom.**

———

This is a perfect example of how Myth #7 creates power struggles in relationships. **For a man who buys into this myth, even the most** insignificant interaction becomes about guarding against what he perceives as threats to his freedom, rather than about cooperating with the woman he loves. When his wife asks him a question, he feels he will lose his freedom if he answers on the spot. When she suggests an idea for how he can handle a situation, he feels he'll lose his freedom if he goes along with her suggestion. When she tries to make plans, he feels he'll lose his freedom if he commits.

In deference to the women reading this section, we need to stop for a moment and answer the question that's burning in all of our minds: *What the heck is this "freedom" men are talking about? What do they mean when they say they "need their freedom"? Freedom to do what?*

I've spent many years, both personally and professionally, trying to understand this concern for freedom that men have, and I must admit I am continually amazed at how men actually define the experience of being free in regard to their intimate relationships. Guys, as I've analyzed it, I've come to the conclusion that when you say you want to maintain your freedom, you mean the following:

- *Freedom not to have to answer to your partner*

- *Freedom not to have to explain yourself or your behavior*

- *Freedom not to have to be anywhere or do anything you don't want to do*

- *Freedom not to have to talk to your mate when you aren't in the mood to discuss anything*

- *Freedom not to have to make plans or commitments*

- *Freedom not to feel obligated to take care of your woman's needs if you don't feel like it*

- *Freedom not to have to deal with your partner's issues*

- *Freedom not to have to explain why you need so much freedom*

I must confess that when I read this list, I feel like saying to men: *"You want all of those freedoms? Fine—then go be alone! You can have all the freedom you want by yourself."* All right, so I'm reacting a little dramatically, but isn't that what this list amounts to—a description of being single? When you're not in a relationship, you don't have to answer to anyone or do anything you don't want to do, or make plans, or deal with another person's needs. But when you fall in love, you trade some of these "freedoms" for the joy of sharing your life with another human being. **It's the price you pay for the gift of love.**

This is what perplexes women about men: You want to be with us and love us and have us love you, but you don't want to feel *obligated* to do anything that would take away your freedom. My answer to this is *that the kind of freedom some men are so terrified of losing is really an illusion, a freedom they never had in the first place.*

When it comes to living in this world, very few of us, unless we live alone on a desert island, have the freedom not to be concerned with people or things around us. Each time you drive a car, you're giving up your freedom, because unless you want to get arrested, you stay on the roads, obey the traffic signals, and follow the rules. Each time you go to work, you're giving up your freedom, because you're doing what someone else asks you to do, you dress in a way that has been deemed to be acceptable in your workplace, and you spend time trying to please others, whether it's the client or customer or your coworkers or your employer. Each time you turn on the television, you're giving up your freedom, because your senses are being bombarded by images someone else has created, and even though you do control the channel changer, you're still momentarily seeing things you did not choose to see and hearing things you did not choose to hear.

In this same way, **the moment you enter into an intimate relationship with another person, you are relinquishing a certain amount of your freedom.** From that point on, someone else is going to react to what you say and do, have expectations of you, need things from you, project her issues onto you, and affect you with her moods, energies, personality, and desires. *That's what a relationship is—letting yourself be affected by someone else.*

True freedom in a relationship is not about what you get to do or not do now that you're with someone else— it's being free to love without fear, to receive without resistance, and to give without holding back.

What happens when men believe Myth #7?

•Men use this myth as an excuse to avoid making a commitment.
"Sure, I'd love to have a steady girlfriend, but I'm not the type of guy who can give up my freedom, know what I mean?"

"When I realized Sue wanted to get married, I broke off the relationship. She was trying to chain me, and I'm the kind of guy who needs a lot of space and freedom."

In spite of what these men are saying, it's not losing their freedom that they're afraid of—it's making a commitment to an intimate relationship. Committing to love another person is scary. You open yourself up to being hurt, to being rejected, to the possibility of loss. For some men, the fear of this kind of pain is so strong that they avoid getting too close or making a commitment to a woman. However, they're not about to say, "Look, I'm terrified of commitment, so I can't open my heart to you," or "My last girlfriend cheated on me, and I'm too scared to trust love again." These sentiments would make them appear weak and not in control—and this wouldn't be very manly! Instead, they use Myth #7 as an excuse: *"I'd love to be with a woman if I could find one who wouldn't try to take away my freedom,"* they insist. In other words, the reason they aren't in a committed relationship is because all the women they meet are too demanding and controlling.

The problem with a man who stereotypes a woman as wanting to rob him of his freedom is that he'll overreact to even her slightest attempt to create closeness, and miss the very love that could heal his heart of the pain that caused it to close down in the first place.

The Truth About Myth #7

Women aren't trying to rob men of anything. On the contrary, *we're trying to give you something—our love, our devotion, our loyalty.* All of our efforts to communicate with you, spend time with you, be intimate with you, and work things out with you are not attempts to take away your freedom, but to create the best relationship possible.

Seven Mantras to Combat Seven Myths

There's a principle in metaphysics that says in order to control your mind and create your desired reality, you should replace your negative thoughts with positive thoughts. For instance, instead of thinking, "I can't succeed," you tell yourself "I have everything it takes to be successful." I had the idea that I should end this chapter with a similar suggestion for how men can take each of the seven myths about women and replace them with seven positive characterizations.

I call these the seven mantras to combat the seven myths. The word *mantra* comes from Sanskrit, and means a word or phrase that uplifts and enlightens the soul who repeats it. I thought it might be useful to create seven uplifting thoughts that men (and women) could think to themselves whenever they discover that they're focusing on the negative. For instance, if you find yourself thinking, *"My wife is being so controlling right now,"* you could make a conscious decision to think the mantra that's the antidote for that myth: *"My wife is trying hard to make a contribution to me and to be included."* Doesn't that sound better? It will feel better, too.

Here are seven loving mantras about women:

Seven Mantras to Combat the Seven Myths About Women

OLD MYTH	*NEW MANTRA*
1. *She's never satisfied.*	**She is really committed to making things the best they can be.**
2. *Being with her is so much work.*	**She is really committed to love and to making this relationship successful.**
3. *She wants to control me.*	**She wants to contribute to my life because she loves me.**

---

4. *She is so jealous and possessive.*	***She is really committed to protecting our relationship.***
5. *She is way too emotional.*	***She has such a tender and open heart.***
6. *She's so together—she doesn't need me to take care of her.*	***Even though she is strong, she needs to know I am there for her.***
7. *She wants to rob me of my freedom and smother me.*	***She is committed to creating a great relationship and staying connected.***

For a man to redefine these seven myths about women is a great act of commitment and devotion. Guys, when you decide to practice seeing the best about your partner rather than the worst, you will be giving both yourself and your mate an invaluable gift—to learn what it is like to see and be seen through the eyes of love.

PART
II

WHAT WOMEN WANT MEN TO KNOW ABOUT LOVE, INTIMACY, AND COMMUNICATION

CHAPTER EIGHT

How to Avoid Turning a Perfectly Sane Woman into a Raving Maniac

I consider myself to be a very sane woman. Most of the time I am reasonable, logical, centered, and easygoing. I have a high level of self-confidence and intelligence. I have undergone over thirty years of professional training, study, spiritual practices, and personal therapy, all of which have given me extensive psychological skills that help me deal with life's inevitable emotional challenges. Yet I must confess that in spite of all of this experience and all these attributes, when I am in an intimate relationship, the man I love can make me feel completely crazy!

I love the title of this chapter, and so do all the women I've showed it to, because most of us have experienced this phenomenon time and time again—*one minute we are feeling perfectly calm and sane, then suddenly our mate does or says something that brings out the worst in us, and in the next moment we find ourselves deteriorating into the kind of woman we vowed we'd never become.* It's as if he pushes the exact button that makes us feel insecure or frightened or needy or jealous or angry. **And what's always so frustrating about this process is that our partner doesn't seem to get the connection between his behavior and the undesirable reaction it produces in us!**

How many times in my own relationships have I witnessed the man I love say just the thing that is guaranteed to make me feel like . . . well, like something unmentionable. Even then, I would try to get him off the hook and give him a chance to remedy the situation. "Do you really mean that?" I'd ask, hoping he would realize what he'd said and retract it. Or I'd reply, "That really scares me," or "It hurts me when you do that," thinking that perhaps if he understood the negative effect his expression or action was having on me, he'd reconsider. But no, most of the time my partner was clueless, forging ahead with no apparent awareness of the fact that *the stand he was taking was guaranteed to bring out the worst in me, and stubbornly refusing to respond any differently in spite of my warnings, hints, and pleas.*

Of course, I'm not alone in my frustration. I've talked to literally thousands of women who've described this very same scenario. "I know my husband doesn't mean to hurt me or make me feel horrible," they'll say, "but it's as if he has a list of all the things he can do to drive me crazy, and he just does them one after another, and then can't understand why I go nuts!"

I agree with this comment—I, too, know that most men don't mean to hurt the woman they love and certainly have no intention of doing or saying things that will elicit her worst qualities. But unfortunately, this happens all the time, because men simply aren't aware of what they do that drives women crazy. And that's what this chapter is all about.

Guys, wouldn't you like to know what you can do to avoid turning your wonderful partner into a woman you can't stand to be with? Ladies, do you ever wonder why you go through this terrible metamorphosis from a reasonable and confident person to an insecure, paranoid mess? In this chapter, I'll reveal the answers to you as we look at the biggest mistakes men make in their relationships with women, and what men do, perhaps unknowingly and unintentionally, that can transform a calm, sweet woman into an emotional wreck.

The following is the formula for bringing out the worst in a woman. Why would a man ever want to use a formula like this? Well, he would if he wanted to make a woman unhappy, or to force her to break up with him, or to drive her crazy. Of course, most men do not have these goals in mind, and therefore would never apply the steps in this formula to the way they treat their partner, right? Wrong! *Whether you're aware of it or not, guys, you may be practicing the principles of this crazy-making formula in your relationship.*

Thousands of woman helped me create this list. During seminars, in interviews, and through written surveys, I asked them: *"What can a man do to bring out the worst in you?"* The formula in this chapter is the result of their honest answers and confessions. I think the information is priceless to any man who really loves women and wants fewer hassles in his love life.

Guys, if you've ever wanted to know the secret for making a woman happy, read this list with an open mind and a caring heart. It's **NOT** a *"to do"* list—it's actually a *"not to do"* list, since it will tell you what NOT to do if you want to bring out the best in your partner and have a harmonious and fulfilling relationship with a woman. In previous chapters, I hope you'll follow the suggestions I've been offering. However, this time, I want to say that **I hope you never do any of the following things!**

How to Bring Out the Worst in a Woman

1. **Don't talk to us.**

2. **Don't listen to us and ignore our needs.**

3. **Be rebellious.**

4. **Don't reassure or comfort us.**

5. **Flirt with other women.**

6. **Be distant and aloof.**

7. **Criticize us.**

8. **Be vague and ambiguous.**

9. **Be forgetful and procrastinate.**

10. **Don't pay attention to us.**

11. **Don't tell us what's going on with you.**

A NOTE TO MEN: Guys, you'll notice that I won't be sugar-coating any of the information that follows. I want to be as honest and to-the-point as possible, so that I hope you can see just what it is that you may be doing that has a negative effect on the woman you love. Remember: I believe that most men have no idea how power-fully their behavior impacts us, and really don't understand why women react the way we do. So this isn't about making men wrong—it's about trying to make the interaction between you and your partner more right!

1. Don't talk to us.

We want to discuss some plans with you. You change the subject. We try to make conversation over dinner or while driving in the car. You grunt a few times, but hardly respond.

We bring up an issue that is upsetting us. You tell us you don't want to talk about it.

Men are really good at not talking about what they don't want to talk about. I know what you're thinking—it's not your nature to express yourself; you're not always comfortable dealing with emotional issues; and you really enjoy being quiet, especially when you're stressed out or aren't in the mood to have to respond to anyone, even the woman you love. There's nothing wrong with any of this. **But the fact is that when you don't talk to a woman, it brings out the worst in us.**

I can just see your eyes rolling, and hear you sighing as you say to yourself, "Here we go—the lecture about how we need to talk more." Well, guess what, guys, it's true! It is first on this list because it is one of women's most predominant complaints about men, and the most frequently cited item when women are asked what brings out the worst in us.

When some men hear this, they protest, "What do you mean? I talk to my partner all the time." I'm not referring to talking about the weather or current events or the kids or other neutral topics—it's about responding to a woman's need to have a conversation about something in particular, whether it's planning for the future or dealing with a problem or discussing your relationship.

Here are some of the ways men make this first mistake, along with a description of the unappealing qualities you can look forward to seeing in your woman when you don't talk to us.

What Men Do That Drives Women Crazy
- You *don't respond* when we bring up something you don't want to discuss—you get *silent* or say one or two words, but basically *ignore what we've just said.*

- You *get angry with us* or make us feel wrong for wanting to talk about something, and *intimidate us* into dropping it.

- You are *evasive* when responding to what we ask you, and give us no real information or feedback.

- *You get up in the middle of a discussion and begin to do something else*—watch TV, play on your computer, look through papers on your desk, technically ending the conversation.

- You say we will talk about it at another time, *but never bring it up again from your side*, and when we do, you refuse to discuss it once more.

- You don't tell us what's bothering you, and instead, *pull away, shut down, and get distant.*

How Not Talking to Us Brings Out the Worst in a Woman

- We become *worried and anxious*, afraid of what you might be feeling that you won't tell us.

- We become *insecure* because we don't have the information we need to feel safe, and because we don't feel you care enough to talk to us.

- We feel *needy* because we feel you are pushing us away.

- We appear *pushy and persistent* as we try to get you to talk to us.

- We appear to *nag and complain* as we keep bringing up the topics we want to address.

- We appear *compulsive* as we keep talking, hoping you will eventually respond.

• We become *angry and resentful* that you don't care enough about our needs to talk to us.

What Women Want Men to Know:

When you don't talk to us or respond to us, we feel unloved and not cared for. We know it isn't always comfortable or desirable on your part to talk to us, but the consequences of not talking are far worse.

What Men Can Do:

1. When you find yourself feeling reactive, remind yourself that your woman's intention in wanting to talk is *not to control you, but to connect with you.*

2. *Don't just say nothing—acknowledge* the fact that we are trying to have a conversation, and if you cannot do it at the moment, *schedule a time that works for you.* (See Chapter 9 for more details.)

3. Remember that the longer you put off a conversation, whether it's about making plans or confronting a delicate issue, the more uncomfortable it's going to be when you finally get around to discussing it. *Tell yourself that the sooner you deal with it, the less painful the whole thing will be.*

---

2. Don't listen to us and ignore our needs.

We tell you what we need. You tell yourself it's not that impor-tant.

*We let you know we're not feeling happy in the relationship.
You dismiss it as our being cranky or complaining too much.*

*We explain that we have a difficult week coming up and would
like your help and support. You somehow block the information out
and don't offer one bit of what we asked for.*

Not all, but most women will eagerly give the man we love a
blueprint for making us happy. By the time the relationship is serious, we've told you what we want and need, what makes us feel
secure and what upsets us. Just to make sure you get it, we tell you
over and over again! **But way too often, guys, you don't listen to
us and totally ignore the very needs we've shared with you.**

Men don't listen in small and big ways. Your partner gets up the
courage to tell you she is feeling neglected, and you do nothing at
all about it. Days, weeks, months pass, and it's as if she never said
anything at all. Or she mentions that it would mean a lot if you'd
call her when she's out of town on her business trip, yet you simply
don't do it. Or she asks you to make sure when you baby-sit the
kids during her Wednesday night class that they don't watch TV
too close to their bedtime or they won't be able to sleep, and yet
each Wednesday when she arrives home, the kids are still up and
cranky from too much TV. All of these scenarios add up to the
same thing: **You either don't listen to what we tell you, or you
choose to ignore it.**

————————

Recently, a friend of mine called to tell me some sad news that
perfectly illustrates this mistake men make of not listening, and
how serious its consequences can be. Lynda had been married to
her husband, Irving, for eighteen years. They had raised two children and created what appeared to their friends to be a good marriage. But for the past five years, Lynda had been very unhappy.
Irving wasn't paying enough attention to her and seemed lost in his

own world of work and worries. He'd become moody and depressed, and took his anger out on Lynda and even the children by often losing his temper and in general by not being very pleasant to be with. Lynda and Irving hadn't had sex in ages, and the relationship was basically a mess.

Over and over, Lynda tried to talk to Irving about their problems. In the beginning, she would bring up the topic and begin to discuss her feelings, only to have him change the subject or walk away. As time passed with no changes, she became increasingly frustrated, and every few months she would tell Irving they *had* to have a talk, that things were terrible. Reluctantly, Irving would agree to sit down with Lynda. But each time, the same thing would happen—she would talk and cry and beg him to work with her on the relationship, and Irving would slump down on the couch, stare at his hands, and say nothing. Nothing changed. In the past nine months, Lynda told me, she'd gotten to the point where she had actually threatened Irving with divorce, desperately hoping to shock him into doing something to save their marriage, but even that didn't work.

One day, Lynda finally realized she couldn't go on any longer and decided it was time to tell Irving she wanted a separation. That night when he came home from work, he found Lynda sitting on the couch waiting for him. "Irving," she said in a voice choked with tears, "I've tried and tried, but I just can't try anymore. I think it would be best for us to separate, and I want you to move out."

Irving looked at his wife with total shock on his face. "You want to separate? Do you know what you're saying? I can't believe I'm hearing this. What happened?"

"What happened?" Lynda said in disbelief. "How can you ask me what happened? For five years I've been begging you to work on the relationship, crying to you about how unhappy I was, but obviously you just didn't listen!"

"How can you do this to me without giving me a chance? This is all so sudden. Don't you feel we should think about this?" Irving pleaded.

"I've given you a hundred chances to think about it," Lynda replied. "You can't seriously tell me you're surprised. Where have you been for the past few years?"

Lynda wept with frustration as she replayed this conversation for me. The worst part, she told me, was that Irving was a good man, and she knew, as impossible as it seemed to her, *that he truly hadn't heard what she'd been saying to him for five years*. "How could he ignore my warnings and pleas?" she asked me.

I'm not sure that I know the answer to Lynda's question. Perhaps Irving, like many men, didn't want to hear information that made him feel like a failure; perhaps he didn't have any solutions to Lynda's complaints, and therefore unconsciously chose to ignore them. Or perhaps he just didn't take her seriously, and dismissed what she was saying as mere nagging. But whatever the reason, he didn't listen, and the price he paid was that he lost his wife.

Guys, maybe when you don't listen to your woman's concerns and ignore her needs, the consequences aren't this severe, at least for now. But why make us get to the point of no return before you pay attention to us? Why drive us to being dramatic, hysterical, or threatening before you finally take our needs seriously? You will hate us when we become like this, and we will hate ourselves.

There's an old joke I sometimes tell in seminars when I'm trying to introduce this topic with a little humor:

A woman's been married to a man for forty years. And once a week for the past thirty years, she's told him if he doesn't change, she's leaving. One day he comes home to find her packing all of her belongings into suitcases and moving cartons. "What's wrong?" he asks. "Is there a problem?"

Women find this little anecdote amusing. Men, on the other hand, usually don't laugh. I've often wondered if it's because they don't get the joke, or if it's because they do get it, and they don't like it! But, guys, this is all I'm trying to say: **Don't push a woman to the point where she has to threaten to leave you, or shut down sexually, or turn into a bitch in order for you to finally listen to what she's trying to tell you.**

What Men Do That Drives Women Crazy

- You *don't acknowledge what we say* when we say it, and act like you can't wait until we finish talking so you can forget about it.

- You *invalidate what we say we need* by telling yourself, or us, that we're just being needy or demanding.

- *You hold out on giving us what we ask for until the very last minute*, as if you're seeing how far you can push us or if we'll give up.

- You *minimize the importance of what we need or ask for* by deciding that it's not really crucial, and conclude therefore that it's not necessary for you to respond.

- You act like you hear us and want to fulfill our needs when we express them to you, but then proceed to *ignore everything we said* and make no effort to do anything.

How Not Listening to Us and Ignoring Our Needs Brings Out the Worst in a Woman

- We become *insecure and frightened* because we feel as though you don't care about us.

- We become *needy* because we feel deprived when you don't even try to give us more of what we need.

- We appear to *nag and complain* as we repeatedly ask for the same things.

- We become *angry and resentful* because you ignore our feelings.

- We become *demanding and even threatening* in order to get your attention.

- We act *bitchy* when we realize you are choosing to ignore what is important to us.

- We become *anxious and high-strung*, always wondering if you will come through for us or not.

What Women Want Men to Know:

When you don't listen to us and ignore our needs, we feel as if you don't love us enough to take us seriously, and that you don't care about the effect this will have on us, or about the consequences to the relationship. Ironically, the longer you put off considering our needs, the more needy we become, and the harder it is to satisfy us when you finally get around to trying.

What Men Can Do:

1. Think of listening to us and what we want or need as an *insurance policy* for the relationship. We are giving you the keys to making us happy and, in turn, when we are happy, we will be a much better partner to you.

> **2.** For one week, *try focusing on just one need we express to you*—more affection; more time with the kids; picking up your clothes, etc.—and make an effort to give us a little of what we ask for.
>
> **3.** *Please take us seriously.* We mean what we say, and if we ask you for something, it's not a frivolous request—it's because it's very important to us. And that is because YOU are very important to us.

3. Be rebellious.

We ask you over and over again to please help us keep the bedroom orderly by putting your clothes away at the end of the day. You simply don't do it.

We tell you it bothers us when you read pornographic magazines, and that we'd prefer you didn't subscribe to them anymore. You tell us we're not your mother and to stop telling you what you can and cannot do.

We ask if you'd mind telling us that you won't be coming to bed right away on those nights when you're going to stay up late watching TV in the den, and saying good night so we don't wait for you. You get annoyed, claiming you aren't going to report your every move to us.

This is a touchy issue for you, guys, so I'm going to try to explain this as gently as possible. We've already talked in previous chapters about a man's innate need for a sense of independence, and his fear of losing his freedom. I know how sensitive you are to feeling you need to *"answer"* to a woman, or that you're *"obey-*

ing" her commands, or that she's *"ordering"* you around. But you need to know the truth—**a surefire way to turn a perfectly nice woman into an angry bitch is to let the rebellious part of you run your relationship.**

There, I've said it, and you may very well rebel against me and the information in this section. A primal part of you may react to your feeling that I am telling you to give up, give in, lie down, and let your woman walk all over you. Of course that is NOT what I'm saying at all. **This is not about giving up your freedom, but freeing yourself from the rebel who may be running your life.**

Where does the rebel come from? He originates in the part of every little boy that, at some point, must cut the childhood emotional ties that bind him to his mother, and redefine himself as separate and independent from her, thus becoming a man. This process of separation is essential if a boy is to grow into a healthy, autonomous male, and it necessarily involves a bit of rebellious behavior. In particular, this is true during the teenage years, as a young man strives to be not his mother's son, but to rebirth himself as his own person.

So what's the problem? Well, *in many boys, this separation process never completes itself*—sometimes because the mother hangs on too tightly and makes the son feel guilty for breaking away; sometimes because the son has to step in to fill the role of male in the house if his father is deceased, absent, or abusive, thus becoming very protective of his mother; and sometimes because the son's love is so strong and the family so close that he unconsciously remains emotionally enmeshed with his mother in a way that prevents him from feeling autonomous.

Guess what happens when a man never completes his emotional separation from his mother? He gets to *act it out with the other women in his life,* **particularly his wife, girlfriend, or lover, rebelling against what feels like their control, influence, or authority over him.** Sounds delightful, doesn't it?

Now you may be wondering, is the man aware that he's doing this? Probably not. Is his woman aware of it? Well, let's put it this way: Take a sweet, sensitive woman, combine her with a man who's acting out his rebellion, and what do you get? **A FRUSTRATED, ANGRY, NEUROTIC WOMAN WHO FEELS LIKE SHE'S GOING CRAZY!!**

How can you tell if you're a rebel, guys? Here's a quick true-or-false quiz for you to take. Of course, you don't *have* to take it if you don't want to (ha-ha).

Are You a Rebel?

1. **The word "pressure" is one of the more frequently used terms in your love vocabulary, as in:**

   "Don't pressure me about that or I'm out of here."
   "When you tell me what you want, it feels like pressure."
   "I really hate when you pressure me into doing things like reading this book."

2. **When a woman asks you to do something, you feel an uncontrollable urge to do the opposite.**

3. **You dislike and disagree with the term "rebel," and prefer to think of yourself as an independent man who is unwilling to give up his power and become a "wuss."**

4. **You hate this quiz.**

How did you do, guys? If you thought the quiz was stupid, refused to think about the questions, and didn't laugh even once, then congratulations—you are a bona fide rebel!

Let's get serious for a minute, because there is an important point to be made here: *The problem with being a rebel is that you turn every interaction with your partner into a battle of the wills, a power struggle in which you unconsciously feel you have to prove yourself to be independent and unable to be controlled.* She says, "Let's go away for the weekend," and you feel compelled to say you are too busy to go, even though you secretly like the idea of getting away. She says she's in the mood to make love, and you suddenly feel tired and uninterested, even though ten minutes ago you were about to suggest messing around. She criticizes the behavior of a friend of yours, and you find yourself fiercely defending him, even though you were just thinking the same things she said.

What Men Do That Drives Women Crazy

- You *resist* doing anything we ask you to do, and often *do the opposite*.

- You *disagree* with our point of view just to be contrary.

- You *interpret our requests as pressure*, and overreact by becoming displeased with us.

- You are *suspicious of our affection or expressions of love* and feel they are methods we use to manipulate you.

- You respond to our offers of help, support, or advice as if they are attempts to control you, and *refuse to take what we have to say into account*, even when it makes sense.

- You *hold back from reassuring us or showing your love fully*, because you don't want us to expect it from you as if you're obligated to perform.

How Being Rebellious with Us Brings Out the Worst in a Woman

- We feel *hurt and unloved* because you seem to be battling against us.

- We get *insecure and needy* when you hold back your love.

- We get *tense and frustrated* when you resist our suggestions or inquiries.

- We become *mothering* when you act like a rebellious teenager.

- We become *bitchy* when we feel you force us into a power struggle.

- We get *irritable and controlling* when you refuse to do the simplest things to maintain the relationship.

What Women Want Men to Know:

When you act like a rebel, you set us up to be your enemy. When you treat us like your mother, from whom you must maintain your freedom, it brings out the worst in us. The more resistant you are to us and the relationship, the more we deteriorate, and become exactly what you fear the most.

What Men Can Do:

1. *Pick your battles carefully.* There are times and situations in your relationship with your partner when you should set boundaries, put your foot down, or say "no"—but NOT all the time! Instead of continually

---

having a knee-jerk reaction to your partner's requests or needs and automatically rebelling, choose the moments when this kind of stand is appropriate. Know what issues are really important to you—having time with your buddies, being able to watch TV and space out without being interrupted, not having to straighten up on weekends, etc.—and negotiate about those, but don't simply rebel against anything your mate asks you to do. Otherwise, your relationship will become a battleground from which no one will emerge without wounds.

2. Whenever you are feeling rebellious, remind yourself that *your partner's intention is NOT to control you or make you into a compliant little boy*, but to connect, communicate, create intimacy, make your life harmonious and orderly, etc.

3. *Work on your mother issues*. UGH...I know this doesn't sound appealing, but if you suspect you haven't resolved your feelings about your mother, and may be projecting them onto your mate, take some steps to free yourself of this conditioning from your past. Have a few sessions with a therapist, join a men's group, talk to other family members—*anything that helps you become more aware of your reactions on the inside and less reactive on the outside*.

4. Don't reassure or comfort us.

We tell you we're feeling worried that you haven't been happy with us lately, since you seem distant and unaffectionate. You say we're just imagining things, and tell us to calm down.

Late one night, we confess that we're very nervous about a big presentation we have to give at work the next morning, and ask if you can hold us for a while before bed. You become uncomfortable and say that you really want to catch up on some of your e-mails, and you leave us alone in the bedroom.

While remembering a painful incident from our past, we become emotional and begin to cry. You sit there watching us, but don't say or do anything to comfort us.

If you ask women who is going to be more comforting and reassuring when they are going through a difficult time—their mate or a girlfriend—most of us will admit that it is, indeed, our girlfriend who will do the better job. It is sad but true, guys, that you aren't always so good at reassuring us. **When we're upset, women want to be listened to, embraced, soothed, comforted, and told that everything will be okay. Instead, men often give us advice and instructions, or pull back and leave us alone, or even make us feel wrong for being upset in the first place.**

Remember what we've discussed about a woman's need to feel safe? When we feel frightened or insecure, we instinctively reach out for help, hoping to find some comfort that will diminish our concerns. *So if instead of comfort, we receive coldness or disinterest or disapproval from our mate*, our fear only increases, and we *feel even worse than we did originally*. Whereas we might have been just a little upset to begin with, now we are really upset, not just about the original incident, but about your reaction to us!

This pattern is sadly common in many intimate relationships—
the moment a woman asks for reassurance or comfort from the
man she loves, who's actually a caring, sensitive guy, he suddenly
freezes up, and does the opposite of what she needs. **She needs
him to reach out; he pulls back. She needs him to say encouraging things; he gets quiet. She needs him to tell her it's going
to be okay; his obvious discomfort with her feelings leads her
to believe that things are NOT okay.**

Why do many men seem to have such a difficult time offering the
woman they love comfort and reassurance? There are several reasons:

**1. Men feel they have to solve the problem, and are frustrated
when they can't.**

Have you ever wondered why, when a man sees his woman upset about a problem, he becomes analytical, asking you lots of
questions, offering suggestions and direction, and even becoming
angry with you when he feels you're not responding to his efforts?
This is because **men are solution-oriented**—they are brought up
to feel they are **responsible for fixing things.**

What Women Want Men to Know:

**Men often misinterpret a woman's request for comfort
and reassurance as a request that he fix things for us.**

So when you are hurting, your partner feels responsible for
finding a solution, and his mind will go into problem-solving
mode. Of course, every woman knows that *when we are feeling
scared or insecure, it's not a man's mind we want to interact with,
it's his heart*. What will make us feel better may not seem logical,

but we know it works—hugs, kisses, someone saying, "I understand, honey. I'm sorry you're going through this," or "What do you need from me right now?" Guys, I know when you hear this, it's hard to believe. *"You mean she'll actually feel better if I just hold her and say sweet things, even if I haven't solved her problem?"* The answer is: YES, she will.

Perhaps it will help you to think about how you'd comfort your six-year-old daughter if she were frightened. You'd simply hold her and love her, and that love would penetrate her being and calm her down in a way no words ever could. Well, inside of every woman, even those of us who appear to be the strongest and most invulnerable, is a little girl who gets scared sometimes. Whether we know how to ask for it or not, what we really need at those times is what every little girl needs—strong, secure arms around us to make us feel safe and remind us that we're not alone.

Sometimes, guys, when you feel especially powerless to help the woman you love, remove her pain, or fix the situation, you get angry, seemingly at her. This reaction totally confuses women. "I'm the one who is hurting—why is he angry at me?" we wonder. Of course, you're not really angry at her—you're angry at yourself because you feel like you've failed to protect her, or are failing to rescue her. But if you're not aware that this is going on inside of you, the feeling of anger can "leak" out, and make you irritable, critical, or even mean to your partner. This brings out the worst in us, as we feel the one person we've turned to in our vulnerable moment has turned on us.

2. Men feel guilty for causing a woman pain, and in turn become angry with us.

It took me years to figure out this dynamic, but once I did, it's helped me understand more about why men react the way they do. A woman tells her husband that something he's done has hurt her, or that she's unhappy in some way, and wants some reassurance. But instead of comforting her or saying he's sorry, he actually becomes angry with her, accusing her of being too sensitive, or too needy, etc. What's going on here? He's probably feeling guilty for making her unhappy, or humiliated that she's pointing out something he did he wasn't even aware of. *Rather than admitting to himself that he feels like a jerk, he blames her for "making" him feel that way.*

When we tell you we're scared or upset, guys, and you get angry with us, it makes the situation twenty times worse. **The truth is that we're not bringing it up to blame you or criticize you— we want to feel better, to feel safe and loved again, and we're asking for your help and reassurance.**

What Women Want Men to Know:

Men often make the mistake of hearing a woman's pleas for comfort and reassurance as blame, rather than as a request for love.

What Men Do That Drives Women Crazy

- You *lecture us or give us advice when we're upset,* when what we really need is for you to be understanding and compassionate.

- When we tell you we need some reassurance, you do the opposite and *pull away.*

- You *dismiss our being upset as an overreaction,* and ignore our need for support.

- You get *angry and upset* with us for being upset, thus making us more upset.

- You *make us feel wrong* for needing reassurance, as if it means that we're overly weak or needy.

- You *minimize the importance of our feelings*, and decide they don't deserve to be taken seriously.

- You become *analytical and logical* when what we need from you is love and sweetness.

How Not Reassuring or Comforting Us Brings Out the Worst in a Woman

- We feel *abandoned and rejected* when we reach out for comfort and you respond by being cold and indifferent.

- We feel *insecure and frightened* when we ask for reassurance and you won't give it to us.

- We appear *needy and desperate* when you make us feel we have to beg for a crumb of comfort.

- We become *anxious and high-strung* when we feel you don't understand what we are asking for.

- We become *depressed* when we don't feel safe with you.

What Women Want Men to Know:

When we reach out to you for comfort and reassurance,
and you respond with indifference, detachment,
or anger, it makes us feel as if you don't care that
we are hurting, and that you don't love us enough
to be there for us.

*The more you refuse to reassure us, the more frightened
and in need of reassurance we become.*

What Men Can Do:

1. *Remind yourself that we don't need you to rescue
us or fix things—we just want to feel you are there with
us, and that we aren't alone.* You can't go wrong with
hugs, kisses, sweetness, and other forms of emotional reassurance. If you think you have ways you could help us
with a problem, ask us if we'd like some suggestions.
Sometimes we'll take you up on your offer. And sometimes you'll be surprised to discover that we really don't
want to logically tackle the problem. We just want you
to listen and give us emotional support.

2. When we tell you something you've done has hurt
us and we need some comfort and reassurance, *try to put
your pride aside and reach out to us.* All we want is to feel
connected and happy again, not to blame you or hold on
to the past.

3. *Remember: The most valuable thing you have to offer us is not your advice or your logic but your love.* Your
love has the power to heal our heart, and that's worth
more than any solution you could suggest.

5. Flirt with other women.

Dear Barbara,

My boyfriend of three years has a terrible habit of flirting, and it's driving me crazy. He's always staring at other women when we are together, especially their bodies, and sometimes he even comes on to women right in front of me, although he denies that's what is going on. When I complain about his behavior and tell him how much it hurts me, he insists he's just being "friendly," and "joking around," and accuses me of being "insecure" and "jealous." The problem is that how he behaves does make me feel insecure, so I can't really defend myself. I don't think he'd ever cheat on me, so why does this bother me so much? Please help!

This is only one of hundreds and hundreds of letters I've received over the years from women complaining that their partner's flirting was bringing out the worst in them. Men often laugh when I bring up this topic, as if to say, "Oh yeah, I know women complain about this all the time, but they are really overreacting." Well, guys, I am here to tell you that we are NOT overreacting, and that **this kind of casual regard for how you deal with your sexual energy, as socially acceptable as it may be, is one of the most deadly enemies of an intimate relationship, and a guaranteed way to turn even the most confident, self-assured woman into an emotional wreck.**

A NOTE TO MEN: Before you accuse me of criticizing you, please know that I've talked about this topic to thousands of men and women in my seminars, and I think I have a way of explaining it that you've never really heard before. It's not about who's right and who's

wrong, or who's good and who's bad. Instead, it's about *understanding the effect flirting has on the emotional and sexual energy of an intimate relationship.* **So be open-minded, guys, and let me explain how you may be sabotaging your love life without realizing it.**

Understanding Your Sexual Bank Account

Imagine for a moment that every man and woman has a "sexual bank account." In that bank account is a certain amount of sexual and romantic energy made up of lust, passion, longing, and so on. Just as you are free to do anything you want with the contents of your financial bank account—spend all the money, invest the money, give the money away—you choose what you do with the contents of your sexual bank account.

When you're single, it's as if you invest a little of the savings in your sexual bank account in each potential romantic partner, and then you wait and see if the investment pays off. When a relationship doesn't work out, you stop investing your sexual, emotional, and romantic energies in it. You "withdraw" your energies, and place them back in your sexual bank account, and wait for the next investment opportunity. Of course, just as we all wish we'd find a financial investment that would pay us huge dividends for the rest of our lives, so too when we're single, we are always hoping to discover the "jackpot"—that person in whom we can invest all of our love, dreams, and *"sexual and emotional savings."*

When you fall in love with someone and become seriously involved, live together, or get married, it's as if you've found the investment you've been waiting for. *You make a commitment to invest yourself emotionally and sexually in this relationship on an exclusive basis—no other side investments or short-term proj-*

ects allowed! Day after day, year after year, you make "deposits" (don't laugh!) into your chosen investment. What do these deposits consist of? Intimacy, connection, affection, and love.

What Women Want Men to Know:

Each time you connect emotionally with your partner, each time you share your heart, every conversation you have, every word of love you speak, every expression of your respect and appreciation, each moment of intimacy, each kiss, each embrace, and of course each time you make love—all of these are the deposits you make into the investment of your relationship with the person you love.

Now, guys, imagine that you're happily married. You're an architect at a large firm, and there's a very attractive woman at work who seems to be a little more sociable with you than normal. You feel somewhat drawn to her, platonically of course—after all, she is very nice to look at, and she makes you feel good because she's always smiling at you and complimenting you. So you convince yourself that there's no harm in talking with her frequently, e-mailing brief notes back and forth, and having lunch once in a while. After all, you already have a wife, and this woman is just a friend, right?

WRONG. In spite of your honorable intentions, your interaction with this woman is not harmless at all—**each time you talk with her, e-mail her, pay special attention to her, or interact with her,** *you're making a deposit from your sexual bank account into her account, rather than into your wife's account!* That means you're actually withdrawing "funds," or energy, from an account that you've dedicated to nourishing and sustaining your intimate relationship, and depositing them instead into the account of some woman you hardly know.

What is so dangerous about this? **It's as if you're stealing from your wife and stealing from yourself.** I know this is a strong statement, but think about it for a moment—**when you even occasionally invest your thoughts, your appreciation, your playfulness in another woman who overtly or covertly shows interest in you, you're taking assets that belong to your relationship and spending them somewhere else.**

"Wait a minute," you might say, "it's not like I'm doing anything wrong. I'm not sleeping with this woman. I'm not even touching her. Our conversations are totally polite. So how can you say I'm taking anything away from my wife?" Well, I say it because it's true. I believe that **the kind of male attention and energy and interaction you're sharing with this other woman should only be shared with your wife if you want to keep your relationship as strong, intimate, and passionate as possible.** It may not seem to make a difference at first, but when you share these parts of you with another woman, bit by bit you are depleting funds from your main investment—in this case, your marriage—and before long you *will* notice the negative effects. You will be a little less attracted to your partner; you will feel a little less connected; you will feel a little more constrained. One day, you wake up and don't feel sexually connected to your mate anymore. **The passion's gone, and you may not even realize why until it's too late.**

If you owned a business that you wanted to become successful and remain that way for a long time, would you take your capital out of it and invest it somewhere else? Of course not. So why would you risk withdrawing some of your sexual and emotional energy from your most important personal investment—your relationship with the woman you love—and investing it somewhere else? The answer is that you wouldn't, *unless you weren't even aware that you were doing it.*

And that's my point, guys—most men aren't aware of this subtle, invisible but powerful interplay of energies that constantly goes on in your love life. No one teaches you this stuff when you're growing up. So you go into relationships with the best intentions, and tell yourself that as long as you don't have sex with another woman, you're being faithful to your partner. And that's a good thing. But you need to know *that the effects of your attention and your choices go way beyond what you do or don't do physically.*

How to Tell If You're Making a Withdrawal from Your Sexual Bank Account

Sometimes when I present this information to men, they say, "Okay, I get what you're saying, but what am I supposed to do, walk around with blinders on? The world is full of beautiful women. Are you saying if I even look at one, I am making a 'withdrawal' from my sexual bank account?" No, of course I'm not saying that. But I think it will help if I explain the difference between what I call "noticing" and "indulging."

See, there's a difference between *noticing* that another human being is attractive as she walks by and enjoying the contribution her beauty adds to the world, and, on the other hand, *indulging* in the sexual energy you feel toward her. When a man is just noticing, he is acknowledging the attractiveness of another woman, just as he'd acknowledge the beauty of a sunset or a terrific sports car. He sees it, thinks to himself, "How beautiful!" and then turns his attention back to wherever it was before.

When a man indulges, it's a different story. Indulging starts out by just noticing—a woman at the next table in a restaurant, for instance—but then progresses as you decide to *participate with the woman's energy in a sexual way,* with your stare, or your body language, or your speech, or just in your mind. Guys, it's as if you temporarily forget your sexual commitment to your partner and proceed to have a wild, ten-second sexual orgy with another woman in your imagination. You may not be doing anything physical, but on the astral plane, it's as if you jumped out of your body, flew over to her table, ravished her, and then jumped back into your body. If your mate happens to be at the restaurant with you, and says, "Hey, where did you go? Are you staring at that woman?" you innocently respond, **"I didn't do anything. I'm just sitting here."**

Well, guess what? We know you're not just sitting there. We know that you were indulging and not just noticing, because it felt to us as if you suddenly disappeared for ten seconds or so—and you did. *You see, women are very sensitive to the balance in our sexual and emotional bank account, and we can feel when you make a withdrawal, even a small one.* We may not know the details of what's going on, especially if we're not present, but trust me, we know that there's less of your attention and energy on us than there was before. *And when the balance in that sexual and emotional bank account starts to go down, a woman's sense of safety and security goes down with it.*

This is why most women (unless they are flirts themselves—but that's another book) hate when their men flirt, and may seem overprotective of the relationship. *We instinctively know that once a man starts withdrawing even small amounts of sexual and emotional energy, it will bring out the worst in us.* We suddenly feel deprived of our three most important needs—to feel safe, to feel connected, and to feel valued—and begin to elicit all the characteristics most men can't stand. Of course, this only makes us less appealing to our partner, which in turn makes other women more appealing, and a vicious cycle begins.

You know, I don't have a reputation for being a conservative person in just about any way. I've been a liberal thinker all of my life. So it may seem strange that I take such a strong stand on this issue. My position, however, is *not based on any kind of moral judgment, but rather on my observations of the harmful effect that being casual about sharing sexual energy has on intimate relationships.* It's hard enough to make a relationship work without adding this extra challenge.

What Women Want Men to Know:

When you invest your emotional or sexual energy somewhere other than our relationship, it hurts us more deeply than you can imagine, and it slowly drains the relationship of its vital resources.

What Men Can Do:

1. When you feel tempted to make a withdrawal, even a small one, from your sexual and emotional energy bank, ask yourself: *What is my purpose in doing this? What do I expect to get out of this?* **Remind yourself of your commitment to your partner and, rather than making a withdrawal, make a deposit into your partner's account by sharing your love in some way.**

2. When you see an attractive or appealing woman, think of her not as something you want, but as a beautiful piece of art that you are admiring. *Notice, but don't indulge.* **In that moment, remind yourself of your own beautiful woman and how fortunate you are to have her love.**

Here are the next six ways men can bring out the worst in a woman. I'll discuss each of them more briefly than I did the first five, as some of this information has been discussed in earlier chapters, and some will be covered in chapters to come.

6. Be distant and aloof.

Here's one of the quickest and most effective ways of turning the woman you love into an insecure, needy mess right before your eyes: Pull away, don't communicate, don't respond to her inquiries about what's wrong, and watch the strong, confident, fun-loving person you enjoyed being with deteriorate into a paranoid, neurotic person desperate for reassurance. **Remember: Women need to feel safe, connected, and valued. So, guys, when you shut down and act distant and aloof, it brings out the worst in us.** We feel scared, we feel disconnected, and we feel you don't really care about us.

Some men call this "playing hard to get." I call it thoughtless and insensitive behavior. It's as if you suddenly left the relationship, and we can't find you. We see you, maybe we can even touch you, *but we can't feel you because, emotionally, you have vanished*.

Sometimes men aren't even aware of why they become aloof, and really don't do it intentionally. There are dozens of reasons a man might put up emotional walls and distance himself from the woman he loves, from resistance to intimacy, to fear of getting hurt, to childhood issues, and many more. Guys, women understand that you may be in the habit of shutting down without realizing it. So we try to reach out and bridge the gap in any way we can, because we know the longer you remain closed off, the worse we will feel.

Nothing good ever comes from this habit of closing your heart to your partner. It brings up every abandonment issue a woman has; it sows the seeds of mistrust, so we can't fully relax; it elicits our deepest insecurities, so that you get turned off to us and become even more distant. Eventually, if it goes on long enough, we vanish too, and you lose us and the relationship.

What Men Can Do:

When you find yourself shutting off and "leaving us" emotionally, try to find your way back. Don't lie to yourself and pretend that your distance is harmless, because it isn't. We know you are gone, and we are hurting. If there is a problem, communicate about it, but don't just go numb. Use the techniques in the next few chapters to help you reconnect and reestablish the intimacy.

---

7. Criticize us.

What do some men get out of constantly criticizing their partner? Do they really believe that we will "improve" if they assault us with judgments and continually point out what we are doing wrong? Do they somehow feel that the tough-love approach will help us shape up and become a better person? Do they seriously think that by chastising us about our weight, how we dress, how we take care of the house, or our friends, cooking, books, etc., that we will be inspired and motivated to change?

Exchanging healthy feedback and constructive suggestions is a part of a good relationship, as we'll see in our next chapter. But guys, *if you're the critical type (and you know who you are), be pre-*

pared to turn your woman into the very thing you dread! The more you tell us we aren't doing it right, the less confidence we have and the worse we do. The more you judge how we look, the worse we will feel about ourselves and the less we will work on improving our physical appearance. Bit by bit, your constant criticism will chip away at our self-esteem until we walk around starved for the smallest crumb of your approval. Sounds disgusting, doesn't it? Well, it's the inevitable result when you play the critic.

When a woman lives in constant fear of her partner's criticism, she becomes chronically insecure and nervous, as if she's walking on eggshells.

Most highly critical people were harshly criticized and judged themselves as children. They were told it was "for their own good" to receive such relentless feedback, and unconsciously they may still believe this and thus attempt to improve their partner by criticizing her. **But no growth ever occurs through fear—it is through love that we feel safe enough to change, to blossom, to shine.**

What Men Can Do:

When you feel like criticizing your partner, ask yourself, "What is my intention in communicating this information right now?" Is your intention to help correct a problem in the relationship, ask for something you need, or request a change in your mate's behavior? Or is it simply to unload your anger or resentment on her? If you are trying to give some feedback or express an emotion, perhaps there is another way to share your feelings that might sound less judgmental. (See Chapter 11.)

8. Be vague and ambiguous.

Here's how to transform me from a patient, calm woman into an anxious, irritable one: *Don't give me a straight answer about anything; refuse to make specific plans; never fully commit yourself to any agreements we make because you want to "leave things open"; respond to my questions with such ambiguity that I am not sure what you actually said.*

This is the magic formula for driving me, and most women, totally crazy, and unfortunately it's one of men's favorite methods of communication. Many of you are experts at being vague, and not letting us know what you're actually thinking, what you're actually planning on doing, and when you're planning on doing it. The more you evade being specific, the more exasperated we get.

This pattern is such an important one that I've devoted a lot of time to it in Chapter 11. In my surveys and interviews with women, this complaint came up over and over again as one of the most common things men do that make women completely crazy. So I'm going to do what men do all the time, and be vague here, and tell you I will deal with this issue later!

9. Be forgetful and procrastinate.

"Did I tell you I'd call the plumber? I guess I must have forgotten."

"Your parents' party is this weekend? I *thought it was next month sometime."*

"Look, I told you I will talk to John about his grades. I just don't want to do it right now."

"I believe you when you say we discussed your feelings about this a few months ago—but I just don't remember the conversation."

These are all comments men make to their partners that drive women crazy. I'm sure every woman recognizes these statements from moments in her own relationship—when the man has forgotten to perform a task or keep an appointment, when he is putting off doing something he promised to do, when he doesn't remember discussing something that was important to us.

Here's what really upsets us, guys: We know that if your boss told you to be in his office at noon, you'd be there. You wouldn't show up a day later and say, "Did we discuss some kind of appointment? I must have forgotten." We know that if you're a sports fan, and got tickets to basketball finals, you wouldn't get the weekends mixed up and say to your friend, "The play-offs are this weekend? I thought they were next month." And we know that if you'd met with an investor who told you he was considering putting a million dollars into your business, and all he needed was a one-page description of your company's goals, you wouldn't say to him, "Look, I'll do it, okay? Only not this week." And yet this is exactly how you often treat the woman in your life.

How does a woman feel when you are forgetful and procrastinate? **Like we aren't that important to you. Like if we don't stay on your case, you won't remember or get things done. Like how we feel or what we want isn't one of your priorities. Like you don't pay attention to what we say or need. Like you simply don't care.**

All of this brings out the worst in us. When you appear to be forgetful and unreliable, *we become more aggressive, pushy, mothering, and bitchy.* We also become afraid we can't count on you, *and thus get insecure and nervous,* because we feel we can never totally relax and trust that you'll do what you said you'd do. And of course the more a woman exhibits these qualities, the more turned off a man gets, and the less he wants to be responsible to her, and the more he procrastinates, and the more insecure she gets—this is the vicious cycle that's created.

What Men Can Do:

Guys, please don't space out on us! Whether it's because you don't like feeling you have to report to your partner, and thus become rebellious, or because certain things that are important to a woman just aren't important to you, so you decide to ignore them, or because you get lazy and figure we'll remind you eventually, the result is the same: *We end up feeling like your mother or your drill sergeant,* always on your case about doing this or that. Not only do you dislike it when we behave that way, but we hate it ourselves.

Please don't be so casual about your promises, conversations, and plans with your partner. We take them seriously, and so should you. Remember: Women pay attention to all of the love details, and if you said something three weeks ago, believe me, we will remember it, even if you claim the incident has vanished from your memory. **When you keep your commitments to us, we feel loved, valued, and respected,** and in turn we will love and value you even more.

---

10. Don't pay attention to us.

Remember Chapter 6, where we talked about how important it is for a woman to feel valued? Well, I'm going to repeat myself briefly and remind men that *when you don't pay attention to the woman you love, it definitely brings out the worst in her.* When you forget to show interest in our lives and concerns, don't ask us how we are and what we need, and don't notice it when we are unhappy, lonely, overworked, or underloved, we end up feeling invisible, as if we don't even matter much to you.

Go back to Chapter 6 and refresh your memory about this need women have, and how when you neglect it, we become even more needy. In Chapter 9, I'll share some easy and effective techniques for giving a woman the kind of attention that makes us feel totally adored.

11. Don't tell us what's going on with you.

"Didn't she already cover this earlier in the book?" you may be asking yourself. Yes, guys, I did, but I'm bringing it up again, because I can't remind you too many times how important it is for you to share your world, your feelings, and your inner process with the woman you love. *When you exclude us, we don't feel respected, valued, or trusted.* Even worse, we become *paranoid,* wondering what's going on, or worrying that you're hiding something we should know. Inevitably, we are tempted to *pressure you to open up, or to pry* until we find out what's bothering you, behaviors I know you find less than thrilling.

In our Chapter 12 on communication, I'll explain some things you can say to your partner when you really aren't in the mood for a big discussion that will calm us down and get us off your back until you are ready to talk.

———

What's the antidote to these eleven ways a man can bring out the worst in a woman? It's the opposite of everything we've just talked about. So guys, in case you're interested, and I hope by now you are, here's the "to do" list for making your partner really happy.

I know many women are going to copy this list and put it up on the refrigerator so their husbands have to read it every day, or e-mail it to their boyfriends at work, or find other creative ways to make sure the man she loves sees it. Now remember what you've learned so far, guys, and don't get reactive or upset with us if we resort to such blatant tactics. We're simply being creative, committed, devoted, and loving. And, okay, we admit that we thought perhaps you might need a little reminder, just in case this information slipped your mind ... !

How to Bring Out the Best in a Woman

1. **Talk to us.**
2. **Listen to us and care about fulfilling our needs.**
3. **Don't be rebellious—be cooperative.**
4. **Reassure and comfort us.**
5. **Keep your sexual and romantic energies invested in us.**
6. **Stay connected and don't shut down.**
7. **Compliment and appreciate us.**
8. **Communicate with us clearly and concretely.**
9. **Keep your commitments in a timely fashion.**
10. **Pay attention to us.**
11. **Share what's going on with you.**

CHAPTER NINE

How to Be the Perfect Lover Outside of the Bedroom

Many years ago, I took a weekend trip with my partner at the time to a romantic hotel in the country. It felt so good to be away from work, away from everyday pressures, away from everything, and just be alone together, especially in such a beautiful location. By the time I woke up Saturday morning, I felt refreshed, happy, and very much alive. We ate breakfast with the other hotel guests outside on a lovely terrace overlooking the mountains, and when we were done, decided to take a walk around the grounds.

As we left the restaurant and began to stroll down the path arm in arm, I noticed a woman walking in our direction, and as she saw me, her face broke into a big smile. She appeared to be about fifty years old, and she obviously worked on the housekeeping staff of the hotel, as her arms were full of towels. I wondered what she was smiling about, and smiled back. Just as she was about to pass, she stopped for a moment right in front of me and said with a wink: *"Love looks good on you, honey."* Then, she went on her way.

Even today, I can remember exactly how I felt when I heard this phrase—it was as if someone had put one of the deepest truths of my soul into words. This woman I'd never met before had looked at me and seen that my heart was happy, and that I was feeling very loved. "Love looks good on you," she said. And, of course, she was right. Love made me shine, love made me glow, love made me connect with my most essential self. She knew about the miraculous power of love. She knew because she was a woman, and she understood the way being loved makes a woman look.

No beauty treatment, no expensive outfit, no fancy jewels can make a woman look as radiant as when she is feeling truly loved by the man in her life. Nor can any of these things cover up the look of sadness, heartache, and emptiness a woman has when she is not feeling loved. We can tell when we gaze at ourselves in the mirror what our heart is feeling. It speaks to us through our face, through our eyes, and it never lies. And when we see other women, we can see their hearts as well, and we know, just as that woman years ago knew, when a woman is loved, and when, on the other hand, she is hungry for love.

This chapter is about what it takes to put that look on a woman's face that I had that day. It's about how to feed a woman's heart, and how to make sure she is not starving for love. *It's about being a real lover in the true sense of the word, not just in the bedroom, but outside the bedroom, where it really counts.*

I remember reading about a research study that focused on orphanages in Europe that were populated with infants who'd been abandoned at birth, many of them sickly and malnourished. The study came about because the doctors at the orphanages noticed a marked difference in the growth weight of the babies. Some babies seemed to be developing and thriving at a much faster rate than the others, who, mysteriously, didn't seem to be doing well at all. At first the doctors were puzzled. All the infants were fed the same formula and given the same medicine. All were kept in the same nursery, exposed to the same amount of light and the same schedule. Why were some developing so rapidly, and some struggling?

Then the doctors discovered something interesting. Several nurses assigned to certain babies were in the habit of giving the infants more than just the required medical care—they picked up the infants, held them, talked to them sweetly, stroked their heads, and sang songs to them. The other nurses were more perfunctory in their duties, and though they were gentle with the infants, they did nothing more than their job required. Sure enough, when the doctors analyzed the data, they found that *the infants who were being held and loved had a much higher growth rate than the babies who were not touched or talked to.*

What conclusion can we draw from this? It has to do with the miraculous power of love.

Love has an inexplicable power to nourish us
at the deepest level of our being.
It feeds our soul, our heart, even our body.
With it, we thrive. Without it, we become *love-starved*.

From the time we enter this world, we need more than food, water, and air to live a meaningful life—we need love. When our heart is fed with intimacy, affection, and communication, this primal hunger for love is satisfied. But when we are deprived of these things, our heart is hungry, and we become *"love-starved."*

I believe that many men and women are walking around love-starved and don't even know it. They are hungry for attention, for affection, for appreciation, for love, just like those infants who were not touched or nurtured. Sadly, I'm not talking about single people, but about people in a relationship with a partner who, perhaps without realizing it, is emotionally starving them by not adequately feeding their heart.

When we're in a relationship with a man and we're love-starved, we're not getting enough of the things we need to feel safe, valued, and connected, so we feel a deep emptiness inside of us. How do many of us deal with that emptiness? *We try to fill it and ourselves up with other things—food, alcohol, drugs, shopping, work, taking care of people, etc.* The truth, however, is that there's only one thing we're missing, one thing we're hungry for, and it cannot be replaced by experiences that give us a temporary high or fleeting sense of fullness. **What we are missing is love.**

Another way to understand this is to imagine that your heart is like a plant—it needs to be watered in order to be healthy, to blossom, and to stay alive. When your partner waters your heart with love, it becomes full and *"juicy."* You can look at a person and tell if they are well loved, because they have that *juicy* look, as if they have just been watered. They are full of juice, full of sweetness. That's what the woman at the hotel was seeing in me.

On the other hand, people who aren't being well loved, who are love-starved, have a heart that is parched and thirsty. Rather than looking juicy, they appear sort of dry and shriveled up, as if they need watering, which they do. They are thirsty for love.

Please know that I'm *not* saying that if you aren't in a relationship, you are love-starved and all dried up—the truth is that if you're loving yourself and regularly connecting with people you care for, your heart is being fed. What I'm referring to is what happens in an intimate relationship when, in order for the bond between you to remain strong, you need a certain amount of love to flow back and forth. When your heart isn't being fed by a partner who has committed to nurturing and loving you, that's when you feel love-starved.

What Women Want Men to Know:

**Learning how to feed your partner's heart is
one of the most important skills you need to
master in a relationship.**

> **When you feed our heart, it becomes juicy and over-flowing. When you starve our heart,
> the love and passion dry up.**

What Happens to Us When We're Love-Starved

How do you feel when you haven't eaten for a long time, and you're just starving? I know how I feel: *cranky, irritable, impatient,* and *overreactive.* Well, guess what? **When you starve your partner emotionally, she is going to become cranky, irritable, impatient, and hypersensitive. In fact, you're going to turn your partner into everything you hate.**

Joyce and Guy had been married for six years and knew their relationship was in a serious crisis. Joyce used to be a cheerful, enthusiastic, and affectionate person, and when she'd first met Guy, she was sure he was the man of her dreams. But lately she'd felt exactly the opposite. She was always angry, sarcastic, and had totally lost her sex drive. Guy kept telling himself that she was going through a phase, and threw himself even more into his work, but as time went by, the situation only deteriorated, and they both finally admitted that they had better get some help, or they would end up divorced.

I sat there listening to Joyce complain about Guy—that he worked too hard; that he didn't appreciate how much she did around the house; that he spent more of his free time with his buddies than he did with her. The more she talked, the more angry she became, until finally she burst into tears.

"Why are you crying?" I asked Joyce.

"Because I sound like a total bitch," she retorted. "And it's true—that's what I've become. I'm crying because I never used to be this way, and I hate myself, but I don't understand what's happening to me."

"Is she right?" I asked Guy. "Did she used to be nice and now she's a bitch?"

"I guess you could say that," Guy responded with a red face.

"Well, why do you think this has happened?"

"Honest to God, I don't know," Guy answered, and I knew that he was being sincere.

As I asked some more questions about their relationship, the problem became crystal clear to me. **Joyce was suffering from a severe case of "love starvation."** Her husband was a sweet, well-meaning person who hadn't seen his own parents be loving toward each other, and therefore didn't know how to behave in a nurturing, affectionate way in his marriage. He owned his own company, worked long hours, and didn't make time for much else. The result was that, unintentionally, he neglected Joyce. He didn't give her heart what it needed to feel sufficiently "fed"—affection, communication, intimacy, time, all the things we've discussed. And so little by little, Joyce became increasingly love-starved, and increasingly bitchy. Like her husband, she, too, was unaware of what was going on or why she was so miserable. She didn't know how to ask Guy for what she really needed, so rather than expressing her feelings, she acted them out. The result was a marriage in a state of emergency.

When I explained all of this to Joyce and Guy, believe it or not they both felt relieved. Joyce had been worried that something was really wrong with her. Once she had a context for her feelings, and an understanding that she was reacting to feeling love-starved, her panic toned down into concern, and she was able to begin expressing her true feelings to her husband. As for Guy, he'd been terrified that the sweet woman he married had just been a cover for Joyce's true nature, which eventually revealed her to be an angry bitch. Even though he wasn't thrilled to find out he had been unknowingly starving her heart, he felt hopeful about making some changes, because now at least he knew the problem was solvable.

I have worked with thousands of couples like Joyce and Guy, where the man doesn't realize he is starving his partner's heart, and the woman herself doesn't recognize the signs that she is love-starved, and therefore can't articulate her needs to her mate clearly. Even though the situation they've gotten themselves into is frustrating, upsetting, and threatening to their relationship, *it's not their fault—they simply didn't know how to do it differently.*

How many of you were taught how to have a wonderful, passionate relationship by watching your parents' relationship? Not too many, I'm sure. Most of us did not learn healthy relationship skills from our parents, who, believe it or not, were actually our love teachers, as I explain in my book *How to Make Love All the Time.* Whether you realize it or not, **you formed the majority of your love habits long before you moved out of the house to live on your own, and those habits were created by interacting with and observing your parents.**

This is the first reason we unknowingly starve our partner's heart—because, like Guy, we don't know any better. No one taught us the importance of feeding our relationship in the same way we'd feed our child or our plants or anything else that we wanted to grow. Even if we realize how important this is, we probably have never been taught how to actually do it.

The second reason you may starve love is that you may have been emotionally starved as a child, and not received the affection or nurturing you should have. **If you learned to exist on occasional crumbs of love, you may only give crumbs of love to your partner because you don't know how to give any more. Or you may be the one who is love-starved in your relationship, like Joyce, and not even know it simply because it's what you're used to.**

Finally, there are some of us who starve our partner's heart as a way to exert power in the relationship, as we've discussed in earlier chapters. You feel as though your partner isn't giving in to what you want enough of the time, so you withhold your love and affection as a sort of "punishment." When she pleases you, you respond with love. When she doesn't, you pull away. Not only is this an unhealthy dynamic, but it never gives you the result you want—people are not like animals who can be trained to respond to commands by withholding rewards or bestowing rewards. Ultimately, a woman (or man) who is treated like this will get smart and leave.

Why Women Settle for Being Love-Starved

Why is it sometimes so difficult for women to recognize that we are hungry for love?

Why do women often settle for being love-starved, and not let our partner know how much we are hurting?

Why is it so easy for us to sacrifice our happiness and not even realize it?

We all do it at times, don't we, ladies?

- We put ourselves and our feelings second, and we put his first.

- We tell ourselves what we want isn't that important, that it's more essential not to rock the boat.

- We discount our own needs, and convince ourselves that we're just being too demanding.

- We don't admit to him or even sometimes to ourselves that we're not getting enough.

I'm not talking about the normal give-and-take that should exist in any relationship, but rather about **how women become too self-sacrificing with our mates, and settle for being love-starved without even realizing it.**

What Women Want Men to Know:

Women often sacrifice too much of ourselves in the name of love, and we end up love-starved and resentful.

Now, it's not that a woman wakes up in the morning and says to herself, *"I think I'll sacrifice my needs today until I become completely cranky and empty inside."* Most of the time we aren't even aware that we're doing this. But we do sacrifice, more than is healthy and good for us or for our intimate relationship.

Here's one of my favorite examples to help both women and men understand how unconsciously women sacrifice. I call it "The Fish Quiz." It's designed for women to take, and men to learn from.

The Fish Quiz

Ladies: Imagine that you've decided to make dinner for you and your husband, and are preparing fish as the main course. You take two pieces of fresh fish out of the refrigerator, and put them in a pan to be sautéed. While the filets cook, you get the rest of the meal ready.

When you go back over to the pan to finish up the fish, you notice that one piece kind of fell apart while cooking (we'll call it the "messy" piece), and since it's in broken sections, it doesn't look as nice as the other piece, which remained perfectly intact. You remove each piece of fish from the pan and place them on separate plates along with the vegetables and rice you made.

You're standing in front of the table where your husband is already seated for dinner, with one plate of fish in one hand, and one in the other. Now for the quiz: **Which plate do you put down in front of your husband—the one with the "messy" piece of fish, or the one with the perfect piece of fish?**

I've given the Fish Quiz to thousands and thousand of people in my seminar audiences, always with the same results. By the time I get to the part of the story where one piece falls apart in the pan, the women are already nodding their heads and smiling, because they know where I'm going. The guys, on the other hand, are staring at me with clueless looks on their faces—they can't figure out why we are talking about fish in the first place! And when I say, "You're standing in front of your husband with two plates in your hands," the women all start to laugh and clap, and the men are looking at us like we're crazy, or all in on some private joke from home economics class that no one ever told them about.

"How many of you would give your husband the 'nice' piece of fish?" I ask, and all the female hands go up in the air. And guess what—even then, the guys still have no idea what we're talking about, or what the point of all this fish talk is!

The point, to a woman, is obvious: *Most of us wouldn't dream of giving our husband the "messy" piece of fish.* Why? It goes against everything we've been taught, consciously or unconsciously, about how to behave in a relationship. Just the thought of putting the "messy" piece down in front of our man gives us the creeps (unless we're really pissed off at him about something!). We would instinctively take the "messy" piece so he could have the nicer one.

When I tell the men in my audiences to imagine themselves taking the Fish Quiz, and ask them which piece they'd give to their wife, the answers and comments just crack me and the women up:

"First of all, could you explain why the piece that fell apart isn't as good as the other one?"

"I don't understand—what is a 'messy' piece of fish? Is something wrong with it?"

"If both pieces are the same size, what's the difference in who gets which one?"

"I'd give her whichever plate was closer to her in my hands."

"This is why I don't cook—because there is secret stuff women know that they don't tell us, and then we get it all wrong, and they get pissed off."

"I say, just give me one of the plates, because I'm hungry!"

Of course, the purpose of the Fish Quiz is not to teach you the do's and don'ts of the culinary arts, but to make a point about **how naturally women sacrifice without even realizing it,** *and how uncomfortable we can become when we don't sacrifice and think we should.* There is nothing wrong with giving your mate the nicer piece of fish, although frankly, most of them wouldn't even notice the difference. It's a sweet gesture that you make when you love and care for someone. **But it becomes a different issue when we're not just talking about giving up the perfect piece of fish, but giving up your feelings, your needs, your happiness—all in the name of being a "good woman" and sacrificing.**

When men ask if women are somehow "taught" about keeping the "messy" piece of fish for ourselves, they're actually not far off from the truth. The habit of self-sacrifice is inherited. Many of us grew up watching our mothers and grandmothers sacrifice their talents, their interests, their dreams, even their happiness and self-respect in order to be a support system for our fathers, or to keep the family together, or not to make trouble. Often in our society, we celebrate women like this, and glamorize their sacrifice as some kind of wonderful achievement:

"Joe's wife endured so much pain and unhappiness during the marriage, but she did raise three lovely children and helped Joe build a successful business."

"My mother was a saint—she put up with Dad's drinking and whoring, and even abuse, but never complained."

"Grandma was apparently a great painter, but she gave up her art scholarship to study in Paris when Grandpa proposed, and moved to Milwaukee."

The hidden message in all of these comments is clear: These women were great because they sacrificed their desires and happiness for the sake of their husband or family.

Of course, as we saw in Chapter 1, this is one of woman's most beautiful qualities—our ability to put love first, to give everything to those we love. Part of this habit of self-sacrifice comes from our natural roles as mothers to our children. We get up in the middle of the night to feed our baby. We give up our jobs to stay at home and raise our children. We forgo our own hobbies and activities so we can drive our kids to soccer practice and ballet lessons. Of course, *we don't call this sacrifice—we call it love, and it is.*

There is nothing wrong with giving up our needs some of the time in order to make others happy. This is the sign of a generous and highly developed heart. But I'm talking about something else—when we sacrifice too much of the time, and we lose our-selves in the process.

> **Each time a woman sacrifices a piece of her feelings,
> her needs, her own dreams, she gives away a
> piece of herself. The more she sacrifices, the more
> pieces disappear and the less of herself remains,
> until one day she wakes up and feels empty.**

Men, I'm not saying any of this is necessarily your fault. As one guy said to me, *"Hey, I don't ask for the perfect piece of fish. She's the one who tells herself she needs to give it to me."* And you're right. **Often, it is not the man in our life, but the pressure we put on ourselves as women not to appear selfish that causes a woman to be self-sacrificing.** And because we are self-sacrificing, we don't always tell you what we need or how starved we are for love until it's too late.

What Men Need to Know About How Women Sacrifice:

- **We often sacrifice our needs and desires for your peace.**

- **We put aside our own emotions so that you can feel good.**

- **We swallow our feelings, tell you what you said didn't really hurt us, cover up how lonely we are, all to make you feel you are doing a good job.**

- **Unless we are really angry with you, or we have already shut down our hearts, we dread telling you that you've made us unhappy.**

- **We don't tell you how overwhelmed or exhausted we are, wanting so much to please you and make you proud of us.**

What Men Can Do:

1. Pay attention to warning signs that your partner is doing too much, giving too much, and not receiving enough—in other words, that she is love-starved.

Signs That a Woman May Be Love-Starved

She is:

- Irritable
- High-strung and nervous
- Needy
- Chronically tired
- Eating poorly or too much
- Depressed
- Fanatically busy
- Sexually turned off and disinterested
- Emotionally distant
- Numbing herself with drugs or alcohol

Don't wait for your woman to fall apart or blow up or break down to be concerned about her. Remember, we probably won't tell you how bad things are, how stressed out we feel, how emotionally exhausted we've become on our own. Look for signs that we're giving more than we're getting, that we're sacrificing too much. When you notice them, follow some of the other suggestions in this book.

2. Ask her how she is doing.

You may not even notice how many times a day your wife or girlfriend asks you how you are doing, how you are feeling, how your day went, and other questions designed to make sure you're okay, to determine if you need anything she can give you. But if you're like most men, you probably don't check in with her like this. Ask her how her meeting went, how the kids behaved, how her car is running after its checkup, how her headache is, how she's feeling about the conversation she had with her sister yesterday— ask her about anything!

One common mistake guys make is assuming *that if they can't fix the situation, why bother asking their partner about it.* As one man said to me, "I know I can't do anything about the problem my wife is going through at work, so I guess I don't ask her how she's doing, because no response I give her will make a difference."

> **Here's what you need to remember: Even if she tells you she's not doing too well, and you can't say anything to make her feel better, just the fact that you asked will feed her heart and make her feel more loved. Your concern will always make a difference.**

3. Ask what you can do for her.

Women are used to feeling we have to do everything ourselves, from taking care of the house to looking after the kids, making the plans, organizing and coordinating everyone's schedule, and buying and cooking the food, often on top of holding down a full- or part-time job. Even if we complain about this from time to time, usually we silently bear these responsibilities and tell ourselves it's just "part of being a woman." So, when a man asks us what he can do for us, we are surprised, delighted, and supremely grateful. Many women commented on this in my surveys:

> *"When my husband offers to help me put the kids to bed, or straighten up the kitchen, I just melt. He thinks he's just being polite, but it makes me feel he really cares. This may sound strange, but it affects me almost like foreplay—I feel*

so much love for him that, later on, I am definitely more in the mood to fool around, rather than feeling resentful that I had to do everything myself."

"I love it when my man asks me if I need anything. I'm one of those women who isn't good at letting anyone else do things for me, so if left to my own devices, I won't ask for help. So when he offers, I feel like he's really been paying attention and notices that I am on overload, and this really endears him to me."

Now, guys, I admit we may not easily relinquish some of our tasks to you, since we secretly feel we can do them better, but we *will* be so appreciative that you offered, and our heart will definitely feel fed.

How We Starve Love and Relationships

We've talked throughout the book of the many ways we make our partner feel unloved and unappreciated, and all of these starve the relationship of the care it needs. Here are a few more common ways you may be starving your partner and your relationship without even realizing it.

1. Neglecting Your Partner and the Relationship Until There's a Big Problem

None of us would get in the habit of waiting to fill up our car until it totally ran out of gas. Yet that's the approach many people, especially men, often take in their love life—you wait to give the relationship attention until there is a problem. It's not that you don't care—it's that somehow *your love life gets put on the bottom of your priority list after work, hobbies, exercise, and whatever else seems important.*

As we've seen, men do not put love first, or sometimes even second or third. It's almost as if you try to put off dealing with the relationship for as long as possible, just like waiting until your gas gauge is almost empty before filling the tank. However, this habit can have the same result in your love life as it can with your car—before you know it, you've run out of gas.

Guys, I know it's not always easy, and certainly not always fun, to put time and energy into feeding your relationship. You'd probably rather watch a game on TV, or surf the Internet, or even work overtime—anything to avoid hearing your woman tell you what she's not happy about. *But the more you feed your partner's heart, the more juicy the relationship will become,* and before you know it, you'll *want* to be intimate and connect because it will feel so darn good.

I've said this before and I will say it again here for emphasis: **Don't wait until your partner is about to walk out the door to finally listen to her complaints. Don't wait until she is so love-starved that she's shut her heart down. Don't wait until your relationship is in an emergency state to pay attention to it. Do it now.**

At the end of our life, none of us is going to say, "I wish I spent more time working on my career. I wish I'd spent more time watching TV. I wish I'd gone to the gym more." I really believe we'll say, *"I wish I had loved more. I wish I had let the people I loved know how much I cherished them."*

2. Putting the Kids First

I'm going to say something I feel strongly about that may not be politically correct, but that I believe with all my heart is true: **When**

you put your relationship with your children ahead of your relationship with your partner, you are making a mistake that could eventually destroy your marriage. Being a parent means loving and nurturing your children, but in your good intentions to always give them attention, and always be there for them, you may unknowingly be starving your partner of the love she needs.

I have seen this pattern occur over and over again in marriages where one or both partners focus most of their emotional attention and energy on the kids, making them the glue that holds the relationship together. One day, when the kids grow to a certain age, or when they go off to college, the couple turns to each other and realizes that they are like strangers, and their relationship is dead. How did it die? They starved it of the love, the intimacy, and the connection that all relationships need in order to survive. *They gave everything to the kids, and nothing to each other. And they end up with great children, and a nonexistent marriage.*

I'll never forget a man who came to one of my first weekend relationship seminars many years ago in Los Angeles. Walter brought his wife, Grace, and his four children, who were all in their early to late teens, and told me they were attending in hopes of becoming closer as a family. To look at them, you would have thought they were the perfect couple with the perfect kids.

On Saturday afternoon of the seminar, I talked about how we often starve our partner's heart without realizing it. I noticed that Grace looked agitated, and kept raising her hand, wanting to speak. When I called on her, she stood up and immediately began to cry:

"Everyone thinks we are the all-American family," she began tearfully, "but if I'm going to get anything out of this weekend, I have to tell the truth, to myself and to those I love. And the truth is, Walter, that I'm not very happy. I love you and I love the kids, *but you never put me first*. From the moment our oldest, Jesse, was born, you've put the children first. You give them all of the attention and affection I long for. You tell them how proud you are of them, saying the words I want to hear. They think you are the perfect father, and I guess you are, but you're not the perfect husband. I watch you with the kids, and I feel jealous of them, jealous of my own kids, and I feel miserable and empty inside."

As Grace sobbed, Walter stood up and put his arms around her, and their four kids sat holding hands with tears streaming down their faces. "Walter, did you know Grace felt this way?" I asked.

Walter was trembling as he answered. "I guess I did in the back of my mind, but I never meant to hurt her. I'm sorry, honey," he said, turning to his wife. "I've just been trying to be a good father. I didn't want to make you feel I don't love you, because I do."

"Is she right?" I asked. "Have you been putting the kids first?"

"Yes, I have," Walter admitted sheepishly. "My dad was never home when I was growing up, and I guess I've been trying to make up for it. So I've been Super Dad. I wanted to prove we could have a great family."

"And you do," I replied. "But the foundation of a great family is a great marriage. What good is it if your kids feel loved but don't see you loving each other?"

Then I turned to Grace. "What do you need from Walter?" I asked.

Grace looked at her husband with vulnerable eyes. "I'm tired of feeling like number two, like I'm not as important as the kids. I want to come first."

I had an idea, and asked the four children to stand up and turn to their parents. "Kids," I said, "let me ask you a question: Is it okay with you if your dad makes your mom number one in his life from now on, ahead of you?"

The kids all smiled and shouted out, "Yes!"

"Okay, Walter," I said, "I'd like you to turn to Grace, and tell her that from now on, she's Number One."

I will never forget the look of bliss on Grace's face as Walter turned to her in front of everyone in the room, took her hands and said, *"Sweetheart, I make a commitment to you that from this moment on, you're Number One!"* The couple embraced, and the rest of the seminar attendees cheered.

"Just a minute, Walter, you're not done yet!" I said. "There's a second part of this that is just as important. I'd like you to tell your children, 'Kids, from now on, Mom's Number One!'"

With his arm around Grace, Walter looked at his kids, and in a really loud voice said, *"Kids, I love you, but from now on, your Mom is Number One!"* Four teenaged bodies rushed toward the couple, and they all embraced. And in that moment, they *were* the perfect family.

This moment has stayed with me in all the years that followed, and I know Walter and Grace would want me to share it with you. On that day, Walter recommitted to his wife and to his marriage. He was a prime example of a kind, caring man who, without knowing it, had been starving his wife's heart by putting his kids first. And Grace, like a typical self-sacrificing woman, told herself that she was lucky to be with a man who was such a devoted father, and that she had to come second, and not complain. Neither of them realized the damage they were doing to the marriage, damage that fortunately wasn't irreparable.

The greatest gift you can give your children is the gift of a happy and lasting marriage. And that's going to take work on your part.

> **Every time you feed your partner's heart,
> know that you are feeding your children's hearts as
> well, for the love the two of you share will overflow
> and bless your whole family with happiness.**

The Love Diet: How to Feed Your Partner's Heart

This is the "Love Diet." I've created it as an easy way to remember and practice feeding your partner's heart and being a wonderful lover outside of the bedroom. It's simple, it's fun, and it will make a big difference in your relationship.

When you study nutrition, you learn about the basic food groups—vegetables, grains, proteins, dairy products—and the importance of having each of these every day. Well, emotional nutrition is the same—feeding your partner's heart means making sure you give him or her all of the basic *"emotional food groups"* each day. What are these? I call them the Three A's: **Attention, Affection, and Appreciation.** They are the secret ingredients contained in the Love Diet that will fill up your partner's heart: *You pay attention, you show affection, and you express appreciation.*

The Three "A"s: Three Ways to Feed Your Partner's Heart

1. **Attention**
2. **Affection**
3. **Appreciation**

If I asked you right now how often you need to eat every day, you'd probably answer that you need to eat at least two or three times a day, with a few snacks in between. Well, I'd like you to think about feeding your partner's heart in that same way with the following Love Diet.

• **Love Meals:** Your partner needs three Love Meals a day. What is a Love Meal? It's a time each day for three minutes when you feed your partner's heart with one or more of the menu items contained in the Three A's: Attention, Affection, or Appreciation. I call this the **3 x 3 formula, three times a day, when you choose to actively love your partner for at least three minutes.** Think about it as three minutes of intimacy. Maybe it is three minutes in the morning together before you get out of bed, or three minutes on the phone in the middle of the day, or three minutes after the kids go to sleep. These are Love Meals. Just like you'd have breakfast, lunch, and dinner, you have Love Meal #1, #2, and #3!!

- **Love Snacks:** Even when you eat several good meals a day, you need a snack once in a while, don't you? Well, the same applies to feeding your partner's heart. Along with the 3 x 3 formula of three Love Meals a day, give your mate several *love snacks* during the day.

  What is a love snack?

- *A kiss on the cheek or the neck when you're passing your partner*

- *A quick call to say: "I love you."*

- *A compliment: "You look gorgeous."*

- *A look or smile that contains all of your love*

- *A note left in your partner's purse or a message left on her cell phone*

Now that you know the basics of the Love Diet, here is a description of its three main ingredients: The Three A's.

1. Attention

One of the most common ways we starve the heart of someone we love is by not giving them enough attention. This is why paying attention is one of the most effective ways to make your partner feel loved and is the first ingredient in the Love Diet.

Paying attention **means being there 100 percent in the moment with the person you love.** "Oh, I already do this," you might say. "We spend lots of time together." But the truth is, spending time together doesn't necessarily mean you're really giving her your full attention. You're talking with her, but you're also playing with the dog. You're sitting next to her, but you're also watching your favorite show on TV. That's not paying attention. And she will feel it. In other words, it doesn't count as a Love Meal!

Giving your partner your attention means being there fully with her. You are not doing anything else. You are not watching TV. You are not opening the mail while you talk. You are not fooling around on your computer. You are giving her all of your attention, even for a few minutes. How? Look into her eyes. Ask her how she's doing. Listen. Hold her. That attention will nourish her heart more than you can imagine.

Paying attention to someone you love like this tells her she is important to you, that you value her, that for those three minutes three times a day, she is the only thing that matters in the world. When you fully pay attention, precious moments of intimacy and passion can occur. This is one of the best forms of foreplay, as we'll see in the sex section.

2. Affection

You may have heard of a famous survey taken in the past five years when thousands of women were asked whether they would rather have intercourse with their husband, or just cuddle. What was the response? Almost 80 percent of the women said they'd rather cuddle than have sex! Men are baffled, not to say disappointed, by these statistics, but women understand them completely. Simply put, *most women are starving for more physical, non-sexual affection from their partner*.

Affection is the second ingredient in the Love Diet. *It means physically connecting with your partner three times a day for three minutes*—holding her hand, embracing her, kissing her, stroking her hair, being physically intimate.

When you are affectionate with your partner, you link your energies on a physical dimension and create a flow between your hearts. Remember our story about the orphans, and how healing affection is for the heart? When you show your mate physical affection, you are feeding her heart in a profound way.

Why do some men have a problem being affectionate? They fall prey to what I call the **"All-or-Nothing Syndrome."** This is a belief that says "If I don't have time to do it all, I will just do nothing" and it's based on the misunderstanding that all sexual sensation has to end in orgasm. (More on this in Part III.) In the minds of some men, they think that if they get aroused, they're supposed to go ahead and have sex. *So if they don't have time to go all the way, they avoid even getting excited, feeling it will be a "waste."*

For instance, a man is lying in bed with his wife in the morning, and she reaches over and starts to cuddle with him. He begins to feel aroused, but realizes he has to get out of bed within five minutes or he will be late for work. So he pushes her away and says, "Not now, honey, I have to get up." She feels hurt and rejected, and can't understand why her husband doesn't want to be affectionate with her. He doesn't even realize anything is wrong. Later that night, when he does have time for sex, she seems cold and disinterested, and he can't understand why.

What's happening here is the All-or-Nothing Syndrome. He felt he didn't have time to do everything, so he wouldn't even hug or kiss his partner, feeling it couldn't lead to anything. But guys, *affection isn't always supposed to lead to something. It is an experience of in-*

timacy in itself. Besides, those Love Meals of affection will have a great effect on your sex life. We talked earlier in the book about the Love Bank each of us has, and not making deposits in the wrong account! Well, **whenever you show affection toward your partner, you are making a deposit in her Love and Intimacy Bank**. How does that affect your sex life? As we'll see later, **the higher the balance in a woman's Love and Intimacy Bank, the more turned on she will be by you, and the more she'll want to make love.**

3. Appreciation

"I know he loves me, but he doesn't appreciate me." I hear this lament from women all the time about their partners. That's because most women are starving for more appreciation from the men we love. When men hear this, they are confused. "How can she say I don't appreciate her? I work hard to support her and the kids; I am faithful; I remodeled the basement for her last year. I do lots of things to show my appreciation."

Guys, what you're talking about is *showing your appreciation* by things you **do**. But what really feeds a woman's heart is *hearing you express your appreciation in words*.

Most women are much more verbal than men, and often things don't feel real to us until they are spoken. Knowing you appreciate us isn't always enough—we need to hear you say it. **We need your words**. Your words of love and praise are like precious jewels to us. We collect them and cherish them, and they make us feel valued and rich with happiness and contentment.

How should you express your appreciation?

• **Tell us what you love about us.**
• **Tell us what you appreciate that we do for you and our family.**

- **Tell us what you admire in us.**

- **Tell us what you're grateful for about being with us.**

- **Tell us what you're proud of us for.**

Often men feel they are appreciating their mates, even verbally, but what they don't realize is they may not be appreciating them for the things they really need appreciation for. In particular, women in my surveys begged me to tell men that they really want and need more **appreciation for taking care of the children and the home**. So many women expressed the need to hear their mate appreciate them for being a good mother, or making the house beautiful, or always having his shirts cleaned and ironed, or keeping his favorite foods in the refrigerator. Working mothers in particular wanted their men to know that they would like to be appreciated for taking care of the children and the home while also holding a part- or full-time job. As one woman wrote:

> *"I need to hear that I'm a great mother and wife, that he appreciates my cooking dinner after I work a nine- or ten-hour day; that he appreciates the fact that I handle the details about the house—from organizing the lawn being mowed to having the car inspected, to taking the dog to the vet or our daughter to the doctor."*

I've found that it's not that men don't appreciate the efforts their wives make in these areas. **It's that often women are so good at multitasking that it appears it's all effortless to us, thus the men just take it for granted and don't realize how hard we are working to keep it all together**. It may look easy, guys, but it's not! You can't imagine how hearing you say, "Thanks for dinner, honey," or "You dressed the kids so nicely for church this morning," or "I really appreciate your remembering to make my dentist appointment," feeds our heart with love.

Gratitude Snack Before Bed

Here's a simple and powerful technique for feeding your partner's heart with Appreciation. I call it a Gratitude Snack Before Bed. It's a way you can express your appreciation and gratitude to your partner for something she (or he) did that day. You get in bed, and before you go to sleep, take a minute to thank your mate for something from the day:

"Thank you for watching the kids tonight so I could go to the gym."

"Thank you for making my favorite pasta for dinner."

"Thank you for calling me at work today—it really cheered me up."

"Thank you for the shoulder rub when I came home. I really needed it."

"Thank you for being so patient with me this morning when I was so grumpy."

It's great to take turns giving each other little Gratitude Snacks. You'll be amazed how much you can find to be grateful for once you put your attention to it. And by the way, don't be surprised if your Gratitude Snack turns into another kind of more physical snack. Love is the best kind of foreplay there is. . . .

Feeding Your Children's Hearts with the Three A's

Your children need their hearts fed just as much as your partner does. The Three A's are a really easy way to remember how to give your kids the love they need. Each day, make sure you're giving them a few minutes each of Attention, Affection, and Appreciation. Pay attention to them exclusively so they really feel you there. Hold them and kiss them, not just when you wish them good morning and good night, but lots in between. Express your appreciation for them—tell them you're proud of them; tell them what you like about them; thank them when they do something that makes you happy.

One of the techniques that works particularly well is *giving your kids a Gratitude Snack Before Bed*, just like I suggested you do with your partner. "Thank you for cleaning your room today." "Thanks for helping Mom do the dishes." "Thank you for playing quietly tonight when I was on the phone." Your children will go to bed feeling happy and loved with very full hearts.

Things That Starve Love and Things That Feed Love

No act in a relationship is neutral. It either feeds your partner's heart, or it doesn't. It either nourishes the intimacy between you, or it starves it. It either brings you closer together, or it separates you further apart. How often we forget this, and don't realize that what we say or don't say, what we do or don't do, is having a profound effect on the person we love.

In my seminars, I always ask my audiences to help me make a chart on the board listing things that starve love and things that feed love. This is a great way for us to see the impact of our words and actions on our relationship. Here's an example of the kind of chart I'm talking about:

Things that starve love	*Things that feed love*
Withholding feelings	Communication
Criticism	Compliments

Flirting	Fidelity
Taking your partner for granted	Expressing gratitude
Acting as a loner	Acting as a team
Building up resentments	Clearing up issues
Withdrawing...................................	Reaching out
Working too hard	Spending time together
Blaming your partner	Taking responsibility for your part

Naturally, there's a lot more that could be added to this list. This is a great chart to look at together with your partner. Discuss the different items, and see if you agree or disagree with the ones I've listed. In fact, I encourage you to make your own chart, either by yourself or preferably with your partner, listing what you've found that feeds or starves the intimacy and happiness in your relationship. Seeing it written down really brings some of these issues home. I know a couple who posted their chart on their refrigerator so they'd be reminded of its contents every day. They wrote to tell me that their relationship had improved tremendously, just because they were more conscious of what they were doing to starve or feed their intimacy.

I came up with the Three A's because men so often would say to me, "I want to be a better husband, but I'm not sure what to do," or "I know my girlfriend needs more attention from me, but I never seem to know exactly what she needs." The Three A's makes it simple: Just pick one—Attention, Affection, or Appreciation—and you can't go wrong. Better yet, combine all three for a triple whammy of love!

Feeding your partner's heart with the Three A's is like a love insurance policy. Do you know that the majority of extramarital affairs happen not because the person is looking for sex, but because they're looking for the Three A's? When women who've been unfaithful are asked about the reasons they cheated on their mates, very few of them say, "Because I met a guy with a nice body," or "I wanted to have sex with my yoga instructor, who seemed very limber." **Most women confess that the reason they strayed outside the relationship was that they were love-starved. They weren't getting enough Attention, Affection, or Appreciation from their mate, and eventually found it elsewhere.**

This isn't an editorial comment on infidelity, but rather a reminder that if you make sure to give her Love Meals and Love Snacks every day, she won't walk around hungry looking for somewhere else to eat!

If you're presently in a relationship, I hope you try the Love Diet right away. Make a commitment to do it for just one week, **three times a day for three minutes using the Three A's, and a few Love Snacks in between**, and you will be amazed at the results. Your partner will glow with love, and you'll feel more in love.

Seven Small Investments That Will Give Men a Big Payoff

So many times throughout this book, I've made the claim to men *that women really aren't difficult to please—it's just that you have to know what to do*. I've also said that men would be amazed if they realized how easy it is to make a woman happy with the smallest acts and simplest gestures. Well, guys, I know you probably still don't believe me, so the time has come for me to lay it out even more plainly than I already have and give you a list of some of the best ways to feed a woman's heart. These are the "little things" she's always talking about wanting you to do for her. I'm here to tell you that if you try them, you will discover that the fabulous results you get aren't little at all.

I call these *"seven small investments that will give men a big payoff."* Imagine for a moment that your investment broker called you excitedly and announced that he had discovered the most amazing opportunity: You would give him $50, and in one day he'd turn it into $50,000! Imagine that you absolutely knew he was telling the truth. What would you do? Of course you'd go for it! You'd jump in your car that instant, if necessary, to bring him the money yourself.

You can see where I'm going with this, can't you?! The suggestions contained in the following list are small emotional investments. They don't take much time or energy at all. Yet, I guarantee you that, in most cases, they will give you big payoffs in your relationship. What might those payoffs be?

- *A woman who is in a better mood*

- *A woman who is calmer and less anxious*

- *A woman who doesn't nag or complain*

- *A woman who is more fun to be around*

- *A woman who thinks you're the best there is*

- *A woman who wants to have sex more than before*

A NOTE TO MEN: Guys, you'll notice some items on the list that follows that you may not enjoy doing that much, like buying and giving your partner a card, or some you might find horrible even to think about, like going shopping with her and telling her which outfits you like when she tries them on. Don't think I'm not sympathetic—I am. But I will remind you again that *the momentary discomfort you may experience doing these once in a while is nothing compared to the joy and satisfaction you will get from having a happy, happy, happy woman on your hands*.

Think of these seven suggestions as foreplay. As you'll see when you get to our chapters on sex, we women get turned on in our heads first. You may be thinking, "Come on, can a card or phone call actually make my sex life better?" YES! YES! YES! **Doing the things on this list will make you irresistible to the woman you love**.

A NOTE TO WOMEN: You know how you're always complaining to your man that you wish he'd do "the little things" to make you happy, but when he asks "Like what?," you don't know what to say? Well, you'll never be at a loss for words again after reading this list. Don't forget to add your own suggestions when you share this with your partner.

1. Give us greeting cards.

Women love cards. We can't get enough of them. Every survey response I received contained a reference to cards. I'm not talking about cards just for special occasions like birthdays or anniversaries, but for any time. Funny cards, romantic cards, pretty cards, homemade cards, simple cards. The more cards, the better.

Why do we love them? They are concrete reminders that you are thinking of us, that you went to the trouble of getting a card. We keep them, we read them over and over, we brag to our friends about them.

I know men's response to this: "I'm not a card kind of guy." Well, my response to you is: *Force yourself.* You do lots of things you don't particularly like to in life, like wearing a tie to work, or obeying the speed limit. All we're asking you to do is buy a little card once in a while. How hard can that be? You don't have to think it makes sense or even enjoy the process. *Just try it.* Go to a store and get a bunch of cards at once, so you don't have to go back all the time. E-mail cards are great too, although the actual physical card in our hand or on our desk can't be beat.

What do you do with the cards once you have them? Well, write something in them, of course. Then you can just give the card to us, or leave it on our pillow, or in our purse, or in our car, or on the refrigerator, or anywhere else we will find it. Women love surprises.

One final word: *Think of cards as foreplay.* Did you know the letters *C A R D S* actually stand for Ceremonious Attention Rewarded by Dynamite Sex? At least you'll have a positive reference to the word from now on.

Here's what I'm trying to say. Women get cards. We feel closer to you. We want more sex. Are you on your way to the store yet? I thought so....

2. Leave us notes.

Men are sighing as they read this. It's the "note on the pillow" suggestion. Yep, you're right. *We love anything you write us in your own words*—a note, a little drawing, a simple "I love you" on a Post-It. It's so personal and so intimate; even better than cards, to tell you the truth. Cheaper, too!

How long would it take you to write us a simple note? Ten seconds? Do you have ten seconds in your day to spare? Do you know what a great investment that ten seconds is going to be? We will be in a great mood all day. We will forgive all kinds of transgressions you've made. We will get out our sexy nightie.

Don't put pressure on yourself, guys, worrying that you're not Shakespeare and can't write anything romantic. A few XXX's will do. A smiley face. A heart. We aren't picky. We just want to know that you made an effort, and that will be enough.

The best present I've ever received from a man was a journal my partner gave me one year for Christmas. At the top of each blank page, he wrote a line or two—something he loved about me, or a beautiful memory we'd shared, or a happy thought for the future. This book is priceless to me. I read it all the time. No gift bought at a store, or expensive piece of jewelry, could rival the journal he gave me. Why? Because it contained his words, and to a woman *the words of love our man gives us are a treasure we keep in our heart forever*.

3. Call us during the day.

Women crave connection. By now, you know that, because I've said it dozens of times. (Women also repeat themselves!) *Connection feeds our hearts, it makes us feel loved, it even turns us on.* We especially love to feel connected when we're not physically with you, because it shows us you are thinking about us.

Here's a one-minute formula for making your woman happy: Pick up the phone in the middle of your day, and call her. Invest sixty seconds in feeding our heart. You don't have to have anything particular to say. We will just be happy to hear your voice. These messages are also wonderful: "I am thinking of you." "I hope your day is going okay." "I can't wait until this weekend when we'll have some time alone." Or, "I'm just checking in." Oh, we just love it when you check in. Checking in is the opposite of disappearing, which we hate.

What happens when you call us? We relax. We smile. We think you're considerate. We think you're wonderful. We make a big deposit for you in the Love Bank, which you can collect later. Now isn't that worth picking up the phone?

For bonus points, check in with us when your plans change and you know we will be wondering what happened. Call when you're going to be late. Call when you think we've been trying to find you and you've been unavailable. Call when you think we might be worried. One of the sweetest things my partner did recently was call to tell me he was going to be on the phone for a long conference call, so if I tried to reach him and couldn't, I shouldn't wonder what was going on. This phone call made my day, because he was being so considerate of my feelings.

Remember, as much as most men hate the phone, women consider it an extension of their bodies! So when you use it to reach out to us via the phone, well, you get the idea. . . .

4. Brag about us in front of other people.

Try this the next time you want to make your woman very happy: *When you're with her and other people, such as friends or family, find an appropriate moment in the conversation to say something wonderful about her.* If the conversation is about restaurants, say, "Veronica is such an amazing cook, I don't even like to eat out anymore." If someone mentions work, say, "Did I tell you Veronica sold more this month than anyone in her department?" If the topic turns to kids, say, "Veronica has a magic touch with our kids. You should see her invent games for them to play. I could watch her for hours."

I won't go on, but you get the idea. Before you say that this seems artificial or forced, let me remind you that your woman probably brags about you like this when you're with others all the time, and you don't even notice it. If she doesn't, she should. *Having one's merits pointed out in public stimulates a primal response in a woman.* It's as if you are a male animal and are letting the other animals know that this is your mate. Animals, of course, demonstrate this in other ways, but you can just stick to the compliments!

When a woman feels you are proud of her, she melts. You get many, many points for this. A compliment in public is worth ten in private. This is definitely verbal foreplay of the sweetest kind.

5. Make plans for us to do something together.

Plans are a turn-on. Plans make a woman feel safe. Plans make us feel you are thinking of us. Plans make us feel very grateful. Big plans, little plans, it doesn't matter. Just make some plans for us together.

Guys, I know your excuses: Women are better at making the plans, so why should you bother? My response? *Because it makes us feel taken care of.* It shows that you are investing in our future with your thoughts, that we are moving forward together.

See, *it's not about the content of the plans at all—it's about the act of making them.* That's why any kind of plans you make are wonderful, whether it's finding a new restaurant and planning a night out with us, or planning to watch a special event on TV with us, or even planning to help us clean out the garage. *As long as you tell us in advance, it qualifies as a plan.* And that's why we love it. Remember that one of the ways men drive a woman crazy is by being vague and ambiguous? When you make a plan with us for a few hours from now or a few days from now or a few weeks from now, we have something solid to hold on to in our awareness, and we feel safe.

Do you want to see your woman turn into a puddle of love at

your feet? Sit down with her and say, "Honey, shall we plan out our weekend?" or "Are there any plans we should be thinking about that you'd like to discuss?" Just use the word *plan* in a positive way. Maybe you can even whisper "Plans, plans, plans" in her ear. Mmmmmm . . .

6. Offer to go shopping with us.

Before you scream with horror, hear me out: You don't have to do this one often, but when you do, it counts for a huge deposit in the Love and Intimacy Bank. Most women love shopping. As I explained earlier, it's a sensual and intimate experience for many of us. So if you offer to share that experience, it will give us a big thrill. There is something erotic about having the man you love there while you try on different outfits, and asking his opinion about which he likes. We get to focus your attention on our body, and you get to stare at it in public.

I recommended this technique to a man I know, and with much resistance, he agreed to ask his wife if he could go shopping with her. Just before he left, Herb called me. "I can't go through with this, Barbara," he confessed. "I would rather have a root canal at the dentist than go to the mall today."

"Listen, Herb," I answered, *"don't think of it as shopping, or you will be miserable. Think of it as an exercise in concentration.* Get into her mind. Focus on everything she is focusing on. If she's looking at the colors of two sweaters, really think about those colors. If she is comparing the shape of different jackets and how they fit her body, look at those jackets as if you were being paid to give your professional opinion. Soon you'll feel a resonance with her consciousness, as if you get her from the inside out. I promise! You can do it!"

I hung up the phone from my pep talk, and waited anxiously to hear what happened. Later that afternoon, Herb called me from his cell phone. "Joy is paying for her purchases," he said, "so I had to call you for a minute and tell you that **it worked!** At first, I wanted to run out of each store screaming, but I practiced focusing on her and trying to understand what she was doing and thinking. And after a while, the strangest thing happened. I started feeling really close to her, and having a good time. She could tell I was enjoying myself—I think she was shocked—and suddenly she got really affectionate with me, giving me kisses each time she came out of the fitting room. I swear, we both were getting turned on.

"Now we're on our way home, and Joy mentioned that since the kids are at friends' houses for the day, we might want to lie down and 'rest.' She never suggests messing around in the afternoon. Suddenly, I love shopping!"

Taking my suggestion about this may require a leap of faith on your part, guys, but try it. For extra points, *pick out something you think would look nice on your partner and ask her to try it on for you.* Even if she doesn't like it, the fact that you were thinking of her in that way will create some very juicy intimacy.

7. Surprise us.

Women love to be surprised by the man we love. Something about it is very sexy. It's unexpected, unplanned, kind of like a sudden seduction. And since we're always trying to do twenty things at once, *surprising us with something sweet and wonderful makes us feel very taken care of.*

When men hear this, they think we're talking about surprising us with two tickets to Paris, or a gold bracelet, or something flashy. But really, guys, any surprise will do. Surprise us by coming home with flowers. Surprise us by going grocery shopping for us before we have a chance to. Surprise us by making the bed in the morning while we're in the shower. Surprise us by feeding the dog even though we normally do it. Surprise us by bringing home take-out food when you know we've had a hard day and probably won't be in the mood to cook. Surprise us by buying a CD you heard us mention we wanted.

Here's a great suggestion: *Surprise us by trying out some of the ideas you've read about in this book!*

————

This is just a partial list of small emotional investments that will give you a big payoff in your relationship. Your own partner probably has her own items to add to the seven suggestions I made.

Why should you take this list and all of the information in this chapter seriously? Why should you give it a try? Because to do so is to **demonstrate your commitment** to your relationship and your partner.

What Women Want Men to Know:

True commitment isn't about a ring, or a piece of paper, or how many years you've lived together with a partner. *It's the way you treat the person you love every single day.*

I've noticed that men often think of commitment as an internal stand they've taken, a decision they've made—you're committed to a woman in your heart, you're committed to caring for her and your family, etc. *Women, on the other hand, being the manifestors and creators that we are, look for signs of commitment on a daily basis, and use those signs as evidence that we are loved.*

True commitment isn't something static—it's a way of behaving in your intimate relationship from moment to moment. Each time you do something to express your love, you demonstrate your inner commitment. Each time you ask yourself "How can I feed my partner's heart?" you strengthen that inner commitment. And the more that commitment grows through the actions of love you take, the more connected and passionate you and your partner will feel with each other.

What all of this comes down to is: *Don't wait to start making love to your partner until you get to the bedroom.* Lovemaking begins whenever you choose to pay attention to her, to appreciate her, to touch her with sweetness. In this way, true lovemaking always starts in the heart. Sometimes it may end up between the sheets, and sometimes it may not, but when you are feeding the heart of the person you adore, you are making more love for both of you, and this makes you a wonderful lover in the truest sense of the word.

What Women Want Men to Know About Communication

Nothing is more frustrating than sitting across from the person you love the most in the world, and realizing that, at times, you simply can't talk to him or to her without some kind of tension or upset developing. If you've ever been in love, I'm sure you're all too familiar with this feeling. *"Why does it have to be so hard?"* you ask yourself. *"If we love each other so much, why can't we understand each other?"*

I've spent the past thirty years searching for the answer to that question. The truth is that falling in love, having sex, and figuring out how to live together all look like the easy parts of a relationship when you compare them to the ongoing challenge of trying to cre-

ate consistent and harmonious communication with your partner!
So many of the problems, disagreements, and struggles that couples encounter stem from the fact that we don't know how to talk
to each other in a way that works. We all do our best, but often it
isn't good enough, and we're left wondering if it's even possible
for men and women to learn to speak each other's language.

In my book *Secrets About Men Every Woman Should Know*, I
told women how men think, listen, and express themselves, and
suggested techniques for learning how to talk to the man you love.
Now, it's time for me to do the same favor for men. I wish every
man could read the following chapters before his first relationship
with a woman. That's because they contain everything women
have told me over the years that they want men to know about how
to communicate with us. The topics include:

- **Five Secrets About How Women Communicate**

- **Ten Male Communication Habits That Drive Women Crazy**

- **What Women Hate to Hear Men Say**

- **What Women Love to Hear Men Say**

If you're in a relationship, this is an important section of the
book to discuss together. Ladies, I think you'll find the following
pages contain some really effective ways to explain to your mate
what you've been trying to say about communicating with each
other. And, guys, after reading these chapters, you won't ever be
able to complain that you don't understand how women communicate!

CHAPTER TEN

Five Secrets About How Women Communicate

Five Secrets About How Women Communicate

Secret #1: Women love to talk because it creates connection.

Secret #2: Women express our thinking and feeling process out loud.

Secret #3: Women communicate with details.

Secret #4: Women use talking as a way to release tension.

Secret #5: Women minimize how upset we are.

Communication Secret #1:
Women Love to Talk Because It Creates Connection

A woman is sitting on the couch with her sweetheart after dinner. He picks up the remote control, ready to turn on the television, and she turns to him and says, *"Honey, let's just talk for a while."*

Instantly tensing up, he asks: *"Why, is there a problem?"*

Does this exchange sound familiar? If you've ever been in a relationship, I know it does! This scene is replayed millions of times each day in households all over the world as women try to talk to their partners, and men try to avoid the conversation at all costs. For many men, *"Let's talk"* are dreaded words. They hear them, and immediately sigh, grunt, grit their teeth, and prepare for the worst. Whether they respond with *"What's the problem?"* or *"Do we have to?"* or *"Oh boy, what's the matter now?"* or *"Let me sit here in peace, I worked hard all day,"* the message women receive is the same: **"I don't want to talk to you."**

No matter how much we understand about men, no matter how many times we go through this, women still feel hurt and confused when a man responds in this way. Why? Because we love to talk, especially to our partner. When we talk with you, it creates intimacy, it creates connection. *We don't have to have a reason to want to talk other than this—the desire to feel close to the man we love.* This is why it baffles women when we suggest talking and men react by asking, "Why, what's wrong?" or saying, "Uh-oh, here we go again," as if the only reason to talk to the one you love is when there's a big problem.

What Women Want Men to Know:

**Women don't need to have a particular reason to talk to the man we love.
There doesn't have to be a specific purpose or goal.
We want to talk to you simply because we love to connect with you.**

Guys, this is one of the most important secrets about how women communicate that you need to understand. **For a woman, talking is a way of loving, connecting, exchanging energy. The process of communicating itself is the goal, rather than any particular outcome**.

I once heard an amusing analogy to how when a woman says "Let's talk," a man wants to know what the purpose is. Imagine a man says to his wife: *"Let's make love."* And she answers: *"Why, do you want to make a baby?"*

If a woman responded this way to a man's request to make love, he'd think she was very strange indeed. But isn't it the same thing? Although making love *can* have the goal of getting a woman pregnant and creating a child, we usually do it just for the sheer joy of doing it, and not with a particular outcome in mind. In the same way, although having a conversation can have the goal of clearing up problems or exchanging important information, often its purpose is in the process of connecting with words, and not for any other reason.

Now I admit that sometimes when women say "Let's talk," it is indeed a precursor for dropping a verbal bomb of complaints and criticisms on our partner. I warn women against doing this in *Secrets About Men Every Woman Should Know*, and suggest that instead they give their mate a verbal "preview" of what they'd like to talk about, and ask if now is a good time for the discussion. But ladies, if you're in the habit of pouncing unannounced on your partner with negative feedback, he will dread any invitation to converse, fearing that what's coming will always be unpleasant.

Here's an important secret about women for both men and women to understand:

> **Women are *process-oriented*.**
> **It's in the process of an experience itself that we find**
> **meaning, whether or not we accomplish a specific goal.**

Women are what I call *process-oriented*. We gain value out of the process of doing things and focus on that as much as any goal we might achieve. That's why two women can sit down and say "Let's talk" and not have an agenda in mind, or why a mother can play with her child for hours without having to achieve anything or teach her anything, or why we can take a day to ourselves and appear to do nothing, and yet emerge feeling refreshed and inspired. It's why we know that just being with someone we care for who is in pain will make a difference, even if we don't say anything helpful, or why writing in our journal will make us feel more clear and calm, even if we don't come up with solutions to our problems.

So for instance, when I say "Let's talk for a while" to my partner, much of the time I may have absolutely no goal in mind other than to share the process of communicating with him. *It's almost as if I am saying, "Let's make love," only with words, not with our bodies.*

I want to take a moment and address something men ask me all the time: **Why do women love to talk so much?** Well, perhaps it's because we understand that one of the best ways to create intimate connections between ourselves and our sweethearts is with **words**. *Words are bridges that allow us to travel from our private world into our partner's, and him into ours.* They link our silences together, so we can know the person we love from the inside out, and he can know us.

I believe that words are necessary because they take the formless energy that love is and wrap it into packages. *They furnish our feelings with concrete form so they can be passed on to our mate.* Each expression of caring, of appreciation, of gratitude becomes a beautiful present we offer our beloved. And each time we share something about ourselves, our thoughts, our feelings, it's as if we're giving a piece of ourselves to our lover. **In this way, talking is a form of making love—verbal intercourse if you will, which is why women find it a form of foreplay.** (More about this in Part III.)

Why Men Don't Enjoy Talking Like Women Do

If women like to talk so much, then why do men often not like to talk in the way that women do? Men often have a difficult time with how much women like to talk **because men are primarily** *goal-oriented.* **They find their value not just in participating in the process of an experience, but in achieving a specific goal, a measurable outcome.**

> **Men are *goal-oriented* and *solution-oriented.***
> **They like to feel that what they are doing, whether**
> **it's communicating, spending time with someone,**
> **or engaging in an activity, is going to *accomplish***
> *or achieve something specific.*

Here are some of the reasons men don't always like to talk in the way women do:

1. Conversations without an apparent goal often make men very uncomfortable because they seem inefficient.

This is why men say (or at least think!) the following things when they're talking to women:

"Is this conversation going anywhere?"
"Is there a point to this discussion?"
"Could you please cut to the chase?"
"What is the bottom line here?"
"Where is all of this leading to?"

Notice the emphasis on words or phrases that have to do with getting to a goal. **This is because men communicate best when they have a focus for the conversation. They like to know what the purpose of a discussion is, and what a woman wants or needs from them.**

Unconsciously, men may feel pressured to perform, to "do it right," but when they don't feel they are clear on the purpose of a dialogue, they don't know what "it" is. **This is why men often don't like to get involved in a conversation with their partner without being informed of an agenda. To proceed with a discussion without knowing its purpose may seem inefficient to the male mind, which wants to accomplish something useful.**

Women, on the other hand, don't need a focus to enjoy talking—just the process of participating in a conversation with someone we care about fulfills our deep need to connect. And as we'll see in our next Communication Secret, our style of talking may appear to be the opposite of focused! So we can't always understand why our man seems uncomfortable when we want to have a conversation, and we interpret his resistance to talking with us as a sign that he doesn't care or doesn't want to be close.

2. Men don't like doing what they feel they aren't good at.

For many men, the inner world of feelings isn't as familiar as the world of the mind. From the time they are little boys, men aren't encouraged to feel and express emotions as much as women are. One result of this is that men often don't have the same *emotional confidence* that many women have. *They may not be able to get in touch with feelings as rapidly as women do, or put those feelings into words on command.*

Remember: **Men like to feel competent and successful and have been trained to define themselves through these values. So naturally they don't like doing something that makes them feel inadequate, unskilled, or insecure. And talking about feelings and emotional issues definitely falls into this category.**

Can you see why, when a woman turns to her lover and enthusiastically says, "Darling, let's talk about us and our relationship," he cringes? *What she thinks will be an intimate love fest, he dreads as a long session of emotional aerobics!*

I'll never forget a conversation I had with a boyfriend a long time ago about why he got so upset every time we had a "talk." For months I had been trying to figure out why he hated having conversations about anything relating to "us." Finally one night, in a fit of frustration, he blurted it out: *"I can't keep up with you!"*

"What do you mean?" I pleaded, not understanding what he was trying to say.

"I mean I can't keep up with you in our conversations, with your pace and how fast you figure out what you want to say, with your willingness to talk about all of your feelings, with any of it. I feel like an amateur running a race against an Olympic athlete."

I remember feeling awful at the time, but not fully understanding what this man was trying to tell me. Many, many years have passed since then, and looking back, I know exactly what he meant. This was a very intelligent man, but in the realm of emotional communication, he didn't feel confident, so he avoided going there with me as much as possible. No wonder he hated to talk about our relationship.

Does this sound familiar? This is why men often find talking with their mate "exhausting." Women think they are just making excuses when they say this, but guys, I know you're not. It can really feel like a marathon that you don't want to be running.

3. Men internalize their thinking process and only communicate the end result.

"Why doesn't my mate share more of his process with me?" women ask me in frustration. *"I never know what he's thinking."* When I give women what I believe is the answer, they aren't always happy with what they hear: *"He doesn't share more of his process because he doesn't want to."* Why not? **Because men often prefer expressing themselves only when they are clear on exactly what they're feeling or thinking, and not before. They internalize their thinking process and wait to talk about it until they've come up with a solution or opinion they are sure about.**

I call this *"mulling."* Men like to mull things over inside, silently and in private. For instance, if you're a man reading this book right now, you'd be more likely to think about a particular point for a while before discussing it with your mate if she's nearby, or with a friend, if you're reading at his house. You might nod your head, maybe even mutter "Hmm," but probably not say much out loud. However, I have a feeling, if you're a woman reading this book, you've already been making comments to your mate or whomever else is around. That's because women think out loud. (See Communication Secret #2.)

Men often feel unprepared to have conversations with their partner because she wants to talk NOW, and that doesn't give you guys time to "mull." Of course, women don't realize you're mulling something over, or need more time to think about it before discussing it with us—we just end up feeling like you don't want to talk to us. More about this later.

What Men Can Do:

Guys, we know we like to talk more than you do. We know you aren't always comfortable with emotional topics. We know you'd often rather just be quiet. But we love you and need to connect with you through communicating.

1. Even if you don't think you're very good at talking about feelings, *it's better to do it poorly than to not do it at all.* It's just like anything else: The more you practice, the easier it gets.

2. When a woman wants to talk, *ask her if there is anything specific she wants to cover.* If there is, you will now know the agenda, and can feel more comfortable. If she says that there's nothing in particular—she just wants to talk—believe her! She's simply trying to create some intimacy, and perhaps even feel closer so she can be more in the mood for some physical loving.

Communication Secret #2: Women Express Our Thinking and Feeling Process Out Loud

"When my wife talks to me, she's all over the place. I know she's a smart woman, but she can sure sound like a scatterbrain."

"I love my fiancée, and I try to be attentive to her needs, but whenever she starts to talk, she goes on and on and on—I feel like she's never going to stop."

"I've been trying to make an effort to be more supportive when my wife is upset, but to be honest, half the time I have no idea what she is talking about. It's like she's telling me every thought that's in her head."

Let's be honest about something that baffles men: Why do women sometimes sound so confused, scattered, and dramatic when we express ourselves, and yet insist that we're very clear about what we're saying? Why do we seem to him to be going on and on about nothing, and yet afterward, we seem to feel better? Are we aware that we're repeating ourselves? Do we realize that we switch subjects twenty times in five minutes?

The answer to all of these questions is found in Communication Secret #2: **Women express our thinking and feeling process out loud.**

Ladies, you know what I'm describing here. You and your husband are having breakfast, and you decide to tell him what you have planned for that day:

"Honey, could you make sure you leave those two suits out on the bed, because I am going to the cleaner's this morning. I know you need them back for your trip next week, so I figure I'll get them there before noon, and pick them up tomorrow. Actually, if I'm going to the cleaner's, I might as well return the videos we rented over the weekend, since it's nearby. Oh, but you didn't watch the one you really wanted to see yet, did you? That's right—well, I'll leave them here for another day. Oh, I almost forgot, did I tell you Steve and Arlene called yesterday to let us know their house sold? Isn't that great? That reminds me, I never wrote Arlene a thank-you note for the flowers she sent for our anniversary. Where did I put my organizer? I know I had it here last night. Anyway, about the cleaner's, is there anything else you need me to drop off?"

What is the woman in this scenario doing (besides driving her husband crazy)? She's expressing every thought she has out loud, allowing one to flow into the other. To her partner, it may appear that she is just rambling. But as any woman knows, she's not rambling, she's doing what I call *spiraling*.

I came up with the term "spiraling" after studying the difference between how men and women think. In my lectures, I like to explain it by comparing the male and female thought process to our sex organs, because it's an easy and amusing way to remember this information. Imagine for a moment the female sexual area— our womb. It's actually circular in nature, kind of like a spiral. Well, I believe that women's minds reflect the circular nature of our womb in the way they work—**we think in a spiral.** Here's how it works:

We express something we're thinking about. Then that thought reminds us of another topic, and we begin talking about that. Soon, we're reminded of something we've been trying to figure out, and we switch to that subject. Round and round we go like this, going from one thought and feeling to another. It may seem to the untrained observer (male, of course) that we've forgotten about what we were originally discussing, but we haven't. If you listen for a while, eventually we will cycle back to exactly where we started— **that's why it's called spiraling.** And, we may repeat this process several times in the course of one conversation!

Why does communicating this way work for women? Because we are process-oriented.

What Women Want Men to Know:

Hearing ourselves talk helps women get clear on what is going on inside of us.

> **The process of expressing our thoughts out loud actually allows us to figure out what we're thinking and feeling.**

Women's habit of spiraling drives most men crazy. Why? Well, back to my analogy of how men and women think (see, *I'm* spiraling now!)—if a woman's way of thinking reflects the circular nature of the womb, then to understand a man's way of thinking, we should refer to his sex organ. Let's see—it's straight, it points in one direction. **That's why men think in a linear fashion and like to get to the point!**

When a man listens to a woman "spiral," he often assumes we're a little, well, "disorganized" in our thinking. "After all," he thinks, "when I talk I say what I need to say; I get the job done. I don't wander all over the place and waste everyone's time." To a man whose mind operates by trying to "get to the point," women sound undisciplined and excessive when we spiral.

Why Women Sound Undisciplined to Men When We "Spiral" Out Loud

1. We don't edit anything.
2. We jump from one point to another, and don't seem to be thinking logically.
3. We repeat ourselves...and repeat ourselves...and repeat ourselves.
4. We can appear to be very high-strung and emotional.

Guys, what women want you to know is that when we spiral out loud, we are not rambling; we are not confused; we are not stuck; we haven't forgotten one word of what we've said; we know we are repeating ourselves; we realize we are jumping from topic to topic; we're aware that our emotions fluctuate. To us, it all makes sense because we are processing our feelings and thoughts out loud. And when we are all done, we will feel so much better!

Other women understand, of course. You'd never hear a woman say to her girlfriend in the middle of a long conversation: *"How much longer is this going to take? Is there a point to all of this? You know, you've said the same things over and over!"* Just the thought of women talking to one another like this makes me laugh. We wouldn't, because we understand spiraling. Men, however, can find the habit women have of thinking out loud to be very bothersome, and often don't react well.

What Men Do Wrong:

1. You assume we're confused.

Just because you can't follow the logic of how a woman is expressing herself, guys, doesn't mean she is confused. However, in your attempt to be loving and helpful, you talk to us as if we're a child, or worse, like a patient in a mental hospital, explaining things in a methodical, logical voice, hoping we will see the light. This really annoys us, because we're not confused, even if we happen to say we are—we're processing our thoughts and feelings, and eventually, in this conversation or another, we will get clear. But when you interrupt our spiraling process, the whole thing is just going to take longer!

2. You cut us off because you think there's no end to it.

I will admit that women can go on and on ... and on, as we spiral round and round, sort of like a verbal whirling dervish! The truth is, we enjoy processing ourselves out loud. It actually helps us to release tension (more on this later). **However, guys, often you don't even give us a chance, and cut us off before we really say what we are trying to say.** Sometimes you don't even wait for us to say much at all, and abort the process with a comment like, *"Is this going to be another one of your marathon confession sessions?"* or *"I don't have time for this."* Your fear, of course, is that if you don't stop us, you could be there until sunrise. I'm not saying this could never happen, but when we feel you sitting there anxiously waiting for us to come to some conclusion, it only makes us more nervous, and prolongs the process.

3. You take what we say literally.

"And how else am I supposed to take it?" you might ask. Well, my suggestion is to just **let us talk it out without responding right away to every inaccuracy**. For instance, a woman says, "I am feeling so stressed out. We never have fun anymore. I feel all I do is work, work, work." You hear this and think, "Wait a minute, we just went to the movies last weekend. She's not being accurate. She's exaggerating." And you say, "Honey, that's not true. We do lots of fun things together. We just went to the movies last week."

Now you're disagreeing with her about the accuracy of how she feels rather than listening to what she's trying to say beneath the words. We end up feeling that you don't care, that you are insensitive, and that we can't talk to you.

4. You get frustrated because you don't hear a definitive conclusion or result.

Since men are goal- and solution-oriented, it's frustrating for you to spend time talking with your mate, and when it's all over feel nothing has been accomplished. Perhaps she still sounds upset. Perhaps she's repeating the same thing she said at the beginning of the conversation. Don't be misled by this. Even when it appears that the conversation didn't go anywhere, believe me, it did. Just the fact that you sat there with us feeds our heart, calms us down, and you may be surprised to find that an hour or a day later, we suddenly seem to get clear about something we were trying to understand.

What Men Can Do:

1. Talk to your partner about the concept of spiraling. If she agrees that this is how she often likes to process her thoughts and feelings, *try just listening with no attachment to any result.*

2. If you're concerned that your partner will take too much time spiraling through what she has to say, *let her know what kind of time limit works for you rather than impatiently cutting her off.* We'd rather have a brief conversation with you than none at all.

   For instance: *"Honey, I would love to hear all about your day. I have about ten minutes before I have to take a shower, and you have my complete attention."*

Communication Secret #3:
Women Communicate with Details

The following is a true story told to me by one of my best friends, Angela, about a conversation she had with her fiancé, Howard. "This incident must go in your book!" Angela insisted, and when she shared the details, I had to agree.

Angela and Howard were having dinner at an upscale restaurant in New York City. The waiter brought them a bottle of wine they'd ordered, and poured a glass for each of them. "Let's make a toast," Angela said.

"Okay, cheers!" answered Howard, clinking his glass against hers.

"Howard, that's not any kind of toast," Angela complained.

"It seemed fine to me."

"But every time we toast, you say 'Cheers.' It's so impersonal. A toast with your lover needs to be more intimate," she explained.

Howard sighed, and tried again: "Here's to you, honey."

" 'Here's to you'? What is that supposed to mean?" Angela asked.

"It means . . . I don't know what it means," Howard replied impatiently. "It's just a little toast, for God's sake. What's the big deal?"

"The big deal is that a toast should be romantic. You're supposed to say sweet things to the woman you love that will make her feel good."

"All right, what kinds of things am I supposed to say?" Howard asked somewhat sarcastically, knowing if he didn't, Angela would tell him anyway.

"Well, here's what I'd like to hear in a toast," Angela replied. *"Sweetheart, I am so lucky to be with you. You make me feel so good. I can't imagine my life without you. You are the most won-*

derful woman in the world. I don't want anyone else but you. I never even dreamed I could be this in love."

Howard raised his glass, getting ready to toast Angela. Her heart began to beat a little faster in anticipation of the words she was finally going to hear. And then, with a big smile, Howard said, "Ditto."

As Angela recounted the end of the story, I gasped, "No, he didn't!"

"Yes, he did," grumbled Angela.

"What did you do?" I asked.

"I looked him in the eyes, raised my glass and said, **'Ditto my ass!'** "

———

I laughed so hard when Angela relayed this story because it was such a perfect example of how men and women communicate differently, as well as a great illustration of our third communication secret about women: **Women communicate with details.** We include details in what we say to others. We want details when others communicate with us. The more details, the better!

Men, however, are different. **Most men simplify the exchange of information and like to cut to the chase. So they avoid details, and instead give an overview.** And that's all they want from us, too—an overview. For instance:

- When our boyfriend tells us he had lunch with a friend, we ask "Where did you eat? What did you order? What did you talk about?" We want details. If, on the other hand, we told him we'd had lunch with a friend, he'd simply say, "That's nice."

- When our husband asks us how our day was, we offer him details of everything from where we went, whom we spoke with on the phone, what thoughts we had, you name it (not that he actually wants to hear them!). When we ask him how his day was, he says, "Fine."

The reasons for this difference go back to what we discussed earlier, that *men are goal-oriented and women are process-oriented. For men, the goal of the conversation is to pass on the pertinent information. For women, the goal of communicating is the process of conversing itself.* So sharing the details of our thoughts, our feelings, our experiences is a way we reach out to make dozens of little connections between us and the man we love. This is also how women communicate with each other, by sharing the details of our lives. In this exchange of information, we create intimate bonds with one another.

If you listen in on the conversation between two male friends, however, it's a different story altogether. Many less words are spoken. Sentences are more generalized and less specific in content. The goal is achieved—the guys talk and say whatever they needed to—but it usually takes much less time than when two women talk!

So when you put men and women together, you often get this result:

She thinks he's not talking enough. He thinks she is talking too much.

This is what was happening with Angela and Howard. To Howard, toasting his fiancée with "Cheers!" was sufficient. *But Angela wanted details.* She wanted to hear how he felt in the moment, why he loved her, specifics that would create a special moment of intimacy between them. Obviously, "Ditto" wasn't what she had in mind!

What Men Do Wrong:

Here's one of the big problems that develops when men don't understand this secret about women: You misinterpret our attempts to get you to tell us more as prying, and you become annoyed at our habit of sharing so many details in conversations, and think of us as chatterboxes. Then, guys, you react by:

• Cutting us off when we're talking

• Acting totally disinterested

• Getting irritated with us for asking you too many questions

---

What Women Want Men to Know:

Men misinterpret a woman's interest in the details about his life as our attempt to interrogate him or invade his privacy and our habit of sharing the details of our life as an attempt to take up too much of his time, rather than understanding that in both cases, we are trying to connect.

Guys, when you conclude that women simply talk too much or want you to talk too much, you're missing the point. In our own way, we are trying to love you, to create more intimacy, to strengthen the bonds of connection between us.

What Men Can Do:

Women don't expect you ever to be as interested as we are in the details of various topics, or even to express yourself in as much detail as we do, but any effort you make will be so appreciated:

---

1. When we're sharing details with you, *try listening with love*. You know you'd do this if one of your small children was telling you all about his day, or if you were a sports fan and a friend was recounting the events of a game. Instead of thinking, "Jeez, she's going on and on!" tune in to how we are reaching out to you and sharing ourselves.

2. *Try giving us more details when you communicate with us.* Remind yourself that we're not trying to irritate you—*we're trying to create intimacy.* The closer we feel to you, the more we will want to be physically intimate when the time is right!

Communication Secret #4:
Women Use Talking as a Way to Release Tension

- *She's just had an argument with her mother on the phone and is very upset. She comes into the bedroom and wants to tell her husband all about it.*

- *She had a difficult meeting with a client. On the way back in the cab, she calls her boyfriend on his cell phone, hoping to pour her heart out to him.*

- *She's nervous about putting the house up for sale and moving. Just before she and her husband fall asleep, she starts talking about it, going over all the pros and cons for the twentieth time.*

According to statistics, most women live longer than most men, and I believe one of the reasons could be that women talk so much! All right, I'm kidding—kind of. But maybe there is some truth to this theory, because women do have a secret technique we employ for releasing tension and combating stress that most men don't use: **We talk about what is bothering us, and then we feel better**.

This is one of the most natural ways women deal with stress. We talk, sometimes over and over again, about our fears, our upsets, our worries, our hurts. We go over the same issues twice, three times, ten times, as many times as it takes until we feel calmer and less concerned. Our female friends understand this, and would never say to us, *"Didn't we go over this yesterday?"* or *"How many times are you going to say the same thing? I heard you the first time."*

Men, however, don't always understand this secret about women. That's because they have a very different way of handling their tension. **Whereas women externalize our worries, men internalize theirs. We spiral through ours out loud; men keep theirs to themselves.** And so, guys, when your partner repeatedly talks about her worries or anxieties, *you make the mistake of concluding that we are more upset than we actually are.*

What Men Do Wrong:

As we discussed earlier, guys often assume that because women repeat ourselves in talking about our upsets, we aren't making any progress in resolving them. But this is not the case. In fact, it's the opposite.

What Women Want Men to Know:

For women, talking something out over and over again eventually dissipates the stuck energy around it.

Each time we hear ourselves bring up an issue or state a fear out loud that fear becomes a little weaker, and our understanding of it becomes a little more powerful, until suddenly, it doesn't have a hold on us anymore. This is why two women can spend an hour on the phone, and if a man listened in, he might think they were just complaining, and not helping each other at all. But at the end of that hour, I promise you that both women would feel clearer, stronger, and less under the spell of whatever had been bothering them.

When men don't understand this communication secret about women, you often make the same mistakes I listed under Communication Secret #2. But let me repeat a few of them for emphasis:

- You become frustrated or exasperated with us, sometimes cutting off what we're saying because you feel you've heard it before.

- You listen with impatience, feeling as if we're taking too long to express ourselves, rather than listening with compassion and support.

- You lecture us, as if we're a confused child—why else would we be going on and on about the same stuff?

- You mistake our processing our emotions for our being a basket case. We're not falling apart—we're releasing the emotions that have been locked up inside so we can feel better.

What Men Can Do:

1. **The next time your woman is upset or stressed and she starts talking about what's bothering her, remind yourself** *that it's not really the content of what she's saying that's the issue—it's the process of running out her feelings that's going to calm her down.* **Focus less**

on whether or not you've heard her say these things before, and more on being there for her. Hold her hand, put your arm around her, listen.

2. When she's done, *tell her you hope she feels better having talked about it, and that you are there for her whenever she needs to talk again.* (This counts as a huge deposit in the Love and Intimacy Bank!)

3. Try doing this yourself the next time you feel stressed or anxious. Maybe you'll see why we like talking so much!

Communication Secret #5: Women Minimize How Upset We Are

Women are harmonizers. Because we put love first, we value harmony and go out of our way to create it, especially with the man we love. This is why we always want to communicate, to clear things up, to work on the relationship—because we so desperately want things to work, and want to make our mate happy.

Our intention to create harmony is a good thing, but some of the effects of it are not always so good, either for us or the relationship.

What Women Want Men to Know:

In order to keep the peace, women often don't express how upset we really are.

> **We don't stand up for ourselves,
> and we downplay the severity of our dissatisfaction
> with our mate.**

This isn't something we do consciously. Rather, it is a primal instinct to maintain harmony at all costs. We may edit our unhappy feelings so successfully that we even forget about them ourselves.

The problem occurs when men, and who can blame them, take us at our word, and don't realize how upset we actually are about a particular situation because we minimize it when we communicate with you. For instance:

We say: "I've been thinking about the fact that we haven't had sex for a while."

We mean: "For months, I have been terribly unhappy about the fact that we haven't had sex."

We say: "Do you think we should get some more baby-sitting help for the kids?"

We mean: "I am going crazy taking care of the kids and feel totally overworked."

We say: "No, I don't really mind that you can't come to my sister's wedding with me."

We mean: "I am so disappointed that you aren't coming to the wedding, and feel like you're not taking this relationship seriously."

I know as men read this, they're throwing up their hands and saying, "How the heck am I supposed to know she's unhappy if she doesn't tell me?" Of course, you're right—it's not fair to expect you to read our minds. But as I wrote in an earlier section, men don't always get how dissatisfied a woman is even when she does make it crystal clear. So yes, women need to learn to be more honest about our "not nice" feelings, but guys, you need to pay attention to what we're trying to say, and not wait until we are utterly miserable to get the hint.

What Men Do Wrong:

Men often minimize a woman's communications about her unhappiness, probably in hopes that they won't have to deal with it, or that it isn't as bad as it seems. You could say this is a form of denial—if I don't pay attention to it, maybe it will go away.

- You misinterpret serious grievances as mild complaints.

- You tell yourself that we still seem loving and sweet, and thereby discount the severity of what we are trying to say.

- You dismiss it as PMS.

Guys, please remember what I am about to say: **It is a safe bet for you to presume that a woman is probably much more upset than she appears to be.** If she says she's a little irritated, she's probably very pissed off. If she says she's a little anxious, she's probably very worried. If she says she's unhappy, she's probably miserable.

One way to look at it is to think of a woman's complaints as smoke. When you see smoke, you'd better look for the fire. *If we say something is wrong, it is usually ten times worse than it appears.*

———

Let me share a true story about a couple I know well. Ruth and Spencer have been married for eight years and have three small children. When they met in graduate school, they were one of the most romantic couples I'd ever seen. You couldn't imagine them being any more in love.

Spencer became an orthodontist and soon developed a highly successful practice. He and Ruth bought a large, expensive home in a prestigious neighborhood, and when the kids came along, created what appeared to be the perfect life for themselves. Ruth gave up her marketing job to be a full-time mom, and the children thrived under her loving care.

One night last year, Ruth called me in tears. "Barbara," she confessed, "I'm miserable, and I don't know who else to talk to."

"What's wrong?" I asked. "Did something happen?"

"That's just the problem—I don't know what's happened. I've been feeling really weird for some time now, and I told myself I was just tired because of the kids, or that I'd feel better when we finished remodeling the house, but today I realized I can't hide from the truth anymore. I am just so unhappy in this marriage."

"What's going on with you and Spencer?" I inquired. "Is he feeling the same way?"

"I have no idea how he is feeling," Ruth answered angrily. "I feel like he totally neglects me, like I've become a good friend or something. We haven't had sex in about two years, and every time I try to initiate it, he has some excuse—he has to get up early, or he has a headache. Lately, I've just stopped trying. We've just drifted apart, and whenever I attempt to talk to him about this, it's like he just doesn't hear what I'm saying. I've told him I'm not happy, that I think we need to work on our marriage, that we should go to a counselor, that I miss having sex with him, but none of it seems to sink in. I care for him, but I don't feel in love anymore."

"Oh, Barbara," Ruth sobbed, "what am I going to do? I don't want to get a divorce, but I can't go on like this."

My heart broke for Ruth as I listened to her confess her unhappiness. I knew Spencer well, and he hated confrontation of any kind. I could just imagine his total discomfort every time Ruth brought up the topic of their marital difficulties. And yet surely he must realize how bad things were. I told Ruth I'd try to find an opportunity to speak to Spencer, and encouraged her to hang in there.

Two weeks later, Spencer called to say hello and mentioned that he was going to be at a conference in my town the next day. I asked if he'd meet me for coffee during one of his breaks, and he happily agreed. When I arrived at the restaurant, he greeted me warmly, and we spent a few minutes catching up on mutual friends.

Now it was time for me to broach the subject. "How's everything at home?" I asked casually.

"Pretty good," Spencer answered. "Of course, it's been really hard for Ruth with the remodel, not to mention that the kids are a handful. But I guess it's this way for all parents."

"Are you guys getting along okay?"

"Well, we don't spend enough time together alone. That's my fault—I have been working so hard lately, and don't get home until seven or eight at night. By then, I'm exhausted. But Ruthie is really understanding, and has been very sweet about it."

"Sweet?" I thought to myself. "Is he serious? She's miserable!" So I tried again, this time a little more boldly:

"You know, Spencer, one thing I've learned about women in my work is that you can't always tell if they're unhappy. We're so good at trying to get along with everyone. It sounds like Ruth is pretty stressed out. Do you think she might be more upset than you realize?"

Spencer thought for a moment, and then said, "No, she's pretty strong, and I think she's handling the stress well. I admit, I haven't been easy to get along with lately, but she's a real trouper."

We finished our coffee, and I said good-bye to Spencer. The

whole way home in the car, I shook my head in amazement. How could he think his wife was just a little stressed when the truth was she was considering leaving him? How could he be so clueless?

Of course, I knew the answer: *Ruth's attempts to communicate her unhappiness with Spencer were too subtle, too polite for him.* She didn't scream or yell; she didn't threaten; she didn't blame him. She just shared her loneliness and anxiety, and Spencer made the mistake of dismissing the smoke and not looking for the big fire that was blazing out of control right in his own home. Ruth and Spencer are still together, but each time she calls me, she is a little closer to leaving him. My fear is that unless she directly threatens, he won't get the message in time, and that it's already too late to salvage the marriage.

What Men Can Do:

When your partner tells you she's upset, or communicates about something she's unhappy with, PAY ATTENTION. Rather than rushing through the conversation, *ask her to tell you more about how she feels. Assume there is more going on than meets the eye.* I know this suggestion sounds totally unappealing, but wouldn't you rather put out a few tiny flames than be faced with a huge raging blaze?

Even when we insist that we aren't that upset about something, try to get us to talk about it. Just the fact that you are willing to listen to us will make us feel so much better. Remember: *When you connect, rather than disconnecting, we will feel loved, our heart will be fed, and we'll be able to let go of whatever was bothering us that much more quickly.*

CHAPTER ELEVEN

The Top Ten Male Communication Habits That Drive Women Crazy

Here they are, the top ten male communication habits that women complain about. I created this list based on my research and interviews with couples, the surveys I received, and the discussions in seminars with literally thousands of women eager to share their stories about communicating with men.

Ladies, this is an important chapter for you to read and understand. Maybe you've been feeling frustrated or less than satisfied in your relationship, but you aren't sure why, and when your mate asks you what's wrong, you haven't been able to articulate exactly what's bothering you. The information in the following pages will help you pinpoint potential trouble spots in your own relationship and communicate them to your partner, so you can argue less and love more.

Guys, the information contained in this list will be priceless to you. It will save you countless hours of tension, sulking, disagreements, and nagging. It will reveal what you might be doing without realizing it to create tension in your relationship and bring out the worst in the woman you love.

Please know that this Top Ten list isn't meant to be a form of criticism. I believe that most guys are unaware of these communication habits, and that's all the more reason it will be so useful for you to learn about them. And just so you don't think I'm saying it's all your fault, let me remind you that I included a similar list when

I wrote *Secrets About Men Every Woman Should Know*, informing women of what communication mistakes we make with men.

When I was compiling this list, I was interested to discover that many women had actually come up with descriptive names for their husbands or boyfriends when they exhibited the behavior of one of the ten habits. For instance, one woman said that when her husband bottles up feelings and then explodes, she thinks of him as "Volcano Man." Another woman whose partner tends to go silent on her told me that she and her girlfriends refer to him (privately, of course!) as "Invisible Man" when he behaves that way—"Guess who showed up this morning? Invisible Man!"

Women use these admittedly not very flattering nicknames to deal with the angry and hurt feelings we often experience when men act out these ten habits. I thought I'd borrow this idea and use it to help get my points across. You'll notice that each of the ten male habits includes the name of a character that corresponds to the behavior. Here's the list of the Top Ten male communication habits that drive women crazy, along with their ten counterparts. After showing this chapter to the man in her life, I hope no woman will ever have to meet them again.

The Top Ten Male Communication Habits That Drive Women Crazy

1. Men are vague ....Mystery Man
2. Men avoid discussing things............Slippery Man
3. Men withdraw into silence ....Invisible Man
4. Men don't tell us what they
   want and need ....Secret Man
5. Men bottle up feelings and
   then explode..Volcano Man

---

6. Men walk out in the middle
   of a discussion.....................................Vanishing Man
7. Men order us around.......................Commando Man
8. Men make fun of how we feel........Sarcastic Man
9. Men lie to avoid dealing with
   something unpleasant......................Chicken Man
10. Men anticipate the worst and
    get reactive...Reacto Man

#1. Men Are Vague

He won't be specific when you ask him questions.
He hates to be pinned down by verbally committing to anything.
He dodges all of his partner's attempts to get a clear answer out of him.

Ladies, allow me to introduce you to **Mystery Man**, the person your partner becomes when he communicates in a vague and ambiguous manner. Mystery Man is an exasperating character because you're never quite sure what he is thinking or feeling. It's not that he doesn't talk to you, because he does—it's just that afterward you're not quite sure what he actually said.

Mystery Man is an expert at communicating without actually giving out any information. For instance, Martine is trying to have a conversation with her husband, Brian, about his fourteen-year-old daughter who lives with them part-time:

MARTINE: Brian, Charlotte was smoking in her room again last night. I said something to her, but she got very sassy and slammed the door.

BRIAN: I'll handle it.

MARTINE: Well, what are you going to say? You've already talked to her a dozen times about this.

BRIAN: I'll deal with it, Martine.

MARTINE: I know you will, but it would really help me if I knew what tactic you are going to take so we're on the same team. And I'd like to know when you're going to talk to her so I don't interfere by giving her more feedback before then.

BRIAN: Look, I'm going to do it, okay?

Brian became Mystery Man—his responses were vague, he gave Martine no details, no specifics, nothing to answer any of her questions or deal with her concerns. She can't tell if he is upset with her for bringing his daughter's smoking to his attention, or if he just doesn't care that much about it, or if he is taking it seriously. *In other words, she has no clue what is going on inside of him!*

Here's another common example of this communication habit:

A woman is trying to discuss plans for the weekend with her boyfriend.

"Do you like the idea of taking a drive to the country on Saturday?" she suggests.

"That sounds interesting," he replies.

"Well, should I do some research on places to go?"

"You can if you want to," he says in a detached way.

"Well, it sounds like you don't want to go—you don't seem very excited," she says.

"I didn't say that," he answers.

How does this conversation make her feel? Like she wants to scream! He is being so vague that she has no idea how he really feels about the weekend, or what she should do.

Guys, do you have any idea of how much time your partner spends trying to figure you out? We'll call up a girlfriend and ask her opinion: *"Okay, last night he said this. Now what do you think it meant?"* or *"Based on his response to our last conversation, do you think I should bring the issue up again now, or wait a while?"* Why are we asking her, you might wonder? **Because when you're vague and non-committal, you don't tell us what's going on, and we can't read your mind.**

Here's an analogy that might help men understand why women hate it when you're vague in your communication: Imagine that a friend calls you and says he wants you to join him for a hike in the mountains. You enthusiastically agree, and he says he'll pick you up the next morning. He arrives as planned, and you begin your drive. "So where are we going?" you ask him.

"You'll see—it's a really nice place," he answers.

"Well, is it far?"

"Not that far."

"Well, how long is the drive?" you question.

"Not that long—we'll get there eventually."

By now, you'd be totally exasperated with your friend for being so vague and unresponsive to your queries. You couldn't enjoy the ride, because it is colored by so much uncertainty. Well, guys, this is how women feel when you don't give us even a vague map of what you're thinking or feeling or planning.

Why Men Become Mystery Man
Why are men vague in their communications?

1. Being vague is a safety mechanism.

As we've seen, men don't like to be wrong or to make mistakes. Sometimes they are unconsciously vague in their communications as a way of protecting themselves. **If they're not sure of an answer, or haven't figured out how they feel about something, they respond in a vague and ambiguous manner—that way, if they're wrong, a woman can't hold them to what they said, because they didn't actually say anything specific.** This is why Brian wouldn't give Martine details about how he was going to deal with his daughter—he probably didn't know himself, and rather than admit that, he became Mystery Man.

2. Being vague is a form of independence.

Remember how important his sense of freedom is to a man? **Being vague in communication is like an insurance policy for a man's pride and ego.** If a man is vague in what he says, he leaves himself room to change his mind, and his mate can't criticize him for it. If he doesn't give her much information, she can't scold him for not doing something, or pin him down. The less he says about himself, the less he commits himself, the more free he feels.

How Mystery Man Turns Us into Interrogation Woman

Conversations with Mystery Man leave a woman frustrated and anxious because we never get the information we need to feel safe or put an issue to rest. We become impatient, unable to move forward until Mystery Man gives us more input. The result is that we end up feeling *scared, left out, insecure, and angry*.

Inevitably, Mystery Man brings out a certain part of us men hate: **Interrogation Woman.** *"You never told me when you're going to call the accountant—could you give me a date?"* *"Have you* *thought any more about our vacation?" "Why don't you tell me what happened at work to upset you so much?"* The emergence of Interrogation Woman is inevitable when a man insists on being vague—**we want to feel safe, we want to be able to make plans and decisions without waiting forever for you guys to make up your mind, and we need details!**

What Men Can Do:

1. Try not to be so evasive, and give your woman some information when you're communicating. *If you don't feel ready to make a decision, or aren't sure how you're feeling, at least say something.*

Example: Instead of saying, "I'll handle it," Brian could have said to Martine, *"I'm not sure how I want to handle my daughter. I'm going to think about it for a few hours, and I'll let you know what I decide."*

2. *Stop thinking of your woman as the enemy you must hide information from.* **Remember: The less we know, the more anxious and insecure we become, and then you get to deal with Interrogation Woman.**

Sharing information is a way of showing us that we are on the same team. *We don't need to know every detail, just give us an overview.*

#2. Men Avoid Discussing Things

He's never in the mood to talk.
He tells you this isn't a good time, only no time seems to ever be good.

He procrastinates about making decisions and leaves you wondering what's going on.

Ladies, do you know this guy? Of course you do—it's **Slippery Man!** Watch how skillfully he slips and slides out of conversations, skillfully avoiding having to deal with you, your concerns, or the things he's promised to do.

Slippery Man is a master of sidestepping the issue, because he doesn't want to deal with it. To listen to him, you'd think he was the busiest man alive. He never has time to talk about what's bothering you; there's always something pressing at work or in his life that is distracting him from being able to confront whatever it is that he's avoiding. *Since Slippery Man isn't the confrontational type, at first he appears to be cooperative in the relationship—that is, until you figure out that he's cleverly manipulating you by just not being available.*

Slippery Man is actually a close relative of Mystery Man, and their motivations are similar. Like Mystery Man, Slippery Man is trying to avoid being pinned down, making a mistake, or feeling he's being controlled by a woman. You might say his slippery nature is a form of passive-aggressive behavior. He doesn't directly confront you—he just slips away.

How does Slippery Man operate?

1. He refuses to deal with issues when they come up.

Slippery Man's motto is: *Never deal today with what you can put off indefinitely.* He is an expert at putting things off and always has an excuse for why now isn't a good time to deal with something. *"Let me think about it,"* is one of Slippery Man's favorite lines. The problem is that the issues, decisions, and concerns end up going into a sort of emotional Never-Never Land. You know they're there, but you can't quite get to them.

2. He doesn't keep a woman updated on his process.

Guys, imagine that you're a football fan, and are listening to a game on the radio. For some reason, the announcer isn't giving out much information. He won't tell you what quarter it is, he won't tell you the score, he won't tell you how much time is left in the game, or how many yards it is to a first down. Instead, he just vaguely talks about football in general, describes a little bit of what's happening on the field, and keeps wandering off of the topic. Naturally you'd be angry and frustrated. "I want the score!" you'd yell in frustration. "Why won't you give me any information?"

Well, this is how women feel when you become Slippery Man. **We want a progress report on any issues we've been discussing or decisions we have to make as a couple.** *We need updates.* Without them, we are left in the dark.

Let's say a month ago, you promised you'd look into finding us better medical insurance before ours expired. As the weeks go by, you don't mention anything to us, and because women are timekeepers (Chapter 3), we're aware that our insurance comes up for renewal very soon. We try to talk with you about it, but you brush us off: "I told you I'd deal with it. I'm really busy this week."

How does this make us feel? *Totally insecure.* We don't know if we should go ahead and look into the insurance ourselves, or keep bugging you about it, or what.

How Slippery Man Turns Us into Nagging Woman

Slippery Man is an expert at leaving a woman hanging. We can't make plans, we can't resolve issues, we can't move forward, we can't finalize decisions, all because Slippery Man is avoiding communicating with us. And so naturally, we can't help it, to our great dismay we turn into **Nagging Woman: We bug our mate to talk to us; we chase** you around to try to get closure on decisions we need to make; we keep bringing up unfinished business over and over again until we sound like a broken record. Of course all of this becomes a terrible vicious cycle—*the more we try to pin you down, guys, the more pressured you feel, and the more slippery you become!*

When a woman is with Slippery Man, she feels taken for granted. He doesn't care if we are inconvenienced by his refusal to make a decision; he isn't concerned that he's holding us up by procrastinating. Yet, when Slippery Man decides he's ready to talk, he expects us to be cheerfully attentive and open to the conversation. *Ultimately, Slippery Man sets a woman up to become a frustrated, angry nagging bitch who acts and feels more like a man's mother than his wife.*

What Men Can Do:

1. *Don't avoid your partner when we want or need to discuss something.* If you can't talk about it at the moment, let us know when you can. Don't just leave us hanging.

Here is an easy-to-remember formula for lovingly dealing with your partner when you aren't able to have a conversation. I call it *The Three R's:*

What to Do When You Aren't in the Mood to Talk: The Three R's

1. *Recognize* her desire to communicate with you.
2. *Respond* in some way.
3. *Reschedule.*

For instance, you'd say: *"Honey, I realize it's important to you to figure out what we're doing with our families over the holidays. I know you're trying to get it organized in advance. I just feel swamped right now. Why don't we find some time Saturday when the kids are at soccer to discuss it?"*

2. *Give us updates* on things you know we're waiting to hear about. For instance:

"Listen, I know I promised to check into our insurance. To be honest, I haven't a chance. I plan to take care of it this week."

"I've been thinking about our conversation a few days ago regarding painting the bedroom, and I guess I'm still kind of torn about it. Part of me thinks it's a good idea, but I keep wondering if we should wait and see if we're going to sell the house. What do you think?"

Even if you haven't completed a task you said you would, or aren't sure how you're feeling about something, *we will be so grateful for any information you give us.*

#3. Men Withdraw into Silence

You share your deep feelings, and he just sits there staring at you. He says nothing when you ask what he thinks about something.

When you notice that he seems upset and ask him what's wrong, he acts as though he doesn't hear you and doesn't respond.

What woman hasn't been driven to the depths of emotional despair by an encounter with **Invisible Man? That's because Invisible Man often responds to a woman's attempt to communicate with silence**. Talking to him feels like dropping pebbles into a well that has no bottom—you wait to hear them make contact, to hear a splash, but all you get is silence. That's what happens when you try to converse about important topics with Invisible Man. He just vanishes.

Sometimes being in a relationship with Invisible Man feels like you're in love with ghost. He's with you, but he's not. You can see him, but you can't feel him. He acts like he's present, but he doesn't say anything:

You and your boyfriend are driving to dinner, and you notice that he seems to be in a bad mood. *"Is something wrong, honey?"* you ask. Silence. He keeps driving.

You say to your husband at breakfast: *"I was thinking we really could use a vacation sometime soon."* Silence. He stares at his newspaper, and says nothing.

You've been explaining to your partner why you're uncomfortable when he spends so much time talking to his ex-wife on the phone. He's been listening without saying a word. *"Well, is there anything you want to say about all of this?"* you ask him. He shakes his head no. Silence.

What's going on in Invisible Man's head during these encounters? Who knows? Perhaps he's not in the mood to talk, so he doesn't even bother to answer. Perhaps he's not sure how to answer you, so he says nothing. Perhaps he feels worried or guilty or confused, and can't put his feelings into words, so he just sits there. Of course, these are all guesses, because Invisible Man, by definition, isn't going to tell you.

Guys, imagine that your car isn't running properly, and you bring it into the repair shop for an assessment. You leave it there for a few hours, and when you return, you approach the manager:

"Well, did you find out what's wrong with my car?" He just stares at you and says nothing. "Excuse me, perhaps you didn't hear me. I asked if you knew what was wrong with my car?" He looks away and starts shuffling through papers.

How would you feel? Furious, I'm sure.

Here's another example:

You work for weeks on a presentation your boss requested, and finally turn it in. A few days pass, and you haven't received any feedback from him. You make an appointment to see him in his office, and when you arrive, he's sitting at his desk.

"Listen, I hadn't heard anything from you about the presentation, and I was wondering if you've had a chance to take a look at it?" you ask. He sighs, and says nothing. "Is there a problem with it?" you inquire, feeling more anxious. "Do you need me to redo it?" He sits there bending a paper clip with a blank look on his face.

How would you feel, guys? Probably terrified that you were about to be fired. I am sure you see the point I'm trying to make: *It's simply not okay not to respond* to someone when they are speaking to you. *It's rude, it's insensitive, it's disrespectful.* I'm sure you'd feel that way if these scenarios happened to you. Well, guess what? This is just how your partner feels when you become Invisible Man.

Here's the thing I want to tell men about silence:

Silence isn't neutral. It contains a message just as powerful as speech. It isn't the absence of information. It's just the ab-

*sence of words. It isn't the absence of a response to your partner.
It's an empty response.*

When a woman's partner reacts to her attempts to communicate
by being silent, she doesn't come away feeling "He said nothing."
She comes away having heard a message that hurts her heart:

What a Woman Hears When a Man Doesn't Respond

1. What you said isn't important enough for me to respond to.
2. I don't care enough about you to answer.
3. That was so stupid, it doesn't deserve a response.
4. My response will hurt you so much that I am keeping it inside.

How Invisible Man Turns Us into Panicky Woman

Do you want to see a woman's emotional state deteriorate
within just a few minutes? Then give her the silent treatment. Be
distant, disconnected, and aloof. Say nothing. Then watch her turn
into **Panicky Woman**.

When do we panic in our lives? When something happens that
is sudden, that frightens or confuses us. That's how women feel
when, out of the blue, Invisible Man shows up. One minute we are
sitting there with our partner and he seems to be fine, and suddenly
we say something that he's not happy with, and poof—he vanishes, and Invisible Man takes his place. Where has our sweetheart
gone, we wonder frantically? Then Panicky Woman emerges, feeling abandoned, scared, and lonely.

Of course, when our husband or boyfriend sees Panicky

Woman appear before him, he becomes even more invisible. Panicky Woman always makes men want to flee in the other direction as quickly as possible. *The more invisible he becomes, the more we panic, the more he wants to flee, and the terrible cycle begins.*

The irony about Invisible Man is that he can make a woman feel invisible too, as if we have also disappeared, as if he hasn't heard a word we've said, as if he's seeing right through us. One woman wrote that "it feels like he slams a door in my face." And it does feel like that, and worse.

What Men Can Do:

1. When your partner is trying to communicate with you, no matter how you feel, say something. Don't just vanish on us into thin air.

Here are some alternatives to silence:
"I hear what you're saying. Thanks for telling me. I need to think it over for a while."

"This is a bad time to talk to me. I am very distracted. Let's talk later."

"I know you need to talk, but I feel unprepared now. I need more time to give you the response you want."

"I'm noticing myself feeling resistant to discussing this. I think it's because I am tired and just wanted to chill out after work. Can we talk after dinner?"

"I realize this is important to you, but my mind feels overloaded right now and I'm having a hard time

> *concentrating on what you're saying. I think I'll*
> *feel better after a nap/a meal/exercise."*
>
> 2. **When you notice that you're turning into Invisible Man,** *make a concerted effort to reconnect with your partner in some way.* **Reach out and touch her, ask her questions about what she's saying.** *Remember: Nothing positive is going to come from your silence, and it's only a matter of time before Panicky Woman shows up!*

#4. Men Don't Tell Us What They Want and Need

You know there's something he's trying to say, but you can't figure out what it is.

When you ask him if there's anything he needs from you, he says there isn't, but you know he isn't telling the truth.

He seems uncomfortable about something you've said or done, but insists when you question him that everything is fine.

Meet Secret Man: He is so sweet, so charming, so easy to get along with. But you're only seeing half of the picture, ladies, **because Secret Man expertly conceals his needs and desires from you so you'll never know what's really going on inside of him.** He keeps them a secret, maybe even from himself, and try as you might, you can't get him to share that secret with you.

You may think you're making Secret Man happy, but you can't ever be sure, can you? That's because with Secret Man, what you see isn't necessarily what you get. He seems to be satisfied, but is he? Whenever you ask him if there's anything more he'd like from you, he insists that there's not, that you're perfect. This makes you suspicious, because you know very well that you're far from perfect. Does he really feel that way? Is he a dream come true? Or is he hiding something?

The answer, of course, is that Secret Man is a master of keeping secrets. He keeps what he wants a secret. He keeps what he's unhappy with a secret. He keeps his needs a secret. And guess what? *You're supposed to discover these secrets all by yourself.*

Men like this who don't ask for what they want and need emotionally and sexually in a relationship are usually testing their partner, unconsciously, of course. *"If she is the right one for me,"* he thinks, *"if she really loves me, she will figure out what I need."* So he sits back and waits for you to prove yourself. Naturally, ladies, you will fail, because you aren't a mind-reader. Then, each time you disappoint him by not doing what he wanted you to do, or by continuing to do something that bothers him, he bitterly concludes to himself that you aren't the one after all, and therefore he can't really give you his whole heart.

This is what's at the root of Secret Man's withholding behavior—*his fear of being hurt and disappointed.* Ironically, it's this fear that sabotages the relationship and sets his partner up for certain failure. **The less a woman can figure out what he needs, the more she disappoints him, and the more he withholds.**

Secret Man was probably emotionally jerked around by a woman or women at some point in his life. That's why he tests you. *"Is she too good to be true?"* he wonders. *"Could a woman really love me this much?"* But he's afraid to find out the answer, so he doesn't give you a chance.

Here's one of the most frustrating things about Secret Man: It's not that he doesn't try to communicate. In fact, he often thinks he is expressing his needs and desires, and is surprised that you didn't figure out what he was trying to say. **The problem is that his attempts to express himself are so subtle, so gentle, so timid that**

they're practically nonexistent. They're more like hints than actual requests. For instance:

You ask your partner if he's in the mood for Chinese food. He says, "Sure." Then you add, "Or we could go to that Mexican restaurant we heard about." He replies, "Mexican sounds nice." Unsure of his preference, you say, "Well, which one do you want to try?" He says, "Whatever you want, darling."

Since your mate doesn't seem to care, you choose the Chinese restaurant. Later that night after you've come home from dinner, you notice him foraging around in the refrigerator. "Are you hungry?" you ask with surprise.

"Kind of," he answers, munching on some old pizza.

"Didn't you get enough to eat at the restaurant?"

"Well, Chinese food never really fills me up," he responds.

Suddenly you get it—he didn't want to go to the Chinese restaurant at all. When he said "Mexican sounds good," you were supposed to figure out that this was his version of a big YES, even though it sounded noncommittal.

This isn't a serious incident that could break up a relationship. But just imagine how many times in a week Secret Man doesn't let you know how unhappy he is, what he would like more from you, or if you're satisfying him in bed! How frightening it is to a woman knowing that her Secret Man is probably storing up lots of resentful and disappointed feelings. If Secret Man isn't careful, one day all of that suppressed emotion explodes, and he turns into Volcano Man, the next character you'll read about.

How Secret Man Turns Us into Detective Woman

When a woman loves Secret Man, we're operating in a void of information much of the time. What is he really feeling? What does he really need? Am I pleasing him or not? These questions haunt the woman whose partner doesn't express his concerns and desires, and turn us into **Detective Woman.** Detective Woman is *always on the lookout for clues, hints, any signs that will tell us more about what is going on inside of our lover.*

How do we know Detective Woman has taken over? **We watch our mate like a hawk. We analyze every little thing he says over and over again. We ask our friends (Deputy Detective Women!) what they think of what our man did or how he re-acted, hoping to gain insight from their observations.** It's not relaxing to be Detective Woman, because we're always afraid we'll miss that one big clue that will unveil the truth about our beloved. Of course, he notices that we seem tense all the time, and concludes that we're not happy with him, and becomes even more secretive!

The problem is that our Detective Woman's tactics are based on experience dealing with our partner. Secret Man won't give us feedback up front; however, if we happen to stumble upon the truth, he'll tell us that we're right. **So we play lots of emotional guessing games, and ask suggestive questions like:**

"Do you happen to be feeling like I've been calling you too much, and you're needing some space?"

"Did the way I talked and talked last night about my problems at work overwhelm you?"

"Would you feel more comfortable if my sister didn't come to stay with us next week as planned?"

When our partner says "yes" to one of our inquiries, we feel so successful, as if we've solved the mystery of his heart. But this whole pattern becomes exhausting after a while, as we try to piece together the puzzle of who he is without any help on his part.

What Men Can Do:

1. *Give your partner a chance to please you by telling us what you want and need.* When we do something you enjoy, say, *"I really loved it when...."* When you're not happy with something or are concerned about an issue, don't just hope we figure it out on our own, because we won't—let us know by saying, *"I wanted to clear up something that is bothering me...."*

2. *Be specific and give us details when you communicate about your needs and preferences.* Only say *"Whatever you want"* or *"It doesn't matter to me"* if those things are true! Remember: Women think of love as our job. So the more information you give a woman, the more we can make an effort to fulfill your desires.

3. When you notice that we've become Detective Woman, please give us a break and help us out! You know when we're trying to figure out what you're feeling, so *don't make us work so hard.*

#5. Men Bottle Up Feelings and Then Explode

He fumes over something he's upset about, and then blows his top.

He stews silently because he's annoyed with you, but doesn't say anything until all at once he loses his temper.

You have no idea he's angry, because he hasn't said anything, until one day when you ask him a simple question, and he explodes.

Call out the bomb squad, put on your protective gear, and stand back because you're dealing with **Volcano Man**. Ladies, you know him well—**he bottles up his feelings, insists he's fine, until all at once, when you least expect it, he explodes.** Only then do you realize that his anger and resentment have been ticking away, and it was only a matter of time until it blew up, usually injuring you and anyone else who's around in the process.

Of course, Volcano Man doesn't realize the damage he's caused, because he always feels better when he finally lets off steam and gets his feelings out. He may even be in the mood for sex after he's had a tantrum (YUK!) and wonder why you're not that interested. Perhaps if he weren't so self-indulgent, he'd notice the wounds his anger has inflicted upon you, and realize why you look so shaken.

Who is Volcano Man? He is a guy who doesn't know how to deal with his own stress and tension, and takes it out on those he loves. He is usually someone who grew up with a Volcano Mom or Dad who taught him that the only way to deal with emotions was by shouting, intimidating, and threatening. Inside, he is a very scared little boy who's made an unconscious decision to scare off those who would hurt him with his anger before they have a chance to be angry with him.

Volcano Man doesn't communicate with his partner: *He fumes, smolders, intimidates, and badgers.* If a woman attempts to talk about something with him he doesn't want to address, he responds with piercing glances, dirty looks, and nasty comments. When these don't stop us, he reverts to raising his voice in order to shut us down. This tactic usually works to scare us off, because most women don't like to be yelled at.

Let me be blunt for a moment, guys: **There is nothing macho, powerful, or admirable about being Volcano Man.** Someone who can't control his reactions is weak, not strong. Someone who uses intimidation to avoid dealing with his partner's feelings is a coward, and not the boss.

How Volcano Man Turns Us into Tiptoe Woman

Being in a relationship with Volcano Man is like walking through an emotional minefield—you hold your breath, try to avoid stepping on a charge, and pray that you won't get blown to bits. That's why Volcano Man turns his partner into **Tiptoe Woman**. The name speaks for itself, doesn't it? *You spend your time, energy, and effort tiptoeing around your partner, hoping you won't say or do something to "set him off."*

It's impossible for a woman to live with Volcano Man and not become high-strung, paranoid, timid, and terrified. Lovely qualities, aren't they, ladies? But that's what happens to you when you live in fear of the next insult, the next argument, the next drama.

What Men Can Do:

1. If you think you're living with Tiptoe Woman, this may be a sign that you're more of a Volcano Man than you've wanted to admit. Ask your partner if you exhibit the symptoms we've mentioned. Try talking about your feelings, worries, and concerns before they build up and explode.

2. If you suspect you are a true Volcano Man, please seek professional help. It's really difficult to heal that much anger on your own, and a good therapist or anger management specialist can work with you to resolve the issues underneath the anger. You deserve to be free of the prison of your rage, and so does your partner.

#6. Men Walk Out in the Middle of a Discussion

You tell him you want to talk about how little time you've spent together lately. He gets up and leaves the room, proclaiming, "I can't deal with this right now."

You've been arguing about the credit card bills, and you begin to cry. He says, "I can't talk to you when you fall apart like this," and walks out of the house.

You feel like you're finally making progress in a discussion about your kids, when suddenly, he jumps up and announces that it's too much for him, and walks into the den to watch TV.

I don't think there's a woman out there who hasn't had an encounter with **Vanishing Man** at least once or twice in her life. One minute he's sitting there before you like the sweet, loving partner you know he is. Then suddenly, he's gone. Sometimes he explains why he's leaving before he does, which doesn't make it any better but at least you know what's going on; sometimes he pops up from his chair like a piece of toast in a toaster, and with an unhappy comment hurries away; and sometimes, before you even realize what's happened, he's fled the room in silence. No matter how he exits, the result is the same: *You feel hurt, abandoned, and angry that he didn't stick it out.*

What causes this disturbing phenomenon? It's almost as if men have a *Tolerance Meter for Emotional Discussion*, and when the needle hits a certain point on the meter, they reach their limit, their tolerance expires, and they decide that the time for conversation is up. Perhaps this is why Vanishing Man seems to pull his vanishing act with such suddenness, and little warning. Maybe even he doesn't realize it's about to happen until it does.

Some men have a low Intimacy Threshold—their tolerance for emotional discussion lasts a mere few sentences into the conversation, and presto, they're gone. Others can hang in there until one of their hot buttons is pushed: He's fine until his partner starts crying, or uses a certain phrase, or gets a particular look on her face, and he's instantly into his discomfort zone, with vanishing not far behind. Still others are really good at talking with their partner most of the time, unless they're affected by extenuating circumstances—they're really tired; they're under extra pressure at work—and then their propensity for vanishing increases.

Vanishing Man may not have the intention of upsetting his partner, but unfortunately his disappearing act is one of the worst breaches of relationship etiquette that there is. Walking out on your partner when you're in the middle of a discussion or argument is rude and hurtful.

Please understand, guys, I'm not saying that one should sit there in relationship hell hour after hour if no progress is being made in a discussion. There's a moment when calling a time-out or taking a break to calm down is appropriate. But that's not what Vanishing Man does, even though he may think that's what he's doing. He's just bailing out without giving his partner much warning.

Why do perfectly nice guys suddenly turn into Vanishing Man? We've talked about the reasons for this throughout the book—*men get impatient with long, emotional spiraling discussions; men feel blamed or controlled by things women say and don't want to hear any more; men come to an impasse in their ability to process the information being communicated in their conversation and need time to mull it over; men get claustrophobic talking about intimacy and feel the urge to flee.*

The problem with vanishing is that it short-circuits the conversation. There can't be any resolution or closure with only one person in the room.

How Vanishing Man Turns Us into Orphan Woman

How do women feel when we're suddenly faced with Vanishing Man, or more accurately, when we watch Vanishing Man as he leaves the room? We feel abandoned, deserted, orphaned. That's why we become **Orphan Woman.** Like a parentless child who sits and waits for someone to come and take him home, we sit watching the door, hoping that Vanishing Man will return, throw his arms around us and say, *"I'm sorry, darling. I just got frustrated. I shouldn't have walked out on you. I'll never leave you like that again."* All right, maybe that's expecting a little too much, but we'd settle for "Sorry I got so upset" and a kiss on the cheek—anything to feel connected with our sweetheart again.

It's difficult not to become Orphan Woman when our man vanishes on us at such a vulnerable time. We feel hurt, frightened, and very much alone. *And in a strange way, we may also feel like a failure*—we've failed to heal whatever was amiss between the two of us; we've failed to keep our man open and willing to work through our difficulty; we've failed to keep him there with us. Remember, women put love first, and crave connection and harmony at all costs. This is why most of us hate arguments. So we would have sat there all night, if that's what it took, to resolve a conflict and get to the point where we could kiss and make up—anything to heal the separation between ourselves and our partner. Instead, our partner has vanished, and *we feel cheated out of the opportunity to make things right.*

What Men Can Do:

Please don't suddenly walk out on the woman you love in the middle of a discussion. Try to hang in there and use the many techniques you've learned about in this

book to come to an understanding, to resolve your issues, or to at least be kind while you're disagreeing.

Guys, if you feel Vanishing Man beginning to manifest inside your head, or your Tolerance Meter approaching the limit, don't just get up and leave.

What to Do When You Feel Like Vanishing

Let your partner know that:

- *You realize the conversation is important.*

- *You want to continue and clear things up.*

- *You've reached a point where you aren't going to be very productive or helpful for much longer.*

- *You would like a time-out or break for an hour or for the evening.*

- *You absolutely commit to resuming the conversation again at an agreed-upon time.*

#7. Men Order Us Around

He barks orders at you as if he's your boss.

He talks to you as if you're a child who doesn't know what she's doing.

When you make a suggestion, he says you don't know what you're talking about.

Maybe he's watched too many John Wayne movies. Or maybe his

hero is The Terminator. Or maybe he is just a bossy son-of-a-gun. Meet **Commando Man**. Try talking to him, and watch him pull rank on you as he insists that he knows best. Try doing something your way, and be prepared for the list of instructions he'll give you to make sure you do it "right." Try giving him feedback—on second thought, don't give him feedback, unless you're ready to be lectured about how much more experience, wisdom, comprehension, and everything he has than you.

Commando Man loves to dominate and control. He will order you around and expect you to comply with his commands and certainly not challenge them. After all, he is Commando Man, and he knows the right way to do everything. As for you, well, you are supposed to be grateful for his guidance.

Conversations with Commando Man are one-sided. Actually, they aren't conversations at all, they're more like discourses. He talks, and you're supposed to listen. When you're in a relationship with Commando Man, there's only one authority in the family, and that's him, of course. So it's frustrating to try and communicate with him, because unless he wants to discuss something, he simply will refuse to do so.

A relationship with Commando Man is hard on a woman's sense of self-esteem. That's because he has an annoying habit of:

- *Putting you down in front of other people*

- *Treating you in a condescending manner*

- *Acting as if you're less important than he is*

- *Scolding you as if you've done it all wrong*

- *Raising his voice when he talks to you so that you'll back down*

Here's the strange thing about a man like this: *He really doesn't see that he's acting like Commando Man.* In his heart, he truly cares about you, and he believes that he's just trying to help you, teach you, train you, support you, and yes, be a man for you. **What he doesn't realize is the more he treats you with this kind of disrespect, the less passion and attraction there will be between you. Why? Because ultimately, a woman isn't going to be turned on by someone who acts like her "superior officer."**

How Commando Man Turns Us into Passive Woman

When a woman is treated like a child, she begins to feel like a child. When she's criticized and scolded for not doing things right, she loses her confidence. When she's told what to do and how to do it, she loses her initiative. And that's what happens when a woman lives with Commando Man—she becomes **Passive Woman**.

Who is Passive Woman? She is someone who has learned all the skills necessary to get along with Commando Man: She doesn't make waves; she forgoes her own judgment for his; she acquiesces to his way of doing things; she doesn't challenge him even when she disagrees with what he does or says. *In order to survive emotionally and avoid living in a nonstop emotional war zone, she has surrendered.*

Passive Woman may not appear to be passive with anyone else but her partner. Her friends and colleagues may think of her as strong, confident, and empowered—the opposite of passive. But they don't see her when she's interacting with Commando Man. If they did, they probably wouldn't recognize her.

What Men Can Do:

If you're a Commando Man reading this, you probably aren't going to take my advice. But just in case, here's what I'd like you to think about: Ultimately, behaving

---

like Commando Man in a relationship will smother the spirit of the woman you say you love.

At first you may feel she's just being a good wife or cooperative spouse, but in time you'll notice that the warmth in her eyes has grown cold, and that what you've told yourself was her respect for you is actually just fear. You may not lose her physically, but you will certainly lose her emotionally, for her true self will be buried underneath the debris of her self-esteem that shatters each time you treat her as if she isn't as good as you are.

Does even a tiny bit of this ring true for you? Do you feel even a small twinge of guilt? Then please get some professional help, alone and as a couple, so you can have the kind of healthy, loving relationship you both deserve.

#8. Men Make Fun of How We Feel

"Oh you poor thing, I hurt your feelings and made you cry."
"Oooh, you're angry at me, I can tell by that pout on your face."
"Don't tell me—you have another doctor's appointment. I feel like I'm living with a medical encyclopedia."

He thinks he's so funny, this guy. He never takes anything you say seriously. Even when you're upset, he tries to talk you out of your feelings. Meet **Sarcastic Man**. He's a regular barrel of laughs—except that you're not always in the mood for laughter. **But that's the only way he knows how to deal with feelings, by making fun of them. And that means making fun of you.**

Sarcastic Man seems harmless at first, because he's always joking. How angry can you get at a guy who's so amusing? *The prob-*

lem is that he never wants to have a serious conversation. In fact, he avoids confrontation of any kind at all costs. When you bring up an issue, he pooh-poohs it, like it's no big deal. When you tell him you need to talk about something, he says you're being silly. When you get up the nerve to tell him you're angry, he minimizes the importance of what you're saying and dismisses it as foolishness.

Underneath all of this behavior is Sarcastic Man's fear of real conversation, real emotions, real intimacy. His sarcasm is an attempt to make an issue or complaint go away because he's just too scared to deal with it. For this reason, trying to communicate with Sarcastic Man is an uphill battle. Simply put, he doesn't want to face anything unpleasant. Unpleasantness makes him very uncomfortable and tense, so he uses humor to cover up his anxiety. The problem is that you end up being the brunt of the joke.

How Sarcastic Man Turns Us into Serious Woman

The strangest thing happens to a woman who's in a relationship with Sarcastic Man. The more he acts like everything's a joke, the more somber you get, until you turn into **Serious Woman.** You say things like, *"Come on, stop joking around about this"; "I'm serious—we really need to talk"; "This is important to me—it's not funny."* When you try to communicate with Sarcastic Man, you always end up defending yourself, because he is a master at diminishing the importance of what you're trying to tell him. And is it a surprise that you also end up feeling very controlled? That's because sarcasm is really a passive-aggressive form of anger and power. It is meant to throw you off center and make you feel you are ridiculous for even attempting to express yourself.

Being with Sarcastic Man is bound to make you feel disrespected by your partner. Even though he does it in an amusing, supposedly lighthearted way, his sarcastic comments are actually thinly veiled put-downs designed to send you the message that you are too sensitive, too emotional, and therefore your emotions aren't worth taking seriously.

What Men Can Do:

Imagine how you'd feel if you went to your boss and said, "I need to talk about the project I'm working on," and he responded sarcastically, "Oh, is my little employee feeling a teeny bit overwhelmed? You poor thing." You'd feel angry and insulted. That's how your partner feels when you respond to her feelings, needs, and requests with sarcasm.

When you catch yourself trying to make light of something that's going on between you and your partner, stop and remember that this is the woman you love. She has something important she wants to talk about. Guess what? *It doesn't matter if it's important to you or not.* If your child came to you crying about his lost ball, you wouldn't answer him sarcastically and say, "What a crybaby—it's just a stupid ball." So why would you talk to your lover this way?

Listen to what she has to say, use all of the other techniques you've learned here, and *drop the sarcasm.*

#9. Men Lie to Avoid Dealing with Something Unpleasant

He tells you he has to work late, when he's really meeting with his accountant to talk about some failed investments.

When you ask him if he's hungry, he says has a stomachache, but doesn't tell you that he actually already ate with a friend who he knows you can't stand.

You tell your boyfriend you'd like to spend the day with him on Sunday, and he says he can't because he is going to be preparing for a big week at the office, when the truth is he's agreed to help his ex-wife do her taxes.

You're in love with a really nice guy. He doesn't have a mean bone in his body. So why is it, then, that you keep catching him lying to you? *Because he's* **Chicken Man,** *someone who in an attempt to cover up things he thinks will hurt or upset you, gets in the habit of telling you lies.* We're not talking about big lies here—most of the time they're little ones. In fact, Chicken Man would be disturbed to read this section, and would insist he isn't lying, he's just omitting information as a way of protecting you. But let's be honest: **He isn't trying to protect you; he's trying to protect himself.**

Chicken Man is in the cover-up business. *He is always covering up anything he thinks would make someone angry with him.* That's because Chicken Man is usually also Sensitive Man, someone who desperately wants to please everyone. This, of course, is an impossible task, so Chicken Man spends a lot of time running around like a chicken with its head cut off, trying to cover all his bases and make sure no one is disappointed. To do this, he has to lie.

The problem is that Chicken Man really isn't covering up anything—we can feel it when he's lying or hiding something, and it makes us paranoid. When Chicken Man finds out he invested his money poorly, he hides it from us and lies about meetings with the accountant. We, of course, like all women, can feel something is wrong, and when we call his office and he's not there, we assume he must be cheating on us. When Chicken Man nervously turns down our offer of food and says he doesn't feel well, we can tell he's not being honest, and our imagination goes wild. When Chicken Man acts evasive and uncomfortable about making plans for Sunday, we have no idea what he is hiding, but we can smell it, and spend the day alone feeling awful.

Here's the irony about Chicken Man's attempts to protect us from the truth: **His lying, evading, and covering up make us more upset than we would probably be if he just told us what he is afraid to tell us.** At least if we knew what was going on, we could deal with it. But with no information, all we are left with is a nervous anxiety that will not go away, and the parade of negative thoughts that runs through our mind.

In the end, Chicken Man creates the very result he works so hard to prevent, because the truth always comes out, and once it does and we discover he was lying, we feel angry, disappointed, and betrayed.

How Chicken Man Turns Us into Crazy Woman

You're talking to the man you love, and he's hiding something. You can tell by the nervous tone in his voice, the way he keeps changing the subject, the fact that he won't make eye contact. The problem is that you have no idea what he is hiding—is it something huge and terrible, like an affair with another woman, or is it something small and insignificant that he's embarrassed to discuss? There is no way to find out, but one thing is for sure: He *is* lying, and it is driving you crazy. You have turned into **Crazy Woman.**

Remember: One of a woman's basic needs is to feel safe, but when we're interacting with Chicken Man, we feel the opposite: paranoid, mistrustful, on edge as if we're waiting for the blow to fall. We become Crazy Woman, who is always on the lookout for evidence of calamity. The lie Chicken Man tells is the smoke. We can smell it, but we're not sure how big the fire is. So we end up frantically searching every conversation, every interaction, every moment together for any clue that will reveal what's going on.

When we turn into Crazy Woman, we manifest Chicken Man's worst fears. "Look how anxious and frightened she is," he thinks.

"I definitely can't tell her about my investment / my ex-wife's taxes / my dinner with a friend." What he doesn't realize is that it's his well-intentioned but inappropriate dishonesty that's making us crazy in the first place.

What Men Can Do:

1. *Guys, please don't lie to us.* It makes us crazy. It brings out the worst in us. And it wears away at the trust in our relationship. Tell us the truth, even if you're afraid we won't like it. Perhaps we won't, but remember: *We will like it even less once we find out you lied, and we will.*

When you share the truth that might be upsetting, communicate your concerns to us, *and let us know you realize how we might feel:*

"Honey, I wanted to let you know that on Sunday I promised I'd do my ex's taxes. I know you won't be thrilled with this, and I'd much rather spend the day with you, but I thought I'd help her out since it's the first year she has to do them by herself. Please know it doesn't mean anything, and I will come over as soon as I'm done."

Will we be happy that you're going over to help your ex-wife? No, but we'll feel a lot better knowing what's happening than having to figure out why you are avoiding seeing us and are acting so weird.

2. Give your woman a chance to show you how much we love you and how compassionate we are. *When you tell us the truth, you give us the opportunity to rise to the occasion and be our best. When you lie, you make it inevitable that we will be our worst.*

> **3. If you notice that Crazy Woman has shown up, ask
> yourself if you've been Chicken Man lately. You may
> discover some things you've been withholding or
> avoided sharing with us.** *When you open up and commu-
> nicate what's going on with you, we will calm down, al-
> though it may take a little time, so be patient.*

#10. Men Anticipate the Worst and Get Reactive

*You tell him you want to talk, and he accuses you of trying to
ruin his day by starting a fight.*

*You get tears in your eyes during a discussion, and he tells you
you're getting hysterical, and he can't deal with it.*

*He claims he can't share his feelings with you or you will fall
apart, citing an incident from four years earlier.*

It's a no-win situation, isn't it? Anything you say will set him off.
Any attempt to communicate will be interpreted as your having a
nervous breakdown. Anything you've ever said that has hurt him will
be thrown back in your face, over and over again. Yes, it's **Reacto
Man, the guy who's an expert at anticipating the worst before the
conversation's even gotten started, and getting upset in advance.**

Did you know Reacto Man is psychic? At least he thinks he is—
he is certain that he can predict just how a conversation will go:

"I know if we start talking, it will go on all night."

*"I know what is going to happen—you'll start crying and accuse
me of being a jerk."*

*"Every time we discuss this, we go through the same thing, so why
even bother?"*

Reacto Man isn't living in the moment—he's reacting to something that may have happened in the past, or something he is afraid will happen in the future. Maybe he used to have an emotionally messed-up girlfriend, or high-strung mother, and assumes every discussion with you will turn out badly. So the minute you try to talk to him, he's in a time warp. In a way, he's having a conversation with himself. What you say or do really doesn't make a difference. **Why? Because he's already made up his mind about what will take place, and therefore decides to abort the discussion whether you like it or not.**

A favorite method of Reacto Man is *to recall the worst communication moments he's ever had with you, and hurl them back at you as his reason for not wanting to talk.* Maybe once three years ago, during a terrible argument, you got hysterical and stayed up all night crying. Well, even if you want to forget about it, Reacto Man won't let you! He will remind you of it every time you want to have even a simple discussion: *"I know where this is going— you'll be up all night screaming at me and crying!"*

To be blunt, Reacto Man is a stubborn son-of-a-gun. He has a rigid way of approaching challenges or problems, and thus always seems to be on the defensive, ready to protect himself from what he sees as danger. This is why at the slightest sign of too much emotion (or, as he sees it, *any* emotion) he blows up and ends the conversation. *The problem is that there's no way a woman can talk to Reacto Man without being accused of looking like a basket case.* The mere fact that you have something you need to discuss indicates to him that you're already too emotional.

How Reacto Man Turns Us into Reacto Woman

It's inevitable—no matter how hard we try to prevent it, no matter how much we promise ourselves that we won't let it happen, it always does. When Reacto Man shows up, we become **Re-**

acto Woman! Even if we start out feeling calm and centered, after a few minutes of talking to Reacto Man, we're defending ourselves:

"How can you say I'm hysterical? I'm not hysterical!"

"What do you mean, I always get irrational in our conversations? I'm the one who tries to stay focused on the issue, and not blame each other."

"Stop bringing up something that happened four years ago! You're not being fair!"

"Don't tell me to calm down! I haven't even said anything yet except that I want to talk about the weekend."

See what I mean? There's no way around it. **Reacto Man sets you up to react.** If he tells you you're hysterical and out of control, no matter what you say, you sound defensive. If he claims you are going to take forever to talk about something, how can you prove that he's wrong without appearing to disagree? If he brings up the past as evidence that you're irrational, you get pulled out of the present moment. Talking to Reacto Man is a verbal trap from which you can't escape uninjured.

What Men Can Do:

1. *Don't prejudge your partner at the beginning of a conversation by assuming she will react in a certain way, or you will create a self-fulfilling prophecy. If you accuse her of falling apart, she will fall apart. If you tell her she is angry, she will become angry. Give her the benefit of the doubt, and let the discussion unfold.*

2. *Don't exaggerate in order to intimidate her during a conversation.* If she is crying a little, don't call her hysterical. If she is irritated, don't tell her she is enraged. Let your mate express her emotions, and don't stifle them before she can even tell you how she's feeling.

3. *Stay in the present moment during conversations with your partner.* Don't bring up past incidents, reactions, or results. Give her and yourself a chance to work things out *now*.

Guys, I hope you've gained a lot of insight reading about these ten male communication habits. Maybe you recognized just one or two of them as something you do, or perhaps you realize you're guilty of indulging in many of them more often than you'd like to admit. The good news is that now you have the ability to catch yourself when you're becoming Mystery Man, or Vanishing Man, or Volcano Man, and using the techniques I've suggested, you can choose to change your communication tactics, and be the loving, caring man you really are.

A reminder for women: You're not off the hook completely, ladies. Even though I've listed these as ten male communication habits, *I am sure some of them apply to you as well!* Millions of men would attest to the fact that they've been in a relationship with Commando Woman or Invisible Woman or Sarcastic Woman. If you really want your partner to cop to his unhealthy communication habits, admit yours to him, and use the same techniques to learn positive, healthy ways to talk to the man you love.

CHAPTER TWELVE

What Women Hate to Hear Men Say
and
What Women Love to Hear Men Say

Ladies, how many times have you been talking to the man you love, and he says something that really upsets you or makes you angry, only he has no idea why it aggravates you so much? "What's wrong with what I said?" he asks in disbelief. And you're there thinking, "How can he not get it?" Your girlfriends get it. Any female you talked to would get it. *So how come he doesn't get that there are things men say to women that we absolutely hate to hear?*

What about the opposite scenario? You're trying to explain to your partner that you wish he'd express his love more with words, and that this would make you really happy. "What do you want me to say?" he asks you in a bewildered voice. "Well, you know, sweet things," you answer. He stares at you blankly and replies, "Like what?" Your heart sinks in frustration as you realize that this man you adore is totally clueless. And you wonder to yourself, *"How can he not know what I would love to hear?"*

Well, ladies, this chapter is the answer to your prayers! At the request of thousands of women, I've compiled a list that will be an invaluable tool in your relationship with men: the things women hate to hear men say, and the things women love to hear men say. Perhaps all men should be given this list at puberty so they can memorize its contents in order to avoid causing emotional damage to the women who they will love. All right, I'm not entirely serious. But I do think it's a good idea to show this list to any man you care about and any man who cares about women.

I've started off with "What Women Hate to Hear Men Say." After each item, I explain a little about why women hate hearing these particular phrases. This is so men can understand just what it is about their communication that drives us nuts. I follow this with "What Women Love to Hear Men Say," and similar explanations for why these phrases melt our hearts, not to mention get us in the mood for romance. (Translation for guys: That means sex!) I've tried to include as many items on my list as possible based on the most common complaints and requests I've heard from women, but I'm sure you have more of your own. I suggest you write your personal additions down, and make sure to share them with your partner.

Ladies, if your man is open to it, you might try reading through this chapter together. It can be quite amusing, and you can give your own editorial comments as you go along. Women also seem to have fun reading the first list with their girlfriends—you'll see why when you get to it.

Guys, you're about to be presented with priceless information. I didn't hold back in my explanations, because I really want you to get what women are trying to tell you. *For an instant improvement in your love life, not to mention your sex life, I suggest you* **permanently erase** *every item you read on the first list from your vocabulary, and* **immediately include** *every item on the second list in your conversations with the woman you love.*

What Women Hate to Hear Men Say

<u>WHAT MEN SAY TO DISCOUNT OUR EMOTIONS</u>

What Men Say:	*Why Women Hate Hearing This:*
"Just relax."	Telling a woman to *just relax* makes us feel like we're at the gynecologist and about to be probed with something hard and cold! It's a guaranteed way to get us to not relax. *The moment we hear these words, we tense up.*
	When you instruct us to relax, it implies that you think that we're probably overreacting, being dramatic, unreasonable, and not handling something well. Besides, it sounds *condescending*.
"Lighten up."	What a dismissive thing to say! It discounts whatever we are feeling or discussing as being too serious, and too heavy. Translation: *"I don't want to talk about this with you."* Our response: "You lighten up—we're just trying to talk, not do open-heart surgery on you!"
"Calm down."	Like "Just relax" and "Lighten up," but worse—*we feel as if you're addressing us as a mental patient.* "Calm down, Mrs. Jones, your medication is on the way." Hey, we'll calm down if you talk to us about what's bothering us, okay?

Telling us to calm down implies that we are making a big deal over nothing. Well, guess what, guys? If we are bringing it up, it IS a big deal.

"You're overreacting."

Isn't it funny how men tell us we're overreacting when you don't like what we're saying about you, but if we were going on and on about how awful your boss was not to give you that raise, you wouldn't think we were overreacting at all!

What we're doing isn't overreacting, guys—it's called *reacting*. We're experiencing emotions and expressing them. And by the way, *if you keep telling us we are overreacting, then you will see us overreact!*

"You're getting hysterical."

No, actually we were just fine, *but now that you've said that, we're definitely closer to hysterical than we were.*

Guys, your definition of hysterical is when we raise our voice above a whisper, or when one tear falls from our eyes. It would be as if we said to you "You're getting abusive" because you told us you weren't crazy about the new lamp we bought. Listen, we know when we're hysterical, and when you usually say this to us, believe me, we're not hysterical. However, if you insist on saying it a few more times, you will get a very impressive demonstration of hysteria.

"Don't be such a baby."
"Don't be ridiculous."
"Don't be so insecure/ paranoid/emotional."

Gee, thanks for the suggestion. Now we feel so much better. You snapped us right out of our misery. How could we not see how foolish we were being? All right, I'm being sarcastic, but when you say this kind of stuff to us, guys, how do you actually expect us to respond? Basically *any variation on these comments is just name-calling, and it really hurts us to hear the man we love insult us.*

"Breathe."

What are you trying to say, that we're *not* breathing? We're breathing, we're just also pissed off or upset. Women hate when men tell us to breathe. *It sounds so self-righteous, as if you're giving us spiritual instructions.* Hey, our yoga teacher can tell us to breathe; our Lamaze coach can tell us to breathe in our birthing classes; but please, when we're trying to tell you what's bothering us, don't tell us to breathe. Instead, try listening to what we're saying.

"You must be having PMS."

Yes, as a matter of fact, we are: *Patronizing Male Syndrome*! It's a chronic condition women seem to be plagued with on a regular basis, especially when we hear ridiculous comments like this one. All right, sometimes we do have certain hormonal fluctuations, but don't blame the fact that we're upset with you on our body. It's a cheap cop-out to avoid having to talk with us.

WHAT MEN SAY TO AVOID COMMUNICATING

What Men Say:	*Why Women Hate Hearing This:*
"I don't want to talk about it."	Well, I don't want to do the dishes, scrub the toilet, hear you watching sports on TV, change the baby's diapers, or lots of other unpleasant things, but I do them anyway. You don't want to talk about it? Too bad, because I do! Who made you king of the relationship, anyway? When a guy says this to a woman, it feels as if you just slammed a door shut in our face. *It's as if you are saying, "I don't care how you feel. I don't care if you are upset. I don't care about working on this relationship."*
"How long is this going to take?"	This question is usually accompanied by a painful sigh and a look of disdain. *One would think we had just asked you if we could give you an en-*

ema, and not if we could talk to you! The moment you respond like this, we feel insecure and on the defensive. It's like we have to beg for your time, and that makes us feel like we just aren't a priority to you.

By the way, the answer is: as long as it takes. *And your question about how long just added at least ten minutes to the process, because now we are even more upset than we were to begin with.*

"Are we going to be up all night talking about this?"	Well, we weren't planning on it, but now that you have responded to our request with sarcasm and total reluctance, it's certainly going to take even longer than it could have. This question is a close relative to the preceding one, but it makes women even angrier in its assumption that our fantasy for the evening was to fight with you until daybreak.
"I can't deal with this now."	This statement usually is followed by some form of physical exit. You say it, and you split. And we are left standing there hurt and furious. Remember Vanishing Man? This is one of his favorite lines. It's an emotional dead end, and it makes a woman feel hopeless. If you aren't in the mood to talk, there are more polite ways to say that. (See Chapter 11.)

"Here we go again."

You roll your eyes. You throw up your hands in mock horror. You can't believe we want to do this horrible thing, to torture you like this, to... TALK!

Guys, you usually say this right at the beginning of our attempt to have a conversation with you. "Honey," we ask, "can we talk about possibly spending more time together in the next few weeks?" "Here we go again!" you reply. Here we go *where? How do you know where this conversation is going?* What you're really trying to say is "Here she goes again trying to talk about the relationship." That's right, we want to talk about us, because for some strange reason, we happen to love you.

"Now what?"

Another version of "Here we go again," but with even more impatience and condescension. It implies that women exist for the purpose of annoying men with trivialities like, for instance, how the kids are doing, how we're getting along, our sex life, the care of the house, and other topics we try to discuss with you. *When you say this, it makes us feel intimidated and forewarned*, and tempts us to just want to reply with, "Never mind," which is probably what you'd like to hear.

"I'd thought we'd already talked about that."

Yes, we did, eight months ago for seven minutes. Or was it back in 1998? I didn't know there was a quota for how many times we could talk about a subject before we were "done" permanently. Is it like using up Frequent Flier Miles?

Whenever you respond with this phrase, guys, we realize that you are saying you really don't want to discuss something again, that you'd hoped it was resolved. Well, it obviously isn't. This comment makes us feel like we are going to have to talk you into having a conversation, which we hate.

"You've been talking to your friends again, haven't you?"

Do you mean to say that we don't have a mind of our own, and that if we are upset or want to clear something up, we've been brainwashed by our girlfriends? This comment completely dismisses what we're trying to discuss, as if it's stupid and poorly thought out, and thus, not worthy of your time.

CONVERSATION STOPPERS

"Okay, okay, you're right, I'm wrong. Are you happy now?"	No, we're not happy, because *communicating isn't about right or wrong, winning or losing*. It's about connecting, it's about understanding each other, it's about reestablishing harmony. When a man says this, he's missing the whole point of having a conversation. It's not a contest, guys—it's a relationship. What can we say once you've said this kind of thing to us?
"Just forget it."	Oops. We've obviously said something you really didn't like, or stepped into territory you don't want to discuss, or feel we are misunderstanding you, but rather than sharing those feelings with us, you're aborting the conversation. We feel awful, because *you're not giving us a chance to work through whatever is going on*. Besides, we can't forget it, and you know it.
"I'm sorry you feel that way."	In other words, "I hear what you've said and I have no intention of discussing it. I am leaving you with your feelings, and I'm sorry you have them because you are going to be stuck with them for a while since I am not going to deal with them."

This statement is usually said with a tone reminiscent of a funeral director telling the family that he is sorry for their loss. You look at us with sympathy, as if that is supposed to be sufficient, and now you can go back to watching TV.

"I know what I'm doing."

In other words, *we should butt out!* You don't want our input, you don't want to explain yourself to us. You don't care what we think or how we feel. You're going to do it your way, and that's that, so we should shut up and go back to whatever it is that we do in the relationship, like taking care of you and the kids, and leave the IMPORTANT stuff to you.

Yep, this statement pisses us off all right. It cuts off the conversation instantly... or, we can proceed at our own risk.

"I'll handle it."

Another version of "I know what I'm doing," only with an added twist, because it sounds like a command. You are drawing the line in the sand: This is your territory, and we shouldn't cross the barrier. It's a Commando Man kind of statement that pulls rank, and *makes us feel discounted and dismissed.* YES, SIR!

"Don't worry about it."	A kinder but still annoying version of the above two phrases. This one is more patronizing, like the Godfather telling one of his "employees" not to worry about it, that he's taking care of it. We are being dismissed not with a bark, but with a pat on our head.
"If you think I am so terrible, why don't you just leave?"	Talk about jumping the gun, guys. Talk about All or Nothing. What's the message here, that we should either love you the way you are, or if we have a complaint, we should just leave? You just went from 0 to 60 in five seconds. Now you've put us in a position to have to disagree with what you've just said, insist that you're not terrible, and that we're not leaving. *How did we end up consoling you, when we were the one who was upset?*

WHAT MEN SAY TO BE NONCOMMITTAL

"I can't think that far ahead."	Ugh! What a namby-pamby comment, as if it's too much of a strain to make a plan. I'll bet you don't say that to your boss when he asks if you can attend a conference for work. We know what you're doing when you say this, guys—it's avoidance, pure and simple, and it makes us feel unimportant, dispensable, and left high and dry.

"We'll figure it out."	Do you actually think women believe you when you say this in answer to our attempts to make a plan or resolve an issue? We know that you're just blowing us off—in a nice way, of course. I guess we should be grateful that you are at least using the word "we" and appearing to be cooperative, but the truth is, when we hear this phrase, we want to scream in frustration.
"Why not?"	This one needs clarification: We say, "Would you like to come with me to my high school reunion?" You say, "Why not?" It's not exactly a yes, so it doesn't carry any enthusiasm with it, but it isn't a no. Still, it leaves us feeling like we're holding an empty gift box—*you're going along with what we want, but it's as if you really don't care one way or the other.*
	This phrase makes a woman feel like a second or third or fourth choice. It avoids any real commitment.
"Me too."	. . . As in, we say "I love you" and you say "Me too." We say, "I'm so glad we talked about that," and you say, "Me too." This phrase is like eating someone else's leftovers. *You're*

either being verbally lazy by not expressing the complete thought, or you're avoiding saying it and meaning it. It's like a half "I love you." Either way, we feel a little ripped off.

"That's just the way I am."	Here's the ultimate excuse for not having to do anything you don't want to do, for not having to change, for not having to work on yourself or the relationship, for not having to take our feedback seriously. Well, if you're going to avoid showing your commitment, why not be accurate and say: *"That's just the way I'm choosing to be."*

VERBAL BOMBS: SAY THESE AT YOUR OWN RISK

"You remind me of my ex-girlfriend."	No comments necessary on these.
"Have you put on a little weight?"	
"You're turning into your mother."	
"I need some space."	
"Maybe men aren't meant to be monogamous."	

AND THE WORST OF ALL

Silence.........

What Women Love to Hear Men Say

The following are magic words. They don't need any explanation, as we've explained so much about what women need throughout this book. Try these out on the woman you love, and you'll be amazed at what happens. If you want to do something really outrageous for your partner, tell her to close her eyes, and read this list to her out loud. Now *that's* foreplay. . . .

WHAT TO SAY TO MAKE US FEEL LOVED

"I love you."

"I need you."

"I feel so lucky to be with you."

"You are my best friend."

"You're the only woman in the world for me."

"There is no one like you."

"I don't know what I would do without you."

"I can't imagine my life without you."

"You are the answer to my prayers."

WHAT TO SAY TO MAKE US FEEL APPRECIATED

"You are so good for me."

"You make me so happy."

"I appreciate every little thing you do for me."

"I love it when you . . . (something specific)."

"You make such a difference in my life."

"Thank you for everything you do."

"Thank you for ... (anything)."

WHAT TO SAY TO MAKE US FEEL VALUED

"How was your day?"

"Let's discuss this and make a decision together."

"Let's plan ... (anything)."

"What do you think about ... (anything)?"

"Can I help you with anything?"

"What can I do for you right now?"

"What do you need from me?"

WHAT TO SAY TO OPEN OUR HEART

"I'm sorry if I don't always give you what you need."

"I'm sorry about ... (anything)."

"I promise to work harder on ... (something we've been asking you for)."

"Thank you for putting up with me."

"Thank you for being patient with me."

"I know I'm not always easy to get along with."

"Please forgive me for ... (whatever we need to hear from you)."

WHAT TO SAY FOR BIG DEPOSITS IN THE LOVE AND SEX BANK

"I am really attracted to you."

"I want you."

"Your body is perfect for me."

"I want to make love to you later."

"I can't keep my hands off you."

"Let's spend more time together."

"I miss you."

"How can I love you more?"

"Let's just cuddle."

WHAT TO SAY TO BLOW OUR MINDS

"Let's go shopping."

"Let me clean the house for you."

"Wasn't there something you wanted to discuss with me?"

"Let's turn the TV off and just talk."

"Thank you for giving me this book."

PART III

WHAT WOMEN WANT MEN TO KNOW ABOUT SEX

Several years ago, a young couple came to me for help, claiming they were on the verge of a divorce. The focus of their problems was their sex life. According to the wife, she had no desire to make love with her husband anymore and couldn't stand the thought of physical intimacy. Her husband, however, didn't seem to think there was a problem. As she angrily shared her feelings, he sat there with a bewildered look on his face as if he had no clue what she was talking about. I couldn't tell if he simply wasn't interested or if he truly didn't understand.

After a while, I asked him to leave the room, and said to his wife, "All right, woman to woman, what's the problem?"

"Well, I just don't like making love with him," she replied. "I don't like what happens in bed. I don't feel the way I want to feel. It isn't getting any better, and I can't live like this. I'm young and I need happiness."

"What don't you like about having sex with your husband?" I asked her.

"It's hard to put into words," she said slowly, "It just doesn't feel right."

"Let's get more specific and see if we can pinpoint the problem," I suggested. "When was the last time you had sex?"

"Friday night."

"Okay, why don't you describe to me what happened."

"Let's see," she began. "I had just put our daughter to bed, and I was standing at the sink brushing my teeth, when my husband came up behind me and kind of grabbed me and started rubbing himself against me. I thought, 'I guess he wants to make love.' Then he started kissing my neck and acting all excited. He led me into the bedroom and took off my clothes. He was touching me, and he seemed very aroused. And then things progressed, and he was obviously getting more and more passionate and making all these sexual sounds, and I knew what he wanted, and I thought 'Let's get this over with.' Then he entered me and we had intercourse and he finished and it was over."

"All right, on a scale of one to ten, ten being the best and one being the worst, how would you rate that experience?" I asked her.

She thought for a moment and said, "I guess it was a three." I recall thinking, *"Sounds like a three to me, too,"* but I didn't say anything.

Now it was time for her husband to join us. I turned to him and said, "As you know, your wife seems unhappy with your sex life."

"She keeps telling me that," he admitted, "but I can't figure out what the problem is, and when I ask her, she can't explain it to me."

"And how do you feel about your sexual relationship with her?" I asked.

"I'm totally happy with it." He smiled. "Except I just wish she liked it too."

How interesting, I thought—a wife who hates their sex life and a husband who loves it? I must be missing something. I decided to get really specific.

"Your wife told me you made love last Friday night?"

"That's right," the husband answered.

"Could you tell me on a scale of one to ten, ten being the best, and one being the worst, how you would rate the experience of making love with your wife that night?"

"Sure," he replied with confidence. "It was a nine."

When his wife heard this, she turned bright red. "A nine? It was barely a three. See what I mean, Barbara?"

Her husband looked totally confused and insisted, "No, it was a nine."

What was going on here? It was as if they'd had two completely different experiences. I wasn't about to give up, so I said to the husband, "Describe your experience of what made it a nine."

"My wife was standing at the sink brushing her teeth. She'd just put our daughter to bed. I saw her there, and felt turned on. I was in the mood to make love, so I started kissing her neck. Then we moved into the bedroom, and I took off her clothes. Then I was touching her—I guess you'd call it foreplay—and in a little while, I entered her, and then soon it was over, and that was it. It was great—a nine."

As I was listening to this man, I could tell that he really did love his wife and enjoyed making love to her. He seemed like a sweet, sincere guy, and I knew there was a piece of this I still wasn't seeing. Suddenly, I had an idea. I said to him, "Instead of telling me the events that happened—'I did this, I touched her here, I kissed her for this long'—can you tell me *what you were thinking and how you were feeling inside*, from beginning to end?"

He thought for a minute, and he said, "Okay, I'll try. Let's see, I was standing in the bathroom looking at my wife. I guess I was thinking about how wonderful she is with our daughter—she'd just put her to bed so tenderly—and how hard she works to take care of us, and I got this rush of love and just had to go up and hold her."

I looked over at his wife, and noticed she suddenly was listening very intently. "Go on," I told him.

"Then I was kind of hugging her and kissing her neck, and she smelled really fresh and clean, and her hair was so silky—I've always loved her hair—and I thought to myself, 'She smells so delicious,' and I started to get really turned on."

When I glanced at his wife, I was amazed to see that she had tears in her eyes.

"I led her into the bedroom, and I started touching her body. My wife has the softest skin. It's like velvet, and she's so feminine and sexy. I've always been crazy about her. And as I touched her, I felt like I was just melting into a puddle with each caress." Now his wife pulled out a handkerchief and began dabbing her eyes.

"Next, I took off her clothes, and I saw her body and thought 'Gosh, she is so beautiful. I can't imagine anyone as beautiful.' And it made me just want to be as close to her as I could. I just wanted to merge into her." Tears were pouring down his wife's cheeks as she sat forward on the couch, not wanting to miss a word.

"Then, I entered her, and oh, it was the most amazing feeling. I felt like I was home, like being with her was where I belonged, like I never wanted that moment to end. And as I had my orgasm, I felt *'I love this woman so much! I worship her! How could I be this lucky?'* "

His wife, unable to contain herself any longer, leapt off of the couch, threw her arms around her husband and cried: *"That's a 10! That's a 10!"*

I'll never forget this moment. It contained so much revelation for this couple, and for me as well. This man truly adored his wife, but when he made love to her, *he didn't express anything that was going on inside of him—he just did things to her body*. Since she didn't know he was feeling all that love and intimacy, she presumed he just wanted sex, and this turned her off. As soon as she heard him describe how he was feeling, it drew her attention to his heart, and the fact that *he really was making love to her, and not just having sex. And that's what made it a ten*.

What is it that makes lovemaking a ten? It is the love. It's the intimacy. It's the connection between your heart and the

heart of your lover. That's why the husband said he was so happy with their sex life—*he* was feeling the love; he just wasn't doing a good job of sharing those feelings with his wife. That's why she didn't know how to tell him what was wrong—she liked sex, she just didn't feel as though they were making love, but couldn't articulate what she needed from him that would make the difference.

To be a wonderful lover, *you must learn how to make love not just with your body, but with your heart;* how to let the love you feel for your partner flow into your words, into your gaze, into your touch, into your kiss, into everything you do, so he or she doesn't just feel you're loving their body, but that you're loving their soul as well.

This is why it's called "making love"—because when you truly come together in this most intimate way, you are *making more love* between the two of you, and that love will infuse every other part of your life with joy, sweetness, and contentment.

What does it mean to be a lover? It isn't about how you perform sexually or how many sexual techniques you've learned. It isn't about how often you make love, how many different positions you've tried, or how many orgasms your partner can have. Being a lover is about the way you treat your partner all the time, not just in the bedroom. It is the way you love that person— when you are talking a walk, when you are eating a meal, when you are having a conversation, and yes, when you are in bed sharing your bodies. The perfect lover is somebody whose heart is overflowing with love.

The next three chapters of this book are written to help you make your experience of physical intimacy with your partner a ten; to turn mere sex into true lovemaking; and to suggest ways you can be a wonderful lover both in and out of the bedroom. Some of the suggestions you'll read here relate to what you can do in bed. Some of them relate to what you can do out of bed. But all of them have to do with learning to be a true lover in every sense of the word.

This section is not intended to be a complete sex manual—for that, I'd have to write a whole book, and there are many excellent ones already out there. Rather, *what you'll read here focuses on what women want men to know about sex—all the things women told me that they want me to tell you, guys!*

Let's face it—it's difficult for us to talk to one another honestly about sex, and I think it's even harder for women for the following reasons:

1. We're been taught that nice girls don't talk about such things.

2. We're afraid we'll sound pushy or demanding if we tell men what we want, like the "Sexual Traffic Cop" I discuss in *Secrets About Men.*

3. We're afraid we'll sound like we're criticizing our partner, or that we'll hurt his feelings.

4. We don't know how to express what we feel, or how to say it correctly.

Men, I've spent years listening to what women want men to know about sex, and in the following pages I'll tell you everything they've told me. This is invaluable information that will help you be even more of a wonderful lover and partner than you already are. And you're in luck—because I'm a woman! After all, shouldn't you learn about what women want in bed from another woman, and not a man? If I tell you something, you can be sure it's because I KNOW from experience that it's true!

Ladies, these chapters will help you understand more about yourselves, your body, and how to articulate your needs to the man you love. A great way to read this section is together with your partner. You can comment to him as you go along: "That really describes how I feel," or "That point doesn't apply to me," as a way of personalizing the material and opening up a conversation with your lover. Don't forget to add your own comments. It will be much easier than it's been in the past because you'll have the things I've said to help break the ice. Remember: *You are the expert on how to make love to you!*

CHAPTER THIRTEEN

Sexual Secrets About Women

Sexual Secrets About Women

1. Women need to be turned on in our heads and hearts first.

2. Women need to be relaxed and free from distractions in order to desire sex.

3. Women love to be seduced.

4. Women hate to be rushed.

5. What a woman's clitoris would tell you if it could talk.

Sexual Secret #1: Women Need to Be Turned On in Our Heads and Hearts First

Here's the difference between how men and women become aroused:

- **How a Man Becomes Aroused:** Imagine a woman starts caressing her partner. His nerve endings receive the information that an attempt at arousal is taking place and send the information directly to his genitals. Like magic, in a few seconds, his penis responds, becoming erect. Successful arousal has taken place.

- **How a Woman Becomes Aroused:** A man starts caressing his wife as they're getting ready for bed. He's in the mood to have sex. Her nerve endings receive the information that an attempt at arousal is taking place. However, unlike in a man's body, **before this information can get sent to the erogenous zones, it must pass through "Emotional Headquarters" in her brain.**

So a message is relayed from the nerve endings the man is touching to **the Supervisor of Sex and Intimacy** in his wife's head. Who's she, you may ask? *She's the part of a woman who protects her from opening up sexually if she's not feeling safe.* It is the job of the Supervisor of Sex and Intimacy to decide if the information being received by the woman's nerve endings will get transferred on to the erogenous zones in the form of arousal or not.

The Supervisor of Sex and Intimacy in this woman's brain checks all the latest reports that have been stored in her psyche: How's the balance in the woman's Love Bank? Hmm, it looks low. It seems she's been feeling neglected by this man. What's this? Some resentments have built up over the past week. She's been trying to talk to him about some decisions they need to make together, but he's been putting her off. Not good, not good at all.

The Supervisor of Sex and Intimacy in the brain makes a decision—it's not a good night for this woman to have sex. Maybe in a few days if he's nicer to her. She decides not to send the sensory information on to the woman's body. **That means no matter what the man does to try to get his wife aroused, she won't feel turned on.**

Did You Know?

If a woman's heart is closed or feeling love-starved, her man's erotic touch on her body can actually be *annoying instead of arousing*. The same things we love you to do to us when we're in a sexually receptive mood may feel irritating, boring, even painful when our heart is shut off.

What's the woman experiencing as her husband tries to unbutton her blouse and kiss her in order to get her aroused? *Not much at all*. It's not that he's doing anything wrong, or different from how he usually turns her on. It's just that, well, tonight for some reason, she's not in the mood. She pushes him off her, saying, "Honey, I'm tired. Let's just go to bed."

Guys, I bet you didn't know that a woman goes through an extra step that you don't experience in the process of becoming turned on. The fact is, most men can get aroused even when they are not in the mood at all; with someone they don't particularly like; when they are angry at their partner; or under a variety of other unpleasant circumstances—still, their penis functions just fine. That's because they aren't required to have their physical sensations checked for emotional issues before they become aroused.

For women, it's a whole different story. **Our bodies don't just respond to touch and automatically get turned on. Our hearts and heads have to be turned on first—then our bodies follow.** This explains why many women are not in the mood to have sex as frequently as their male partners: *What it takes for us to be in the mood is much more than what it takes for him.*

This is such an important point to understand, guys, and why I always say *a woman's most essential erogenous zone is her heart.*

When you learn how to fill a woman's heart with love, it will overflow into the rest of her body, and she will want you.

What Women Want Men to Know:

**A woman's heart needs to be full before
her body can overflow with desire for you.
Each time you take our hand, stroke our hair, reach out
for a hug, or plant a light kiss on our lips for no reason
at all, it is as if you are saying, "I love you." We literally
feel our hearts fill with joy and contentment,
and when our hearts are full, we can get in the mood
to share our love with you sexually.**

Two Keys to Turning a Woman On: Emotional Foreplay and Physical Foreplay

Remember all the chapters you've read in this book about feeding your partner's heart—doing the little things like giving her cards or leaving her notes; using words to make her feel appreciated; making her feel safe, loved, and valued? What I've really been describing to you is **Emotional Foreplay.** Guys, this is one of women's most common complaints about men: that you skip the Emotional Foreplay, and go directly to the physical.

"The only time my husband touches me is when he wants sex. I'm a very affectionate person, and need more physical affection in general—hugging, hand-holding, cuddling, and not just sex. When he tries to get me turned on and hasn't

` touched me all week, I feel violated and used, and definitely
not in the mood to make love."`

Please, guys, listen to what women have been trying to tell you:
We love you, and want to connect with you physically as much as
possible, but don't wait to touch us and love us until you want to
have sex. When you do, we will not be ready to receive you with
the passion and acceptance you deserve. That is just the way our
psyche is designed.

Here is another way to understand the importance of Emotional
Foreplay: Each of us has a door that opens up into the room of our
sexual passion. A man's door has one lock—you need only one
key to open his door, and that's the key of physical touch. If you
caress a man in the right way, presto—his door opens, and he's
turned on.

Women, on the other hand, have two locks on the door that
leads into our sexual passion—one lock on our body, and a second
on our heart and mind. **So a man needs two keys to open the
door to our body: the key of physical touch, and the key of love
and intimacy; physical foreplay and emotional foreplay.** Guys,
you often try to open our door only using one key, the physical key,
and wonder why you can't get into the sex room! You've forgotten
the other key.

If a man is really good at turning a woman on in her head and
heart by making her feel loved and adored with Emotional Foreplay—whether with words, nonsexual affection, keeping her Love
Bank Account overflowing with deposits, or the other techniques
we've talked about—she may surprise him and open both doors
before he even knows what's happened! You can tell you've been
a success at Emotional Foreplay, guys, when your partner is already turned on before you even get to the physical foreplay. But

most of the time you need to use both keys to open the door of our desire.

Sex Tip About Women: How to Get Your Partner to Want to Make Love with You

1. Keep a big balance in her Love Bank Account. Remember our analogy of the Love and Sex Bank Account? Each time you make a deposit in your partner's account by your loving words or actions, you're ensuring that, when the time comes for her to make a withdrawal, enough assets have accrued so that she feels full and happy and wants to make love with you. *Don't let the balance get too low*, or she simply won't feel interested in having sex as often as she otherwise might.

How do you make these deposits? *Keep her heart fed with the Three A's—Attention, Affection, and Appreciation—and make sure she isn't love-starved. When you let a woman get love-starved, you will end up sex-starved!*

2. Don't wait until you're in bed to start making love. When it comes to creating a passionate and satisfying sex life, what happens *outside of the bedroom* between you and the woman you love is just as important as what happens inside the bedroom. The bedroom may be a comfortable place to have sex, but if you wait until you get there to begin making love, you'll be too late, and your partner will probably have a difficult time catching up with you.

Often it's how you've been treating your partner hours, days, even weeks before you approach her to make love that will determine whether or not she is in the mood. That's why all the hot techniques in the world will be useless to you if she hasn't been warmed up properly.

Imagine that you've decided to build a fire. You don't just throw some big logs into the fireplace, light a match, and expect them to catch and burn for a long time. You shred up some newspaper; you carefully arrange it with some kindling; you let that begin to burn; when it's hot, then you put the logs on.

This is how it is for a woman's body. Each caress, each embrace, each "I love you" outside of the bedroom kindles the fire of desire within our bodies, and slowly, our passion builds until we burn with longing for you. In the same way that you wouldn't expect a fire to be burning strongly after just striking one match and throwing it onto a log, **don't expect us to be "ready" on Saturday night if you have not even touched us or loved us all week long.**

3. Become a master of emotional foreplay.
Don't forget to use both keys to open the door to a woman's desire: the physical key and the emotional key. Use all the techniques and suggestions in this book to keep your partner emotionally turned on, and you are sure to have a passionate and fulfilling sex life.

Sexual Secret #2: Women Need to Be Relaxed and Free from Distractions in Order to Desire Sex

"I don't understand why my wife is so picky about everything when it comes to finding time for sex. She wants to take a shower

*first; she wants to make sure the kitchen is clean; she wants to
check on the kids again. By the time she goes through this ritual, I
just want to go to sleep."*

*"Why does it seem so complicated to get women in the mood to
make love? Don't they ever just get turned on? I feel like there's
some magic formula, only I have no idea what it is."*

It's easy to see why men become frustrated in their attempts
to understand a woman's sexual nature—it's because we're so
different from one another. Guys, I know it's difficult for you to
comprehend why sex often seems like a big ordeal to women
when it's so easy for you. Sexual Secret #2 will help explain
this.

It all goes back to the way a woman's mind works and how different that is from how a man's mind works—**we don't compartmentalize, and men do.** Remember at the beginning of the book,
we talked about the mind as being like a house with many rooms;
men tend to focus on whatever activity is in each room, like the
Love Room, the Work Room, the TV Room, and when they leave
that room of their awareness, they block out whatever is going on
in there. Women, on the other hand, flow from room to room with
all the doors open. Wherever they are in the house of their consciousness, they are acutely aware of what is happening in the
other rooms of their mind.

How does this apply to sex? When a man decides he might like
to have sex, he simply goes to the Sex Room of his consciousness.
He leaves behind whatever is taking place in the other rooms:
work; the kids; household chores; all distractions. He's in the Sex
Room and ready to go.

For women, however, there is no Sex Room. There is the whole house of their mind, of their relationship. This is why women can't just get themselves in the mood to have sex at any time. We have a difficult time turning off whatever else is going on in our lives, in our family, in our day, and throwing ourselves into having sex. *We need to be relaxed and free from distractions.*

Men have an advantage over us here. They can compartmentalize their issues, blocking out what is bothering them so they can still enjoy being sexual. This isn't so easy for women. If our child is sick, it's hard for us to be in the mood. If we had a disagreement with our partner a few hours before, it's difficult for us to be in the mood. If we've left a mess in the den because we're in the middle of wrapping gifts, it's difficult for us to be in the mood. You get the picture, guys. It's really not even about you all of the time.

This also explains how women sometimes behave during sex: *We can become easily distracted by just about anything*: "What's that noise?" "Did you hear the kids get out of bed?" "Ouch, my arm is hurting." "Oh no, I just remembered I forgot to call the dentist's office back." A man's typical response to these comments is "Hmm," as he proceeds ahead with whatever he was doing, hoping you will forget about the interference and continue making love.

The need to be relaxed in order to be in the mood for sex goes one step further. *When a women is tense, she will have a hard time getting turned on.* We know that about ourselves, and so we avoid getting into a situation where we are lying there with our partner too tense to feel anything pleasurable. Often, we will procrastinate about having sex, or ask to cuddle, knowing that if we proceed with lovemaking, it won't turn out well.

Guys, you need to understand this, because you deal with your tension so differently from the way women do:

> **Men use sex as a way to deal with their stress
> and release tension.
> Women want to get rid of their stress and tension
> beforehand so they can get in the mood for sex.**

Sex is one of men's favorite techniques for stress management, and it's one of women's least favorite. Remember: Women want to be fully present emotionally as well as physically during lovemaking, and if we're distracted by stress, that will be impossible. Our technique is to do something else to get rid of the stress, and then, when we're nice and relaxed, we will be ready to make love.

This difference in how we handle tension causes problems in our relationships. A woman is feeling anxious or distracted, but her partner doesn't understand her need to relax or shift gears before lovemaking occurs. Many women complained about this on my surveys, particularly mothers:

"I can't just shift from being a mom all day to being a lover. I need to do something to reclaim myself as a woman, whether it's a bath, or reading a book, or preferably, having intimate time with my husband. Unfortunately, he doesn't understand how important this is to me, and expects me to just be in the mood because he is."

"My husband and I fight about sex all the time—he wants more of it, and I'm not in the mood. It's not that I don't want to make love with him, because I do. But when the kids have been throwing up all day, and the dog dug up the yard again, and I haven't had a minute to myself, it's hard for me to feel romantic. When I tell him this he pouts, as if I'm re-

jecting him. Why doesn't he understand that I need to feel relaxed in order to feel turned on?"

A woman needs to feel like a woman, and not like a mother, in order to be in the mood for sex. That means either the man needs to do something to make her feel like a woman or she needs to do this for herself. This is one of the reasons women often request that their husband spend intimate time with them—it's not about the dinner at a restaurant, or the walk around the block, or the conversation on the couch—it's about grown-up time versus Mommy time. **Those moments during which a woman reclaims herself as a wife and lover are essential to her ability to be in the mood for sex.**

Redefining Foreplay

Men think they know what foreplay means—kissing, caressing, touching a woman's erogenous zones. Well, guys, I'm sorry to break the news, but these things are just the tail end of foreplay. As I mentioned earlier, *for women, foreplay starts hours, days, even weeks before you get into bed!*

1. Anything that relaxes a woman qualifies as foreplay, since the more relaxed she is, the more open she'll be to having sex. That means the following are all forms of foreplay, whether you've ever thought of them that way or not:

- Asking her what's on her "to do" list, and agreeing to complete some of the items

- Offering to clean up after dinner so she can take a bath

- Taking a turn shopping for groceries so she can go to yoga class

- Watching the kids while she takes a nap

- Giving her a foot massage with scented oil

These may not seem like traditionally romantic gestures, but they will have the same effect: She will feel her partner is paying attention to her need to relax, and she will be grateful.

2. Things women do to pamper themselves qualify as foreplay. Guys, did you know that when a woman wants to prepare for lovemaking with rituals such as having a candlelight dinner, taking a bath, or wearing a sexy negligee, she may be doing this for herself and not you? Don't be so quick to complain about these romantic habits. The woman you love knows what she's doing. If these things make her feel sexy, support her in taking the time to do them.

I have a friend who loves to shop for beautiful lingerie. Every time her husband sees her in one of the outfits she's purchased, he makes the same comment: "I wish you wouldn't buy these. It's a big waste of money, because they're going to come off in one minute anyway." "What he doesn't understand," my friend explains to me, "is that I buy these for myself. *The time I take to shop for them; trying the outfits on in the dressing room; putting one on after a bath at night; all these things are a form of foreplay for me. Maybe they don't turn him on, but they sure turn me on.*"

3. Talking about her problems is a form of foreplay for a woman. Why? Because as we saw earlier, expressing our feelings out loud helps dissipate any tension or worries we might have. So guys, when your partner wants to talk and spiral through the events of her day, don't think to yourself, "Do I have to listen to this?" Instead, think, *"This is foreplay. The more stress she releases, the more relaxed she'll become, and the more likely she'll be to get in the mood for sex."*

Sex Tip About Women:
How to Help Your Partner Get in the Mood for Sex

1. Ask her what you can do to help her relax.

Instead of just coming on to your partner when you're in the mood for sex, try to determine how she is feeling. If she is tense, ask her what you can do to help her relax. Put aside the idea of sex, and just be loving and affectionate. Maybe she needs a massage, or for you to hold her and listen to her talk about her day. You may be surprised that after a little while she begins to relax, and suddenly finds herself in the mood to make love after all.

Discuss this whole concept of being relaxed and ask her for suggestions about what helps her feel more relaxed in general. She will probably tell you things you never would have thought of.

2. Find out what makes her feel sexy and feminine.

You may think you know what makes your partner feel like a woman, but why not be sure and ask her? If it's baths, buy her lots of bath oils. If it's candles, make a habit of lighting candles in the bedroom before she comes in. If it's lingerie, surprise her with what she'd like to wear and would be comfortable in, and not particularly your favorite fantasy.

---

3. Redefine foreplay.

Try doing one thing each day that is a nonsexual kind of foreplay. Know that no moment of love, affection, or attention is ever wasted, and the more your partner feels you taking care of her in this way, the more relaxed she'll be when you get into the bedroom. Remember: **The longer the soup cooks, the better it will taste.**

Sexual Secret #3: Women Love to Be Seduced

Women's sexual fantasies often include a man who is slowly and sensitively seducing us, long before the act of intercourse happens. What does it mean to seduce a woman? It means *not* taking for granted that a woman wants to have sex with you, even if you're married or living together. It means *not* showing up in the bedroom naked, getting under the covers, and immediately starting to fondle your partner's erogenous zones. It means *not* thinking that "Are you in the mood to do it tonight?" is an effective way to let your sweetheart know you'd like to make love.

Seducing the woman you love means letting her know,
long before lovemaking begins, that you want her,
that you are attracted to her, and that she turns you on.
It means continuing to court her,
even if you've been married for twenty years.

Guys, something happens to many of you when you get into a committed relationship—*you become romantically and sexually lazy*. It's as if the chase is over, you know you have us, and you figure you don't have to do much anymore to keep us interested. This attitude is the formula for turning a woman off in no time. When you act as though you want us, we feel desirable and want you in return. But when you act as though you've forgotten how much you want us, we stop wanting you.

The mistake men often make is getting caught up in being goal-oriented about having intercourse. You think of this as sex, and everything else—making out, flirting, cuddling—as not "counting." But it's the "everything else" that creates the experience of seduction for a woman, so when you don't see it as valuable, you're missing out on an opportunity to seduce your partner in the truest sense of the word: starting with her heart and working your way to her body.

The Enemy of Seduction: The "All or Nothing" Pattern

What is the "All or Nothing" Pattern? When it comes to sex, it's the idea that **if you don't have time to do it "all"—intercourse—you might as well do nothing.** So many men get caught in this pattern, and without realizing it, sabotage their sex life. That's because the "All or Nothing" Pattern is the enemy of seduction.

Felicia and her husband, Bill, came to me for help with their sex life. Felicia complained that, in her opinion, Bill was avoiding having sex with her, and she was very angry with him.

"Your wife says that you're avoiding sex," I began. "Is that true?"

"No, it's not true!" Bill exclaimed. "Actually, I think she's avoiding sex."

"Well, something's obviously wrong," I replied. "Because you each think you want sex and the other is avoiding it. Felicia, why do you say he avoids sex?"

"Well, whenever we get romantic, he pushes me away and claims we don't have time to do anything."

"It's true," Bill said. "We don't have any time. I started a new job recently and am working a lot of hours. I want to have sex, but there just isn't time for it."

"Yes, there is," Felicia insisted.

"When? When have we had time for sex?"

"Well, for instance, this morning."

"This morning?" Bill said in disbelief. "I was out of the house at seven-thirty this morning."

"Yes, but when the alarm went off, and I tried to cuddle with you for a few minutes, we could have had sex."

"What are you talking about? I only had five minutes before I had to get up," Bill said in a confused voice.

"Yes, I know, but we could have had sex."

I stopped Felicia and said, "Let's define what you mean by 'sex' to your husband."

"Well, when I tried to kiss him, he said to me, 'No, honey, don't get me started. We don't have time to do anything.'"

"What does that mean to you—'no time to do anything'?" I asked.

"It means he doesn't have time to kiss me, to hug me, to touch me for a minute, to be sexual in any way—nothing."

"In other words," I said, **"it's either All or Nothing. You either have time to do everything—foreplay, intercourse, and orgasms, or you don't do anything."**

"That's right," she said. "And since we hardly have any time, we end up with nothing."

I asked Bill if this was an accurate description of his experience, and he said, "I've never thought about it this way before, but it's true—*I don't want to get started if I can't finish*, so I don't even cuddle in the morning. This happens lots of other times, too. If she's trying to be affectionate after dinner, and I know I have to do some work, I'll kind of push her away and say, 'Hey, come on, cut it out.' I feel like she's trying to distract me."

"How does this make you feel, Felicia?" I asked.

"Rejected, hurt, like he isn't interested in me sexually any more."

"But I am!" Bill insisted.

"Yes—but only if you can get everything!" I pointed out.

———

Like many men, Bill had fallen into the All or Nothing Pattern—thinking making love always had to contain foreplay, intercourse, and orgasms. Felicia kept trying to have sex with Bill. It just wasn't the traditional definition of sex that has a beginning, middle, and conclusion.

> **Making love is not about performing certain physical acts. It is about the exchange of sexual and emotional energy between you and your partner.**

Making love can mean holding your partner and giving her a few sweet kisses. Making love can mean stroking her body, noticing that she is turned on, and saying, "Too bad we don't have more time, but I can't wait to see you tonight." Making love can mean calling her on the phone, telling her how sexy she looked in bed that morning, and setting up some time to be together later. Like Bill, a lot of us are ripping ourselves off from moments when we could be making love in different ways just because it doesn't fit our old picture. When you expand your concept of what making love is, you will find innumerable opportunities to seduce your partner.

Part of the problem is that men have been taught that they need to release any sexual tension as soon as possible. So they don't like getting turned on without being able to satisfy themselves. Guys, don't be in such a hurry to get rid of any little feeling of love or sexual energy by ejaculating immediately. Allow that energy to build in your body and learn to pull it up into your heart. You'll find your love for your partner expanding, your desire deepening, and when you do finally make love, you'll experience new levels of joy and ecstasy you hadn't even imagined were possible.

Sexual Secret #4: Women Hate to Be Rushed

Ladies, I know you've had the following experience: You're in bed with your partner and you're both in the mood to make love. He kisses you passionately for a few minutes, and then his hands make their way to your breasts, where he proceeds to stimulate you intently and with great concentration. He spends a few brief minutes on each breast, and then one of his hands jumps down to your vagina, into which he quickly inserts his finger, determining how "ready" you are. If you appear sufficiently lubricated, all foreplay ceases, and he gets on top of you so his penis can enter you. If you're not wet enough, he goes back and repeats steps one and two—a few more kisses; a few more tweaks of the nipples—and then uses his finger to check again. Nope. Not quite done. A little more kissing and breast stimulation, and then once again, that finger probes for moisture. If it doesn't come up with any, this sequence is repeated over and over again.

Years ago, I named this maddening procedure *"checking the roast."* It's a terrible habit men have when they're rushing in bed, hoping to get us "ready" for penetration. We're lying there thinking, "Is he kidding? This is what he calls foreplay?" Each time he "checks the roast," we become increasingly tense and pressured to produce a result, thus ensuring that it's going to take even longer.

What Women Want Men to Know:

When women feel pressured to hurry up and get stimulated, we actually start to turn off, and it takes us even longer to become fully aroused.

I know most men have heard somewhere in their sexual education that women take much longer than men to become fully sexually aroused. This is true. Men can be fully aroused and ready for action in a matter of seconds. Women take . . . well, we take as long as we take. It's different every time, and depends on all of the factors we've been discussing.

Often, guys, you forget this vital piece of information about a woman's body, and get lazy and impatient. **Making love becomes about preparing a woman for penetration, rather than about celebrating each other's bodies and sharing your love.** Frankly, women hate when we feel you rushing and attempting to get us "ready." Guess what, guys? If that's your focus, you'll fail, because you'll only be using one of those keys we talked about earlier, the physical key, and forgetting the really important key to the heart that, to be blunt, will produce more lubrication than any technique ever could.

You wouldn't put your car into fourth gear directly from first would you? No—the car would stall. So why would you take your lover for a "ride" without warming her up first by running through all her gears? I'm referring to sexual foreplay, not the perfunctory kind I just described—a few kisses; a little breast action; check the roast to see if she's done—but really loving and worshiping your partner's body.

On behalf of women everywhere, I say to men: **SLOW DOWN! Stop approaching having sex with your lover as if you're trying to get it over with. This isn't a race. You don't get extra points for finishing quickly. In fact, the opposite is true—the longer you take, the better it will be for her, and for you too!**

Sex Tip: Have Gourmet Sex

Imagine you're eating a delicious and very expensive seven-course meal prepared by a master chef. Would you greedily gobble it down as fast as you could? No—hopefully, you would do what all food gourmets do—you would eat slowly, savoring each bite, allowing time for the food to digest before you went on to the next course.

When it comes to making love, we have a choice between **Greedy Sex** and **Gourmet Sex**. Many men are used to having Greedy Sex. You try to stuff as much pleasure and energy into your genitals as quickly as possible so that our body finally has to release it within a few minutes in the form of a quick orgasm. Instead, try having **Gourmet Sex. Gourmet Sex is a way of making love slowly, allowing a woman the time she needs to become aroused, and allowing a man time to get used to the intense sexual energy—to digest or integrate the energy so he can last longer and experience more pleasure.**

Here's the idea: When you feel the sexual energy building up in your body, don't race ahead to push yourself over the edge into orgasm. Instead: PAUSE...BREATHE...Allow your body to become accustomed to the intensity of the physical sensation before you begin moving or increasing the stimulation again. It may seem like you're doing nothing.

But if you let your awareness sink deeper into the silence between your movements, and focus on the love energy flowing between you and your partner rather than on your own arousal, you will find yourself relaxing.

When you're ready, you can begin moving together again. You'll find that you're now able to handle even more pleasure and stimulation without feeling as if you need to release it, and that the waves just keep getting bigger and bigger. *The better you get at staying in the moment, and the longer you allow the sexual energy to circulate in your body before releasing it, the greater your physical and emotional ecstasy will become.* Sounds delicious, doesn't it? It is!

Sexual Secret #5:
What a Woman's Clitoris Would Tell You If It Could Talk

Most women I know have had that awfully frustrating, teeth-gnashing experience of lying there while our beloved diligently and passionately touches our vagina in the wrong place for a long, long, ever so long time. We squirm hopefully to the left, to the right, forward, backward, hoping that simply by the process of elimination, his untrained fingers will land on our anxiously waiting clitoris. But no, somehow, in spite of all of our yogic contortions, he stubbornly misses just where he should be touching by a few centimeters, and annoyingly grinds into some anonymous spot on our female geography (now totally numb), all the time wondering why we aren't writhing in ecstasy.

At other times, our partner does find our clitoris, but touches it in a way that is guaranteed to be totally ineffective, not to mention frustrating. "Why is he doing *that* to it?" we wonder to ourselves, as we lie there feeling like we want to scream—and not with ecstasy. "What could possibly make him think that would feel good? Do I have to draw him a map with detailed instructions?"

Actually, the answer is "yes"—because men don't have a clitoris, so they don't know what it feels like, or how it works, and unless some bold woman has educated them, they have no way of figuring it out for themselves.

Guys, if a clitoris could talk (I know this is a weird analogy, but bear with me!), the first thing it would say to you would be: **I am not a miniature penis, so don't treat me like one.**

Here's the deal—men often find the vagina quite mysterious. After all, most of its essential parts are hidden from view, and there seems to be a lot going on down there, and so many areas to choose from. Should he touch here, or here? Does this feel good? Does that do anything for us? Exactly *where* is the right spot?

Why all this confusion? Well, think about a penis for a moment. It's big. It sticks out. It has a huge surface area. *And you can touch just about anywhere on it and it will feel fantastic to the owner.* Now, your man knows that. In fact, he's probably touched himself many times, usually without focusing on any particular spot. Pleasuring himself doesn't require much skill. He just grabs the whole thing and he's a happy camper.

This explains why men often think of the whole vagina as a differently shaped penis. **They figure everywhere on it feels good, just like their own sexual organ, and proceed to touch a woman in ways that do absolutely nothing for her.** Oh, how women wish this were true, that we had this big circular sexual organ, and that every spot on it was as sensitive as a penis; but sadly, this is not the case. All things are not created equal, and unlike the generous size and convenient layout of a man's very sensitive penis, most, if not all, of the sexual sensation that produces pleasure for a woman is focused on a tiny, temperamental piece of flesh known as her *clitoris*.

Since you don't have one, guys, here's a brief guide to the clitoris I think you'll find useful.

Secrets About the Clitoris Men Need to Know

Men, imagine for a moment that your penis was only $\frac{1}{16}$ of an inch long. It's partially hidden under folds of skin, and even when that skin is pulled away, you can't really see the whole thing. Now imagine that, unlike a penis, this minuscule sexual organ doesn't always enjoy being touched—in fact, sometimes when it's fondled, it hurts. At other times, it feels numb. And yes, sometimes it feels wonderful, but only when it's stroked in a certain way. Welcome to the world of a woman's clitoris.

I highly recommend that you become well acquainted with the clitoris. Why? *Because that's where all the action is for a woman in terms of intense sexual pleasure*. Guys, you can't imagine how sensitive and complex the clitoris is. Even we don't always know how it's going to respond, so of course it's going to be even more difficult for you. Here are just a few basics to remember:

1. Don't treat it like you would a penis. Although the clitoris is called a vestigial penis, since at conception that part of a female does not develop like it does in males, **be assured that it is not a little penis.** Men make this mistake and handle the clitoris (when they can find it) as they would handle the world's smallest penis, grabbing it, vigorously squeezing it, applying way more pressure, especially at first, than most women like or can stand. *Don't press it like a button, hoping for some magic result.* The only response you'll get will be your woman wanting to smack your hand away.

2. In the beginning, indirect touching is best. Direct pressure on the clitoris isn't what creates the most pleasurable sensation. You can stroke the sides; you can graze your fingers over the top; you can circle around it. Ask your partner how she likes to be touched. Better yet, have her show you. Hopefully, she's an expert on it, and no matter what you think you've learned with previous partners, each woman is unique, so you have to start from scratch.

3. Memorize this phrase: *Variety in the beginning, consistency at the end.* A big mistake men make, whether with their hands or their mouth, is thinking they are supposed to do the exact same thing over and over from the beginning. Most women find this annoying. It seems the clitoris responds best when it's exposed to a variety of touches or sensations. **Don't just stick to one technique from the moment you make contact.**

Although changes are good in the beginning, they are irritating and frustrating toward the end, when women approach orgasm. **Rhythm is the key for women when it comes to, well, coming!** *If your partner seems to be approaching orgasm, don't keep changing what you're doing. Find something that seems to be working and stick to it.*

Have you ever noticed that a woman will grab your hand, or grip your head into place as she nears climax? Men think these are gestures of passion, but what we're trying to tell you is: **Don't move! Keep doing what you're doing.**

There's nothing more frustrating than being almost at the point of orgasm, and the guy decides to be creative and change his technique.

4. Pay attention to the clitoris during intercourse. Forget about everything you've learned watching X-rated movies, where a woman is in some exotic position having a screaming orgasm. This is totally unrealistic. *For most women to come, the clitoris somehow has to be stimulated either directly or indirectly.* Although about a third of women say they are sometimes able to experience orgasm just from intercourse (the inner walls of the vagina have nerve endings, and certain highly sensitive spots), *the majority of us need clitoral stimulation along with thrusting.*

This, of course, is easier said than done. In her frank and educational book *Hot Sex,* Australian sex therapist Tracey Cox makes one of my favorite, humorous comments about sex: *"It's God's fault that couples have so many problems with intercourse. If he really wanted women to enjoy it, he would have put the clitoris inside the vagina. I mean, what was he thinking? The only organ in the body designed exclusively for sexual pleasure, and it's stuck right up there in penile no-man's land."*

The point is, guys, the wild bucking-bronco thrusting routine may get you off, but it probably won't do much for her orgasm at all. *Being a great lover means figuring out how to keep your woman's clitoris involved during intercourse. That means using your hands or your body to keep constant pressure on it.*

One method that really works is called the "Coital Alignment Technique" (CAT). American psychotherapist

Edward Eichel came up with this term in the early 1990s based on his observation that **the in-and-out thrusting model of intercourse was not what helped women achieve orgasm, but that what was necessary was a position that put constant, rhythmic pressure on the clitoris**. With a man on top and inside of her, the women presses her clitoris against the pubic bone region right at the base of his penis. The man's full weight is on her body, keeping his pelvis pressed in place against her clitoris. Rather than moving in and out of her, *he moves with her*, maintaining constant contact with a gentle rocking motion. When you maintain a steady, even pace with Coital Alignment Technique, it's much easier to achieve orgasm for the woman, and it also helps a man last longer.

There are many more secrets about a woman's body and sexuality that men can learn. These are just a few of the ones women asked me to share in this book. Of course, guys, the best teacher will be the woman you love. Tell her you want to know everything there is to know about adoring her body. Tell her you want to master the art of worshiping her. Let your lovemaking become a doorway into a new kind of sexual experience, where mere physical pleasure turns into emotional and physical ecstasy.

CHAPTER FOURTEEN

Women's Top Twenty
Sexual Turnoffs

Here they are—the Top Twenty Sexual Turnoffs women have always wanted men to know about. I compiled this list based on hundreds of interviews, seminars, and discussion groups I've conducted with women over the past twenty years, as well as the surveys I received for this book. They represent the most common sexual complaints women have about men. Many of them are things women feel uncomfortable talking about to their partner, but they told me so I could tell you.

You'll notice some of these turnoffs have nothing to do with sex. They are things men do that turn women off emotionally, leading them to be turned off sexually, and for this reason they're just as important as specific sexual complaints.

This is a great chapter to read together with your partner. If you're a woman, you can make little comments about which of these you particularly agree with, and also let your partner know which turnoffs definitely do not describe him—just so he can feel he's doing something right! If you're a man, be brutally honest with yourself as you read these descriptions. Could they apply to you? If you even slightly suspect you may be guilty of one or more of these sexual turnoffs, make a concerted effort to improve your behavior. Better yet, let your partner know that you think I must have been describing you in a particular section, and tell her you promise to try harder to turn her on, and not off.

Women's Top Twenty Sexual Turnoffs

1. Men who are unfamiliar with a woman's body

2. Men who mishandle a woman's breasts

3. Men who have no nipple etiquette

4. Men who have sloppy sex

5. Men who are bad kissers

6. Men who are too rough

7. Men with poor hygiene

8. Men who are obsessed with how a woman looks

9. Men who judge a woman by her orgasms

10. Men who are pushy about wanting oral sex

11. Men who are obsessed with their own sexual performance

12. Men who have sex with the TV on

13. Men who need to have sex when they're drunk or high

14. Men who don't take time to get a woman properly aroused

15. Men who check out emotionally right after having sex

16. Men with gross personal habits

17. **Men who are obsessed with their own bodies**

18. **Men who don't like giving a woman oral sex**

19. **Men who treat other people poorly**

20. **Men who don't love us**

Turnoff #1: Men Who Are Unfamiliar with a Woman's Body

He touches you tentatively, ladies, as if he is an anthropologist examining some new species of mammal. He gropes around your body parts with uncertainty, as if he's touching them for the very first time, and you feel like an alien being examined on the TV show *The X-Files*. He does the wrong things to the wrong places with such confidence that it makes you wonder who taught him this stuff. "Does he really think *that* feels good?" you wonder, counting the seconds until it's over. Apparently he does, because all the while he appears to be enjoying himself immensely as you lie there praying that he'll get a muscle cramp, or a sudden fit of coughing, and have to stop this torture of ineptness.

Sex is a vulnerable experience for a woman. *So putting ourselves in the hands of a man who acts as if he doesn't know what he's doing is a real turnoff.* Maybe he *does* know what he's doing, but he's nervous about not pleasing us—this makes him super-cautious. **Guys like this check with a woman every ten seconds because they're so worried about doing the wrong thing.** They touch you a few times, and then ask, "Do you like that?" Whether you say yes, no, or maybe, they will ask you again in another few seconds: "How does that feel?" "What about this?" "Would you like me to do more of this or less?" At some point, you are tempted to scream, *"Would you please shut up and satisfy me? Better yet, I think I'll go read a book!"*

Why do men do this? Sometimes it's because they really aren't very experienced or educated about a woman's body, and in this case—especially if they're young—you can forgive them and have fun being their instructor. Sometimes a man becomes too tentative because he had a relationship before you with Bitchwoman, who terrorized him in, and out, of bed, criticizing every move, tearing apart every attempt he made to please her. Or sometimes they're men with heavy guilt issues who freeze up when they actually get in bed with a naked woman.

Guys, *if you don't feel confident about your knowledge of a woman's body, get yourself an education.* Buy some explicit books; study all the pictures and diagrams carefully; ask your lover to give you a guided tour of her anatomy. We're really not that hard to figure out.

Turnoff #2: Men Who Mishandle a Woman's Breasts

"Why does my boyfriend squeeze my breasts like they're fruits he's checking for ripeness? Doesn't he know that this totally turns me off? How would he like it if I squeezed his testicles?"

"Could someone please explain to men that women's breasts don't need to be massaged like the shoulders or the neck do? My breasts don't get muscle cramps; they don't get tense. They don't need physical therapy."

Guys: You grab them; you squeeze them; you jiggle them like they're water balloons. We have one question for you: **If you love**

them so much, why are you doing these terrible things to our breasts?

Why do you mistake our breasts for dough and knead them? When we said we wanted you to *need* us, we meant emotionally, not physically as if we were an unbaked loaf of bread. Our breasts are not dough. Nor are they jugs, bazookas, knockers, or melons. They are a very tender, very vulnerable part of our female form. They do not enjoy being mishandled.

I've never understood why men do this. Perhaps, ladies, they become so enthusiastic upon seeing our glorious breasts that they can't control themselves and squeeze us with delight. Perhaps they saw one too many bad porno films where some obviously male director told the male lead to squeeze Nurse Nancy's size DDDD breasts, that this would turn the viewers on. Well, maybe Nurse Nancy liked it (although I doubt it), but most women don't. *We prefer caressing, stroking, teasing, tickling, gentle rubbing—anything you wouldn't do to dough.*

One more thing: **Women hate having our breasts grabbed first thing when you see us,** even if we've lived with you for years. Here's a hint—say hello; make eye contact; give us a kiss; stroke our arm; hold our hand; but don't grab our breasts as if they're doorbells you need to ring as a greeting.

If you learn to treat our breasts with respect, we will look forward to the times when you visit them. Maybe then we'll use them to do special things to you. Use your imagination!

Turnoff #3: Men Who Have No Nipple Etiquette

While we're in the vicinity of the breasts, we might as well go on to one of women's biggest sexual turnoffs: **men who are very rude to our nipples.** Guys, apparently some of you are very confused. **You mistake our nipples for radio knobs, twisting and turning them as if you're looking for the right channel:** *"Come in, Tokyo!"* (I actually had a man say that to me once while he manipulated my nipples. I think he thought it was funny.) Perhaps you're so used to playing around with your stereo equipment that you just enjoy twisting anything that looks remotely like a button. Men love dials and controls. That's fine, guys, but leave our damn nipples alone!

Then there are those of you who obviously did *not* get breast-fed. You would think that our nipples were dispensing beer, or cappuccinos, or milk shakes—whatever your favorite beverage is—by the **way you suck on them as if you're desperately trying to get some liquid out.** OUCH! It hurts, guys, and we can be sore for days. Not to mention the by-product of nipple abuse—chapped and chafed nipples—which can be very painful, indeed.

Of course, no discussion of nipple etiquette would be complete without mentioning the notorious *"nipple flickers,"* men who think they're playing tiddledywinks with a woman's nipples. What are you doing, trying to see if they will come off? If you flick hard enough, they just might.

Here's the bottom line on women's nipples: We do love having our nipples stimulated. When treated properly, they are a direct line to our genitals. The right techniques can really turn a woman on. *But a woman's nipples are very sensitive, more so than a man's, especially at certain times of the month. What you might like us to do to you, guys, may be way too rough for you to do to us.* **Be sensitive; be gentle; be respectful.**

The best expert on nipples is the woman you love. Ask her what she likes. Some women do like more pinching, squeezing, or biting, particularly when they're very aroused. Some almost never like that, and prefer lighter, more teasing touches or licks. Don't assume you know what she wants until you've done your homework.

Turnoff #4: Men Who Have Sloppy Sex

This is a true story from my days in college:

Back in 1970, I was living in a house off campus with several other students. There was a guy I'll call Alan who rented the back of the house. He was cute and funny, and I had an enormous crush on him. For months I tried to get Alan to notice me, but he always seemed to have another girlfriend.

One weekend, everyone else went to a music festival in the country (this was the seventies), and Alan and I were left alone in the house. This was my chance! I asked him if he wanted to hang out, and he agreed, inviting me into his apartment.

Now imagine this scene: I am sitting on Alan's bed, starry-eyed hippie that I was, and Alan is standing at his kitchen counter in front of an enormous watermelon. "Let's eat this," he suggested. Then, to my surprise, he took out a huge machete, and began to hack away at the watermelon. Seeds and pulp and liquid were flying everywhere. Alan was soaked with watermelon juice, but he didn't seem to notice that, or the mess he was making. He just kept chopping away at this enormous melon with the big knife. I had an odd feeling witnessing this ritual, but wasn't sure why I was so uncomfortable.

Finally, Alan picked up a huge hunk of red melon, and, with a big smile, buried his face into it like a hungry dog devouring a pile of bloody meat. I could actually hear the slurping sounds as he greedily sucked and swallowed the fruit. The juice was dripping down his face, over his hands, and onto the floor, yet Alan seemed to be oblivious to everything but getting that watermelon into his mouth.

At this point, I remember feeling uneasy. I thought about Alan wielding that huge machete; pounding away at the melon; gobbling up the fruit. Suddenly I realized why I was so nervous: *I was next!*

Alan put down the melon rind, and without even wiping his hands, began walking toward me with a sticky grin on his face. This was the cute guy I'd had such a crush on? The one I'd fantasized about as a refined artist and deep intellectual? I had thought I was going to sleep with William Shakespeare, and instead I found myself alone with Attila the Hun!

I won't go into details about what happened next, except to say that having seen Alan's delight as he sliced away at the melon with his machete, and as he sloppily slurped up the fruit, I should have been prepared for his sexual technique—rather, the lack of it. You can use your imagination to fill in the blanks. Don't worry—it wasn't traumatic or upsetting to me in any way—just disgusting; and every time I look back on it, I can't help but laugh. It's a classic early seventies memory. I've been waiting for over thirty years to tell what I call the "Watermelon Story," as an example of Turnoff #4, and finally I have my chance to turn my utterly disappointing experience with Alan into something positive.

———————

In case you haven't figured it out by now, **Alan was a sloppy lover.** He was messy, imprecise, insensitive, self-indulgent, and gross. If you've ever been with a sloppy lover, ladies, you know it. *His movements, his technique, his rhythm are all "off." He's too loose, too casual, too unconcerned about everything.* You end up feeling like that watermelon being slobbered over. YUK!

Men who are sloppy lovers tend to be sloppy about every aspect of sex. They are sloppy kissers (see Turnoff #5); they are sloppy about the way they touch you; they are sloppy about the way they give you oral sex. *For some reason, sloppy lovers love performing oral sex on their partners, except they seem to have taken the idiom "eat her out" literally, and bury their head between her legs as if they are about to have their last meal.* There they remain, greedily slurping away (I can't write this without laughing), unable to make up their minds if they're making love or giving the woman a thorough cleaning.

The irony, of course, is that sloppy lovers think they're wonderful lovers—free, flowing, uninhibited, wild—when the truth is, they're a total turnoff. It's hard to give a sloppy lover feedback; he's usually having such a wonderful time that he doesn't notice the look of horror on your face as he writhes around on top of you.

Guys, if any of this sounds remotely familiar, or if you think Alan was cool to smash his watermelon with a machete and gobble it up like a maniac, you may be a sloppy lover and not realize it. Please, for our sake, clean up your act. Hold back your wild enthusiasm a little. There are two of us there, remember?

As for Alan, I never saw him again romantically after that incident (which I chalked up to experience), and lost track of him after I left college. He's probably an attorney or a stockbroker somewhere. Ladies, be warned: If you meet a guy with a real fondness for watermelon, wear a raincoat.

Turnoff #5: Men Who Are Bad Kissers

"I love my boyfriend, but to be honest, he is a horrible kisser. I think he must have heard somewhere that it's sexy to jam your tongue down a woman's throat. The minute we start to kiss, there's that damn tongue, like some enormous, wet slug flopping all over the inside of my mouth."

"I hate men who kiss with hard, tense lips. They're so rigid and mechanical—I get totally uptight."

"My husband has this awful habit of making noise when he kisses, like a wet smacking sound. Not only does it turn me off,

but it makes me laugh, so I avoid kissing him if I want to have sex."

Kissing can be so romantic, so magical, so sexy, so...disgusting! There's nothing worse than a man who is a bad kisser. No matter what else he does to turn you on; no matter how skilled he is in bed; you always know that he can't kiss, and it just doesn't allow you to respect him as a lover.

Here are a few of women's nominations for the most horrible kisser:

- **Roto-Rooter Man:** You would think this guy gets paid by the inch for how deeply he can thrust his tongue down your throat. Not only that, his tongue never stops moving—sloshing from one side to the other; twirling around; checking out your teeth, your gums, anything it can find to probe. This isn't a kiss—it's an oral exam. Who told him this was sexy?

- **Lizard Man:** Is that a human tongue in your mouth? It feels more like a hard little lizard tongue, rapidly darting in and out. You can practically hear it hiss. Suddenly you feel like you're watching *Wild Kingdom.* Hey, if I wanted to kiss a reptile, I'd buy one.

- **Cleaning Man:** You don't recall asking for a bath. Yet that's what you're getting. Cleaning Man isn't kissing you; he's cleaning your face. For some reason, he thinks you want him to lick your lips, your chin, your nose, your ears, your cheeks with his wet, slobbery tongue. If you let him, he'll use this same technique on other parts of your body—what a delightful thought. Maybe this guy was a dog in his past life, and hasn't completely gotten used to being human. You know you've been kissed by Cleaning Man when, afterward, your face, and possibly other areas, are chapped.

- **Blubber Lips:** Oh my God, someone check this man's pulse. Surely, he must be dead. Otherwise, how could he have such lifeless, limp lips—a mouth that just hangs there globbed onto yours, barely moving? Maybe he's just come from the dentist and has been shot full of Novocaine. That would explain why he seems to have no control over his lips, and can't seem to close his mouth. Or perhaps he thinks you are in respiratory distress, and opens his mouth that wide, placing it over yours because he thinks you need CPR.

- **Jungle Mouth:** If you didn't know any better, you'd think you were in some tropical jungle from the sounds you're hearing: clicking, smacking, squealing, squeaking. And to think they're all coming from your lover's mouth! Kissing Jungle Mouth is like being in a zoo—you never know what you're going to hear next. How are you supposed to concentrate on sex with all these sound effects?

Who is the worst kisser of all? The man who doesn't kiss you. He likes to have sex, but avoids the intimacy of kissing. Maybe you get a perfunctory kiss on the forehead, or the cheek, but nothing like the passionate kiss of love every woman dreams of.

More about what makes a great kisser in our next chapter, on turn-ons.

Turnoff #6: Men Who Are Too Rough

"How do I tell my husband that he touches me too hard? I don't feel like I'm being made love to—I feel like I'm being man-handled."

"Sometimes I wish men would make love more like women. I need gentleness, tenderness, and sensitivity to turn me on. Instead, I feel like I've being given a macho demonstration of how

a man is supposed to look in bed, and frankly, it does nothing for me."

Men don't realize they're being rough. They think they're being passionate, or sexy, or aggressive. But often it just feels rough to a woman. We don't feel like we're being caressed—we feel like we're being squeezed, prodded, and pressed against.

Guys, did you know that because you have more testosterone than women, your skin is thicker and therefore less sensitive to touch? This is why most men enjoy firm, strong touching during sex. A caress that is too gentle may not even register as a touch for you. Women, however, have very sensitive skin. It is thinner and more highly tuned. **So if you touch a woman like a man would like to be touched, it's going to feel too rough to us, as if you're using too much pressure.**

Sure, there are times women enjoy lovemaking that is a little more forceful, especially with someone we trust. But we don't like being thrown around, having our skin rubbed so hard it feels like it's going to peel off, or moved this way and that in an insensitive manner.

Ask your lover to show you how she would like to be touched by demonstrating on you. "How could this possibly turn her on?" you'll think. "I can hardly feel a thing." Maybe you can't, but we can. Try it.

Turnoff #7: Men with Poor Hygiene

How can you think we don't notice, guys? I'm sure you don't intentionally *want* to gross us out. Yet you have these "habits" that are just—how to put it—DISGUSTING! "Doesn't he realize how he smells?" "Doesn't it bother him to live like that?" We ask ourselves these questions, baffled that a perfectly nice man can have such poor hygiene.

Remember: Women get turned on in their heads and hearts first. That includes our eyes and our noses. **It's hard to want to make love to a man whose physical presence turns our senses off.**

I couldn't believe how many comments I received about this on my surveys—not just from single women who date a lot but from wives about their own husbands. So here are just some of women's complaints. *WARNING: These are uncensored, so read them at your own risk, preferably not on a full stomach.*

What Women Hate:

- **Untrimmed, jagged, or dirty nails:** Why would we want you to put those hands anywhere near us, let alone inside of certain delicate places? Nothing turns us off faster than being touched and, suddenly, feeling a sharp, jagged nail or cuticle scraping across our skin. OUCH! And the dirt under the nails is going to condemn you to many sexless nights.

- **Rough calluses on hands:** Same as above. We don't need to feel like we're being exfoliated while you make love to us.

- **Sweaty, smelly, unclean body:** Need I say more? Guys, can you smell yourself? I don't mean the nice, musky smell of a man's natural perspiration that can be a turn-on to the woman who loves you. I'm talking about an unwashed body reeking of stale sweat. I'm talking about guys who do not bathe often enough. I'm talking about Mr. Stinky. And you want to make love to us when you're like that? Why would we want you anywhere near us? *Masculine is one thing—filthy is another.*

- **Dirty, smelly feet and socks:** You are about to get in bed with the man you love. You've been looking forward to making love all day. You both begin to undress. Then, it happens—he takes off his shoes. UGH, that smell! Could it be coming from his feet? You hope it's just his socks, but no; as he removes them, it becomes clear that his feet basically stink to high heaven. Suddenly, you're not in the mood for sex anymore.

Feet can be very erotic and sexy. They can also be totally gross. Perhaps men forget about them because they're the body part that's the farthest away from their face, and it's hard to see them. Perhaps you can't smell them, guys. But we can smell them, and we can see them, and if they're horrible, it's difficult to think of you as a sexy, desirable dream-come-true.

Let's go one step further and talk about toenails. Is it just my imagination, or do guys deliberately file their toenails into sharp, pointy shapes designed to stab us in the legs? If you're clipping your toenails, please file down the sharp edges afterward. Otherwise, at some erotic moment in bed, we get scraped and punctured. And that dirt beneath your toenails has to go.

- **Dirty clothes and underwear:** Why is it that some men think an item of clothing is clean when it can practically walk out the door by itself? How are we supposed to get turned on to you, guys, when you're wearing dirty, rumpled shirts, stained pants— and let's not forget underwear that isn't exactly "fresh"?

- **Bad breath and dirty teeth:** He's in the mood for sex. He approaches us, opening his arms and embracing us passionately. Then he places his mouth on ours for a kiss. Geez, did something die in there? His breath is awful. Doesn't he realize this? Apparently not.

Guys, if you want us to get turned on, please keep your mouth and teeth clean. That means not just brushing once a day, but often; and using mouthwash, mints, or whatever it takes. Make your mouth so delicious that we want to kiss it.

- **Rough beard:** Let's get one thing clear: A woman's sexual fantasy does not usually include having someone run sandpaper over her delicate, tender skin. But that's what it feels like, guys, when you don't shave and then want to make love. *It hurts.* If you don't believe me, take a piece of sandpaper and rub it over your testicles. Nice, huh?

We know shaving is a drag. But so is being scraped and scratched in the middle of sex. Check your beard before you approach us to make love. If you wouldn't like to feel it running across your skin, neither would we. Besides, a man who's freshly shaven is definitely a turn-on.

Turnoff #8: Men Who Are Obsessed with How a Woman Looks

He wants you to have the perfect body with not one ounce of extra fat, but he has a potbelly that makes him look pregnant.

He constantly criticizes your wardrobe and gives you instructions about what to wear.

Before you go out, he checks your hair, your makeup, your outfit to see if he "approves."

I was with a man like this once. I never looked good enough for him. I was too fat; I wasn't toned enough; my clothes were too conservative; my hair never looked right. Do you think this was good for my self-esteem? Do you think it made me feel sexy and in the mood to make love? Not quite.

Women love looking beautiful for the man they love. But when you become obsessed with our looks, we feel like an object, not a

person. Your constant criticism makes us feel scrutinized, devalued, and ultimately turned off sexually. How can we relax in bed
when you've been judging us so harshly?

The thing I've never understood is that often, **the guys who are
the most obsessed with having their woman look perfect are
the ones who look like crap themselves.** Come on, fellows. Before you say anything to us about our appearance, look in the mirror. Maybe you could use a little of the improvement you seem to
be shoving down our throat.

Turnoff #9:
Men Who Judge a Woman by Her Orgasms

*"I feel so pressured by my husband. Whenever we're making
love, he asks me a dozen times, 'Did you come yet? Did you come
yet?' Even if I was getting close, that ruins it for me."*

*"I love having sex with my boyfriend, but I am sick of the pres-
sure he puts on me to have an orgasm. Sometimes I come, and
sometimes I don't, but whenever I don't, he acts like it's a personal
tragedy for him. I hate feeling like I have to have an orgasm in order to make him feel like a man."*

*"My body is really sensitive, and often when I'm having sex
with my husband, I enjoy the closeness and intimacy, but don't
necessarily feel like getting totally aroused and having a climax.
The problem is that he feels obligated to make sure I come even
when I don't want to, and goes at it full force. I practically have to
pull him off me and beg him to stop."*

Orgasms are nice, but they're not everything to a woman. When
we make love with our partner, we treasure the whole experience,

not just ten seconds of pleasure at the end. Some guys, however, become fixated on making sure their partner always comes, even when she doesn't feel like it, or when her body isn't in the mood. They judge her and the success of the lovemaking based on whether or not she had an orgasm—and women hate this.

Having sex is complicated enough for women because of all the things I've discussed—the last thing we need is to feel our partner is lying there counting the seconds until we come. **This kind of pressure is a total turnoff, and actually will prevent us from relaxing enough to have an orgasm even if we want to.**

Some guys get really obnoxious about this—they count their partners' orgasms like pelts they've collected in a hunt. "Oh baby, you came twice. Let's see if you can go for three times tonight." There's nothing wrong with having multiple orgasms if that's what our body wants to do, but we don't want to do it just so you will feel like a big, virile man. Another version of this is guys who rate their partner's orgasms, like grading an earthquake or a hurricane: "That was a big one—a 7.9 on the orgasm Richter scale." Give us a break.

By now you should know that what truly satisfies a woman during sex is the love. It is fulfilling just to be close to our sweetheart, to feel him inside of us, to have our body loved and adored. Sometimes we really want the release of orgasm, but at other times, guys, we are happy just to be with you. A woman's body reacts to so many variables—where we are in our monthly cycle; the worries we have about work; what's happening with the kids—and as we've seen, when our head is distracted, our body may not be able to fully let go. If we're fine with that, then you should be too.

And please, don't ever ask us if we've come yet. If you can't tell, then you already have your answer.

Turnoff #10: Men Who Are Pushy About Wanting Oral Sex

"You know what really pisses me off? When my boyfriend takes my head and forces it down toward his penis to let me know he wants oral sex. Even if I was interested in doing it before, once he gets pushy, I totally turn off."

"If I'm dating a guy who says, 'Hey baby, how about a blow job?'—that's the end of the relationship for me. It makes me feel like a thirty-dollar hooker in the parking lot of a convenience store. I like giving a man oral sex, but not when he puts it that way."

Let's cut to the chase, guys. We know you love receiving oral sex. But when you get pushy about wanting it, we get totally turned off and disinterested. I'm a big proponent of women learning how to enjoy worshiping their partner through the act of loving him orally—in my book *Secrets About Men Every Woman Should Know*, I help women work through their resistance to this, and give explicit instructions that will make the whole experience more enjoyable for both partners. So I'm on your side, guys. But you don't help when you become too aggressive and insistent about it.

Here are some tips for how to get your female partner more interested in giving you oral sex:

1. Keep your genitals clean. Don't laugh—you can't imagine how many women wrote about this in my surveys. When I say clean, I don't mean simply taking a shower once a day. I mean: *Wash yourself completely before having sex.* If your partner gets used to your doing this, she will be more open to orally pleasuring you. Of course, the opposite is true as well—if she expects to feel as if she's pressing her face into a bag of dirty gym clothes, she may not be too enthusiastic about a return visit. It's simple, really. Ask yourself: *"Would I want to put my own face down there before I've washed?"*

If you suspect you've already developed a poor track record in this area, you may need to make an announcement to her that you've turned a new leaf. It can be as simple as, "Let me take a quick shower before we make love. I want to be clean for you." She'll get the message.

2. Don't force her head down toward your penis, *ever.* Do I need to explain this? I hope not. *This gesture brings up all sorts of awful emotional reactions in a woman, from feeling forced, controlled, violated,* etc. It's certainly not the way to get her more interested in oral sex. There are other, more subtle ways of letting her know you'd like some attention in that area.

3. Don't shove your penis deep into her mouth. Guys, have you ever had a penis in your mouth? If you had, you would know how much room it takes up. It's hard for a woman to breathe when her mouth is full, let alone not gag. *Let her monitor the penetration.* Better yet, tell her she's in charge. This will make her feel confident so she can relax without worrying that you will suddenly plunge yourself down her throat.

4. Ask her to read my book *Secrets About Men Every Woman Should Know,* Chapter 5. This portion of the book is famous for converting women who can't stand the idea of giving their partner oral sex into women who are a man's dream come true. I've received more thank-you letters from men about this part of the book than about anything else I've ever written.

Turnoff #11: Men Who Are Obsessed with Their Own Sexual Performance

You're in bed making love with your partner, and he's really into it. He's writhing around; he's moaning; he's passionately doing all kinds of things to you with great concentration. "I should be enjoying this," you think to yourself. But something isn't quite right. Then, you realize what it is—*you feel as if you're in your partner's own personal porno film, and he's the star!* You might as well not be there at all.

Men who are sexual performers are obsessed with how they function in bed. It's not that they aren't great technical lovers—they are. But they are lost in their own, self-created world. **They are more interested in what a great job they're doing than if you are actually pleased.**

Here are some versions of this turnoff:

- **Techno Man:** He is precise; he is skilled; he's read every sex manual there is, and uses every technique imaginable on you while making love. You're in bed with Techno Man. He is a sexual mechanic. *Having sex with him feels more like being worked on than being made love to.* Something about the whole experience leaves you cold.

    Many years ago, I went out with someone who was a true Techno Man. At first, I thought he was a fabulous lover. Soon, however, I began to feel like a demo model in a sex show, as Techno Man displayed his marvelous abilities and wide range of techniques for the audience. Who, you might ask, was the audience? Him! *He was watching himself, performing for himself, impressing himself.*

- **Outer-Space Man:** His eyes are closed; he's lost in unparalleled ecstasy. He's making sounds that sound unearthly. "Wow," you think, "I'm really turning him on." But then, as you notice you're feeling strangely disconnected, it hits you: *He's getting off on himself!* Outer-Space Man is lost in his own world while he's having sex. Is he even thinking about you? Who knows? He could be making love to anyone—that's how anonymous you feel. He's used you to take a sexual trip into Pleasureland alone.

• *Circus Man:* He twists you this way and that, forcing your body into impossible postures that he obviously read about or saw in a bad movie. He arranges you into pretzel-like positions that give you no pleasure whatsoever, although *he* certainly seems to enjoy them. He's Circus Man, expecting you to be a sexual contortionist to fulfill some fantasy he has that makes him feel he's an inventive lover. You lie there, turned off, feeling nothing—actually, you feel pain! Who does he think you are, Gumby?

Turnoff #12: Men Who Have Sex with the TV On

This should be self-explanatory, guys. It's rude; it's insensitive; it makes us feel totally secondary to your sexual experience. Either turn the TV off, put the damn clicker down, and make love to us, or go watch it by yourself.

Turnoff #13: Men Who Want to Have Sex When They're Drunk or High

Let's see: Do I want to make love to a man who is incoherent; not completely cognizant of his behavior; saying and doing stupid things; talking too loud; laughing at nothing; numb to his feelings;

spaced out; lacking in good motor skills; and possibly about to vomit? I don't think so.

Maybe there are some women who regularly use drugs and alcohol in substantial amounts and like being with a man who's doing the same thing. The truth is, there are people who've never made love without being high on something. Either they don't want to or they can't. That's a whole other topic. But for many women, guys, your being inebriated or stoned is simply a big turnoff. *You think you look cool, but you just look stupid. You think you sound intelligent, but you just sound smashed. We can't feel you there with us, so we don't feel safe.*

When a man insists on getting high every time before having sex, it makes a woman feel as if she isn't enough. We want to know you feel high because you're with us, because you love making love to us, and not because you drank a bottle of wine or smoked a few joints. You don't need us to get high that way. And if you don't need us, you might as well be alone.

Turnoff #14:
Men Who Don't Take Time to Get a Woman Properly Aroused

"Why does he think I'm 'ready' just because he's kissed and stroked me a couple of times?"

"My husband's idea of foreplay is asking: 'Do you want to do it tonight?' And he wonders why I don't like having sex with him!"

It starts out all right. Your partner kisses you, holds you, caresses you, and you're beginning to warm up. Suddenly, he seems to feel he's done and ready to move on, and before you know what's happening, he climbs on top of you and begins to insert his penis into your vagina. OUCH!

Guys, if you had this done to you even one time, you'd never, never do this to a woman again. Do you know how small the vaginal opening actually is when it isn't aroused? Much smaller than your penis, to be sure. For most of us, three minutes of foreplay is not enough to make us fully, or even partially, open. Remember what we talked about: Women's bodies take much longer than a man's to respond. I always like using the car analogy—you wouldn't take your car from first to fourth gear without warming it up properly.

One of the reasons many women claim they prefer all other parts of lovemaking to intercourse is that men are too quick to go there. If it's not a pleasurable experience for us, we won't want to do it very often. Soon, we'll avoid it entirely, and you'll wonder why, guys. Maybe it's because you didn't take enough time getting us warmed up.

Let me clear up two major misconceptions men have about the female body that contribute to this problem:

1. The inside of vagina is *not* like a big inside-out penis. I mentioned this in our last chapter, but I'll remind you again: The vagina isn't a big circular penis. Just because you put your penis inside of a woman doesn't mean it automatically feels wonderful to us—especially if we're not open or wet enough. Sure, it feels fantastic for you, guys, because your penis is one big nerve ending. Don't make the mistake, however, of thinking that we'll be in bliss the moment you are inside of us. If we're not properly prepared, being in pain is more like it.

2. Just because a woman is lubricated doesn't mean she is turned on and ready. When guys "check the roast" and feel a little moisture, they often take this as an indication that they don't have to do any more work to prepare their lover for penetration. "She's ready!" they conclude, and proceed to try to squeeze themselves into her vagina. *But being lubricated and being open are two different things.* The vagina can be moist due to all kinds of factors that have nothing to do with arousal: It could be a certain time of the month when, hormonally, we're more lubricated; we could be affected by our diet, by emotions, by medication we're taking. Don't assume just because we're wet that we're ready. **Our body *and* mind need to be open before intercourse will feel good to us.**

Turnoff #15: Men Who Check Out Emotionally Right After Having Sex

You roll off of us, grab the TV clicker, and start watching television; you jump out of bed and go into the kitchen to get a snack; you barely say good night before falling into a comalike sleep: These are the delightful ways men check out emotionally after having sex, and women hate it. We're lying there basking in the afterglow of being one with the man we love, and you're already gone.

It is true that sex has a different physiological effect on men than women—it actually releases chemicals in a man's body that make him sleepy; whereas for women, sex often acts as a stimulant. But that's no excuse for totally disappearing, guys. **When you disconnect so quickly, it hurts us. We feel abandoned, tossed aside, and used.**

Some men check out after sex because the intimacy of the moment scares them, and it's a way of protecting themselves from feeling too vulnerable. Others simply feel as though they've completed one task, and it's time for the next—you leave the Love Room. Whatever the reason, when you pull away physically or emotionally after making love, you're missing out on a precious opportunity to go even deeper into the feeling of love and closeness with your partner.

We don't need much guys, really. *Take just a minute to tell us we were wonderful, to hold us and kiss us gently.* Even if you're about to pass out, let us know: "Honey, I'm going to fall asleep in ten seconds, so thank you, I love you, and good night." Believe me, we will be grateful.

Turnoff #16: Men with Gross Personal Habits

Without further ado, here is a list of items women have asked me to share with men. These are really self-explanatory, guys—at least I hope they are. Simply put, when you do them, they turn us off. Later, when it's time for sex, we just can't seem to think of you in a romantic, passionate way. I wonder why. . . .

Male Habits That Gross Women Out

- *Burping, especially in a loud manner*
- *Farting*
- *Picking your teeth*
- *Playing with your nose hairs*
- *Eating like a slob*
- *Smoking (if she's not a smoker)*
- *Drenching yourself with strong cologne*

- *Talking with your mouth full*

- *Driving a dirty car full of all kinds of junk*

- *Living in a messy house or apartment (for bachelors)*

- *Throwing your fingernail and toenail cuttings on the floor*

Turnoff #17:
Men Who Are Obsessed with Their Own Bodies

You know the type, ladies. He stares at himself in the mirror incessantly, turning from this side to the other to get a good view of his hair, his biceps, his butt. When you're going out together, he's more concerned with admiring how he looks than noticing you. He's constantly working out: going to the gym or using machines at home; chugging down the latest protein drink; watching everything he eats. *Who is he doing all of this for? You? No way—he does it for himself!*

Guys, you may be surprised to hear that men who are obsessed with their own bodies are a total turnoff to most women. There's something about it that gives us the creeps. Perhaps it's the self-indulgence; perhaps it's that we end up feeling like a mere accessory on your arm.

I was with a guy like this once. He spent more time thinking about his own body than he did thinking about mine. Technically speaking, he was built very nicely, and he'd sculpted his muscles using weights so that he looked like the typical image of a male model. The odd thing, however, was that after awhile I found him totally unappealing. Something about his obsession with himself didn't allow me to even appreciate him visually.

Some years passed, and I fell in love with a wonderful man who was the opposite of the Workout King—he didn't really care much about how he looked, and although he was interested in being healthy, he didn't define himself by his physical appearance. My former partner would have been shocked to know that I actually found this new man much more sexually attractive than I'd found him. **But it was true—because the body my new partner was obsessed with was** *MINE!*

Turnoff #18:
Men Who Don't Like Giving a Woman Oral Sex

A friend of mine was recently describing what bothered her the most about her sex life with her boyfriend. "I hate it when he knows I'd like him to pleasure me orally, but he avoids it, and then expects to go ahead and do other things. I guess I feel like: *If he doesn't love me enough to do that, then why should I let him stick his penis inside of me?*"

Guys, I will try to be as clear and to the point as possible about this: *Having a man make love to our vagina with his mouth can be the most intimate, as well as pleasurable, sexual experience there is for a woman. This is the most vulnerable, delicate part of our body; it is the doorway into our womb. When a man worships us there with his mouth, we feel truly loved, accepted, and adored.*

You know how much you love it when we give you oral sex, guys. So of course we love it when you reciprocate. (Some women do have a resistance to receiving oral sex, but that's a whole other topic.) Therefore, when you avoid doing it to us, or do it reluctantly, we feel rejected, judged, and embarrassed. Then, like my friend, when you become all enthusiastic about having intercourse, *we feel cheated.* "How come you get to do what you enjoy, but you won't do what I enjoy?" we wonder.

Why do men have a problem giving oral sex?

1. You think cunnilingus is "dirty." Many men were brought up to think that the place between a woman's legs was dirty. After all, women go to the bathroom down there, as well as menstruate. When you focus on the location of that part of the body, you are overlooking the spirit of the act of oral sex—*it is a way for you to worship the essence of the woman you love.*

2. You are worried about how she smells or tastes. As I explain in *Secrets About Men*, our bodily secretions—semen for men, vaginal discharge for women—will reflect many factors, from the state of your physical health, what drugs or alcohol you imbibe, your diet, and even stress. Assuming a woman doesn't have any infections, the natural scent of the vagina is usually musky and sensual. Sometimes women taste salty; sometimes we taste sweet. Hopefully your partner is scrupulous about keeping herself clean and fresh-smelling, and follows the same advice I gave men about washing before sex. With practice, you can become quite fond of a woman's taste, particularly when you know that what you're doing to her is making her very happy!

3. You've had a bad experience giving a woman oral sex before. If you've ever had an unpleasant experience performing oral sex on a partner, you may be reluctant to try it again. Perhaps you were with a woman who was uncomfortable with it, or inhibited, and you ended up feeling you weren't doing it right. Perhaps you were with someone you really didn't love, and the whole thing felt forced. Or perhaps it hasn't gone well so far between you and your present partner. These negative experiences can turn you off to ever wanting to go "down there" on a woman again. Please give yourself a chance to try once more, this time having learned many new things about women and our bodies.

4. You don't know what you're doing. Many men are reticent to admit that they really don't know how to pleasure a woman orally. *They feel they aren't going to be very good at it, and thus, fearful of disappointing her, they avoid it entirely.* Guys, this is no excuse. Of course, you won't be an expert in the beginning—after all, you don't have a vagina, and have no idea what makes one feel good. But if you give your partner a chance, she will teach you. There are also many excellent books about sex that include chapters on the art of cunnilingus, and if you feel you don't quite have enough information, why not do some research?

A man who enjoys giving a woman oral sex is one of our biggest turn-ons. We will forgive you many other shortcomings if you master the art of loving us orally. And I'll bet you'll get more of the same from us, too.

Turnoff #19: Men Who Treat Other People Poorly

He yells at the other cars on the road, complaining about the way everyone drives.

He gets angry at waiters, parking garage attendants, bank tellers—anyone who doesn't do things the way he thinks they should be done.

He's constantly judging other people, criticizing everything about them—from how awful they look, to the stupid decisions they made, to something ridiculous they said.

You know this guy. He's angry. He's mad at the world. He's chronically pissed off. He doesn't respect others. What a delight it is to be with him.

The bottom line is that women don't like angry men. Angry men scare us; they don't make us feel safe. And when we don't feel safe, we don't get turned on. How can you expect a woman to open up to you in bed, guys, when a few hours before you were insulting the maître d' at a restaurant?

A man whose communication includes heavy cursing, constant insults, and sarcasm eventually becomes unappealing to a woman. There is something so unrefined about someone who can't control his anger, and lets it spew out all over the place. You think this is macho, guys? It's not. It's a big turnoff.

Turnoff #20: Men Who Don't Love Us

In the end, the biggest turnoff is when you don't love us, guys. When we feel you shutting down, putting up emotional walls, ignoring our needs, and pushing us away, our heart closes up to you. *And as we've seen, when a woman's heart closes, her body soon follows.* You could learn every sexual technique that exists; you could become the world's greatest technical lover, **but if we can't feel you loving us, we don't want you touching us. If we can't feel you letting us into your heart, we don't want to let you into our body.**

———

Well, you survived reading about Women's Top Twenty Sexual Turnoffs. Now, in the next chapter, you'll be rewarded with our turn-ons.

CHAPTER FIFTEEN

Women's Top Twenty Sexual Turn-Ons

If you want to know the truth, this entire book has been about how to turn a woman on. *No sexual techniques or skills could have as powerful an impact on a woman as the things we've already discussed: feeding her heart; making her feel safe, connected, and valued; listening to her; talking to her.* Guys, if you read and applied everything else, you probably wouldn't even need this chapter—your partner would be so grateful and feel so adored that she'd melt into a puddle of desire at your feet.

With that said, however, I'm still going to share some of the things women listed as their top twenty sexual turn-ons. Some of these are behaviors that turn us on outside the bedroom; most, however, are more sexually specific, having to do with what a man can do in bed to make his partner happy.

If you're in a relationship, read this chapter together—in bed, of course. Guys, you can ask your mate if she agrees with the items on my list: "Do you like Number One, too, honey?"; or "Does Number Six turn you on like she says?" Perhaps she will personalize the material, and maybe even add some suggestions of her own. Ladies, make sure to emphasize points that you really want him to digest. "Oh, I love this description of Number Fourteen. Mmmmm, that sounds good." Don't forget to compliment him on what he already does perfectly. "You're an expert at Number Two, darling." This will make your man more open to trying some of the other things he'll read about.

Of course, just reading about these turn-ons can be a turn-on. Have fun!

Women's Top Twenty Sexual Turn-Ons

1. Men who make love slowly

2. Men who talk to a woman in bed

3. Men who are good kissers—all over

4. Men who show a woman they love her with their eyes

5. Men who take the time to undress a woman slowly

6. Men who know how to tease with their touch

7. Men who touch a woman's hair

8. Men who love giving a woman oral sex

9. Men who let a woman know they want her in and out of bed

10. Men who understand how to please the female body

11. Men who know how to draw a woman out sexually

12. Men who prepare themselves physically for love-making

13. Men who make a woman feel she is beautiful

14. Men who love to give a woman a massage

15. **Men who caress and hold a woman's hands during lovemaking**

16. **Men who love to cuddle**

17. **Men who treat their partner as they did when they first met**

18. **Men who make a woman feel she's the only one for them**

19. **Men who believe being loved by their partner makes everything else worthwhile**

20. **Men who love us**

Turn-on #1: Men Who Make Love Slowly

We know you want us, but still, you're taking so long to even kiss our mouth. We feel your lips lightly touching our face, our eyes, and we are hungering to feel them finally find our lips. Your hands travel over our body, never quite touching anywhere that you know will drive us wild, and soon we are desperate for your intimate caress. We can feel an ache between our legs, but you hold back from going there, letting our desire build until we can hardly bear it anymore.

This is the description of how it feels to a woman when a man takes his time and makes love slowly. It makes us want you. It makes us long to give ourselves to you. When you allow our body to catch fire slowly, the flames of desire that emerge will be hot and long-lasting; the excitement that builds will be a roaring blaze of passion.

Smart men go slow in bed. They know if they give us the time and space to open on our own, they will not have to coax us. We will want you as much as you want us. Men who understand this secret about women; men who can be patient, tender, and flowing—to you we will give ourselves as we've never given ourselves to anyone before.

Turn-on #2: Men Who Talk to a Woman in Bed

It is wonderful to finally be close to you, alone together in bed. You reach out to hold us, to give us sweet kisses, tender hugs, and soon we relax and feel content. Then, you begin to talk. You tell us how beautiful we are; you say you've missed our body. You whisper things you'd like to do to us. Suddenly, it is no longer enough to just be near you like this. We want to make love with you. Your words have ignited our desire.

Men, do you know how much women want your words? Men are aroused more through vision and touch, but women are stimulated by thoughts and feelings. *Words turn us on. They communicate your passion for us to our brain. They unlock whatever doors we have closed, so we can be totally open to you.*

Think of words like the wind, making waves upon the ocean of feeling and desire. The water is always there in the sea, but it is the wind that moves it, teasing it from stillness until it rises into sparkling swells. **Our longing for you is always there, but it is your words that give it movement, and allow it to rise up in the form of sexual desire.**

Talk to us—before, during, and after lovemaking. Tell us how you are feeling; how we look to you; what you want to do to us; what you want us to do to you; how much you love what we are do-

ing together. Make love to us with words. When you speak these words of love, we feel safe; we feel adored. And we are yours completely.

Turn-on #3: Men Who Are Good Kissers—All Over

Think of a kiss as a gift that you are leaving on your lover's skin—on her face; her eyes; her neck; her shoulders; her back; her belly; her thighs; her hands; everywhere. These light, gentle, unrushed kisses have a magical effect on a woman. We feel the love in them. We know they are not just being offered to get us "ready," but that they are offerings in themselves.

Women love to be kissed—everywhere—not just on our lips. We love tender kisses, teasing kisses, sweet kisses, kisses that don't seem to be going anywhere. Kisses wake up our bodies. When a man kisses us lovingly from head to toe, we feel ourselves begin to open to receive him. It is said that the mouth is a doorway into the soul. *In this way, when we are kissed, a part of our lover enters us. Long before we have actual intercourse, you penetrate us with the love and sweetness in your kisses.*

If you truly know how to place these light kisses on a woman, you could ignore her erogenous zones entirely—yet by the time you were done, you would find her aroused, wet, and hungry for you.

Turn-on #4: Men Who Show a Woman They Love Her with Their Eyes

Nothing is more potent than having the man we love look deeply into our eyes. It's as if we can feel streams of love energy pour directly from his eyes into our heart and then spread to the rest of our body, like hot lava flowing over the earth. One look can turn us on more than any skillful caress. One look can melt us.

Look at your partner as you make love to her. Let her see the desire in your eyes. A man who knows how to look at his partner with a loving gaze will make her feel more completely loved than if he gave her any gift, or professed his devotion with any words.

Turn-on #5: Men Who Take the Time to Undress a Woman Slowly

If you ever watch a well-made erotic film, you'll notice the director always includes a long scene where the man slowly undresses the woman. The camera zooms in on his hands as he unbuttons each button on her blouse, one by one; it shows him taking off each piece of jewelry; it reveals him sliding her skirt down to the floor; then the action pauses as he kisses her while she is still in her bra and panties, not rushing to remove them quite yet. By the time the film reveals the woman as completely naked, the erotic energy has already built to a fevered pitch.

So often we miss the opportunity for this kind of sensual experience by getting in bed already naked with our partner. Men, women love the seduction of being slowly undressed. As you tenderly remove each item of clothing, we have time to allow our erotic self to emerge. If you go slow enough, you may even find we become impatient to devour you, and start ripping our clothes off ourselves—that's how much we can become turned on when you undress us.

Undressing your lover doesn't always have be a part of your lovemaking. Sometimes, though, it is the perfect first scene of your own erotic movie. If you were directing yourself in this film, what would you do? How would you approach her? What would you say as you were undressing her? You'll be surprised at how good you are at this when you try it—and she will love you for it.

Turn-on #6: Men Who Know How to Tease with Their Touch

If you ever watched two women make love to each other, you would notice something very specific about their caresses: *they would use light, teasing touches on their partner's body*, not directly going for the erogenous zones right away, but circling around them; grazing over them; getting close to them but not quite touching. Why would these lovers do this to each other? Because as women, they would know exactly what their partner wanted; exactly what would turn her on the most.

Men would be wise to take a lesson from this. Women love to be teased with touch. **In fact, direct stimulation, especially in the beginning of lovemaking, is far less arousing than teasing.** Women sigh with disappointment when you go directly to their nipples or clitoris—you've just skipped the best part.

Remember the analogy of slowly building the fire with kindling before putting on the big logs? This is also true for touch. The longer you take to tease us, the hotter our fire. Soon we will be begging for you to touch us right on those special spots; we will grab your hand and push it there ourselves. That's how turned on we will be.

Turn-on #7: Men Who Touch a Woman's Hair

This is a simple but powerful suggestion: Touch your partner's hair when you are being affectionate with her, or making love with her. Women love to have our hair stroked and played with. This isn't something most men would know, because normally your hair is quite short. But it is a special, sexy thing men can do to us that drives women crazy.

Some women love having their hair slowly and gently brushed, and consider it a powerful form of foreplay. Others get turned on when you wash their hair for them. Many women say they love when a man is inside of them during intercourse, and he laces his fingers through her hair. Guys, you'll have to discover your partner's secrets on your own. Trust me—her hair is an erogenous zone you don't want to neglect.

Turn-on #8: Men Who Love Giving a Woman Oral Sex

We've already discussed this, but it doesn't hurt to remind you again, guys. As I've said, it is a turnoff to women when we know men *don't* like to give us oral sex. Naturally, then, when a man loves to adore our body that way, we are very turned on to him, and can't wait to make love . . . and make love . . . and make love.

Nothing is more personal and more intimate than having the man we love kiss our most delicate, private place. When we feel you do this with love, with worship, with adoration, you turn our bed into a sacred altar, and turn us into a goddess. What more can I say?

Turn-on #9: Men Who Let a Woman Know They Want Her in and out of Bed

There is something primal and powerful about hearing the man we love say, *"I want you."* Those words make us shiver with delight. They make our body begin to tingle in places that feel oh-so-good. They open up our secret doorways, inspiring us to want you to come in.

Tell us you want us long before we actually begin to make love. The words will penetrate us and, like a time-released capsule, will begin to prepare us for what is to come later. Then, tell us you want us when we get into bed. The words will unlock our lust and longing, and invite us to be your true sexual consort.

Turn-on #10: Men Who Understand How to Please the Female Body

If a man who is unfamiliar with a woman's body is a turnoff, then a man who is masterful at loving a woman is an absolute turn-on. *There is something reassuring about getting into bed with the man we love, knowing you understand exactly how to please us.* It's like going back to a restaurant where we always know the food is going to be fabulous—we can hardly wait for dinner. In the same way, when we know with certainty that our partner is an expert at loving and adoring our body, we can hardly wait to get in bed with you.

Turn-on #11: Men Who Know How to Draw Out a Woman Sexually

Some men have a knack for doing wrong and turning a woman off, even if she originally wanted to make love. Others possess a wonderful talent for making their partner feel relaxed, uninhibited, and playful. When a woman knows that *you* know how to get her in the mood for sexual loving, she trusts you in the most intimate sense of the word.

What does it take to draw a woman out sexually? Everything we've discussed in this book, for starters. Beyond that, each woman has her own special needs that, when they're met, allow her to be her most free sexual self. It's her partner's job to figure out what those needs are. Maybe it's making sure she's had time to herself before she gets into bed with you. Maybe it's lying in bed for a while and talking. Maybe she warms up by giving you pleasure first, and not feeling pressured to be turned on right away.

Learn the secrets that unlock the door to your lover's sexuality. If you're not sure what they are, ask her. She will be happy to tell you.

Turn-on #12: Men Who Prepare Themselves Physically for Lovemaking

Imagine you've invited a guest over for dinner. He arrives in a rush; he's tired and unkempt, smelling as if he needs a shower. Immediately, he begins complaining about his day, and he barely notices all the effort you put into setting the table, arranging the flowers, or preparing a wonderful meal. How do you feel? Like you want to take the dinner and throw it in his face.

Making love with our partner is like inviting a person we love to a feast—and we are the main course! So when a man arrives, having prepared himself for the special event, a woman feels loved and appreciated, and it's easy for her to become turned on.

It's simple, really, guys. Preparing yourself means taking a shower; putting on some cologne; changing your clothes; maybe even preparing the bedroom by lighting some candles or turning on your favorite CD. You don't have to do this every time, but once in a while it makes us feel you value the invitation to share our bed and our body.

Turn-on #13: Men Who Make a Woman Feel She Is Beautiful

I will tell you a secret: *When a woman believes you think she is beautiful, she blossoms. When she believes that you love her face, her body, her scent, her taste, the way she moves, and everything about her, she turns into a Love Goddess. And when she believes you adore making love to her, she turns into a Sex Goddess.*

How can a woman come to know these things? Why, you must tell her, of course—not just once in a while, but all the time. Tell her while you are in bed. Tell her while you are out of bed. The more you let her know how beautiful she is to you, the more she will shine.

I am very blessed, for I have a partner who makes me feel like I am the most beautiful woman in the world. When I walk into the room wearing raggedy old clothes, he tells me that I am adorable. When he sees me after any absence at all—an hour, a day, a week—he looks at me as if he's never gazed upon anything so lovely in his life, and tells me so. When we're in bed—well, that's personal, but let's just say I have never felt as beautiful or desirable as I do when I am with him.

No man has ever given me this gift before—the gift of feeling physically adored. It is a gift that is priceless, one that has transformed me from the inside out. Please give this gift to the woman you love, so she, too, can blossom into everything you want her to be.

Turn-on #14: Men Who Love to Give a Woman a Massage

Touch is the language of love. It is a language with no sound, no rules, no form. Through your hands, your heart speaks to your beloved, expressing feelings in a way mere words cannot. The tender caress of her face, the sensual stroke down her back, the grazing of your fingers across her belly—these gestures transcend the limitations of spoken language and communicate your desire, your need, your emotions more powerfully and more poignantly than words ever could.

Your hands are not just physical appendages. They are transmitters of the powerful life energy that flows through your body. The Eastern system of medicine explains that there are hundreds of meridians, or energetic pathways, that run like highways throughout your body. Life energy moves along these pathways and, according to this system, many of these energy meridians end in your fingertips. *That means your hands can give off tremendous amounts of energy*. This, then, is why touch is so powerful: When you touch your partner, your hands aren't simply stimulating nerve endings that make her feel pleasure; they are actually sending life energy into your lover's body.

One of the most wonderful ways to make love to your partner is to give her a massage. Allow your love to flow from your heart and into your hands, and she will feel as if your hands are charged with electricity, and every caress will be pleasurable beyond anything she has ever experienced before. *When you do this with the purpose of adoring her with your touch, and not simply as foreplay, she will feel your love, your heart, and even your soul flowing into her body*.

Massaging your lover is a way of making love to her whole body. You are the giver, and she is the receiver. This allows her to relax, to open, and to appreciate you for giving her this loving attention—not to mention that it will feel fantastic!

Turn-on #15: Men Who Caress and Hold a Woman's Hands During Lovemaking

The man and woman are in the throes of passionate love-making. He is on top of her and inside of her, moving in a rhythm of erotic ecstasy. Suddenly, he reaches for both her hands with his, palm against palm, intertwining his fingers into hers. She looks up at him and smiles, for what he just did was more intimate than any act of sexual stimulation could ever be.

There is something so personal, so tender, about hands. So often during lovemaking, we neglect our lover's hands in favor of other, more responsive body parts. But those moments in which we touch their hands can be moments of the greatest intimacy.

Women often tell me that they love when a man remembers to touch their hands during sex: kissing them; rubbing his face against them; caressing them; holding them. She can be lost in her world of passion, and he can be lost in his, but when, in that moment, he reaches out for her hand, it is as if he is saying, *"Here I am, my love. I am with you. Feel me loving you."*

Hold your partner's hand while you are giving her oral sex. Hold her hand while she is giving it to you. Hold her hand while you kiss her. Hold her hand while you are inside her, and while you come. Hold her hand afterward as you lie close together, bathed in the perfume of your passion.

Turn-on #16: Men Who Love to Cuddle

Let's get one thing straight. To women, cuddling is NOT a non-sexual activity. It is a form of intimacy, one that, if practiced prop-

erly, can definitely lead to sex. Unfortunately, most men highly un-
derrate cuddling, misunderstanding it as a neutral form of affection, only to be engaged in on mornings or nights when sex is out
of the question.

Guys, you couldn't be more wrong! **Cuddling is a fabulous
form of foreplay.** Why do you think women always say, "Let's
cuddle"? Men hear this as, "I'm not interested in having sex
tonight," but the correct translation is: *"Maybe I'm interested and
maybe I'm not—let's cuddle and find out,"* or *"I don't think I'm in
the mood, but if we cuddle nicely, there's a good chance I could get
in the mood."*

Women love men who love to cuddle. They make us feel safe
and protected, and that they love to be close to us whether or not
we want to have sex. Of course, that makes us want to have sex!
Try adding more cuddling to your life, and you may be surprised to
find out how sexy it really is.

Turn-on #17: Men Who Treat Their Partner as They Did When They First Met

The art of seeing your partner with fresh eyes every day is a
wonderful practice to master. I call this *"seeing with the eyes of
love."* It means treating the person you love as you did when you
first met her. Do you remember? You delighted in each moment
spent together. You couldn't stop telling her how much you loved
her and how lucky you were. You took her out on dates. You
brought her flowers. You gave her cards. You wrote her e-mails.
You did everything you could to make her happy.

You know how to do this, guys; **it means not taking the
woman you love for granted**. Treat her like a woman you want to
seduce. Treat her like a woman you hope will spend the rest of her

life with you. Treat her like a woman you want to make sure no man can steal away. Treat her like your beloved. The more you hold her this way in your heart, the more in love you will feel, and the happier she will be.

Turn-on #18: Men Who Make a Woman Feel She's the Only One for Them

What your woman wants to tell you:

"When I know I am the only one you want, I can give myself to you completely. When I know I am the only one you think about, I can give myself to you completely. When I know I am the only one with whom you will share your deepest self, I can give myself to you completely. When I know I am the only one you will kiss and caress and lie naked with, I can give myself to you completely. When I know I am the only one you will sleep with at night, I can give myself to you completely. When I know I am the only one you want to wake up with each morning, I can give myself to you completely.

"Make me feel like I am your only one, and I will love you like the only one you are for me."

Turn-on #19: Men Who Believe Being Loved by Their Partner Makes Everything Else Worthwhile

What does a woman want more than anything? **To make such a difference in her partner's life that, whatever else he has to put up with, he can deal with because of her.** Nothing can make her feel more cherished, more valued, more loved.

Please know this about us, men—we want to be the one thing in your life that makes sense, the one thing that makes everything else worthwhile. When you let a woman know she does this for you, that she is your solace and your shelter and your sweet relief, we feel we are truly fulfilling our purpose, and we are content.

Turn-on #20: Men Who Love Us

Ultimately, it is the heart, and not the body, that is the source of all true passion. There, in the invisible realm from which all feeling emerges, the ocean of passion lies waiting to be stirred, not by the right touch or by a skillful caress, but by the only thing that can cause passion to rise up—the love from our beloved's heart.

Love us.

CONCLUSION

For me, writing a book is like taking a long and difficult journey to a mysterious place deep inside myself. I know I need to go there, but I am not sure what I will find. I know I am supposed to come back from the journey bearing truth, wisdom, and inspiration for those who await my return, but I am afraid I might not discover anything of real value and will disappoint those I've committed to help. I know the journey will require great strength, perseverance, and emotional courage, as I encounter the inevitable obstacles along the way, both from within and without, but I don't know how to prepare for these battles that have not yet come. So ultimately, as I venture forward, all I can do is arm myself with faith, trusting that I will be guided to the right inner destination, that I will discover what I am meant to retrieve, and that I will find a way to bring it back from the depths of my being, and to share it with compassion, clarity, and love.

The journey of What Women Want Men to Know has been just such an adventure in faith. All I knew when I began was that I wanted to allow the voices of tens of thousands of women I've met, taught, and learned from, to speak through me to the hearts of the men they love. This was my intention as I started out. As with any true pilgrimage, however, so much more has happened than that:

• • •

In the writing of this book, I have come to feel even more love, more understanding, and more appreciation for men than I had when I began. For as I have contemplated your minds and your hearts; as I have spent day after day trying to find the right words with which to tell you what I wanted you to know about loving and understanding women; I have felt you, men, from the inside out. I have spent my life loving men: giving to you; crying over you; reaching out to you; healing from you; learning from you; never turning away from you. Now, in this book, I hope you have felt the sincerity of that love and the fruit of that commitment.

In the writing of this book, I have also come to feel even more love, more awe, and more gratitude for women—including, I might add, myself. Our ability to love is so profound; our willingness to continue trying is so brave. I am more clear than ever that all we want is to experience harmony and oneness with the man we love and to be a source of happiness for all those we hold dear.

When I write, I feel my readers with me, always, in every moment. I feel your pain, your fears, your disappointments. I feel your dreams, your determination, your hunger for the truth. I hope as you've read these pages, dear sisters, you have felt me, too—trying to be your mirror, your mouthpiece, the bridge that connects the wishes in your heart to the heart of your beloved. Did I say the things you wanted me to? Did I tell him what you needed him to hear? That is what I tried to do.

The journey of this book is almost finished for me. Now, with all you've learned, your own journey awaits you—the journey of Love. Like the journey of writing this book, your journey of Love will require great emotional courage, stubborn perseverance, and uninterrupted faith. Sometimes you will feel lost, and not be sure where you are heading. Sometimes you will feel tired and disheartened, and wonder if you should have even started the journey in the first place.

But there will also be moments of great joy, profound revelation, and unimaginable sweetness as Love transforms you like nothing else can. And just as I sit here now, amazed that this book has finally emerged, one day you, too, will emerge from this chapter of your life. And you will realize, as I continue to, that through all of its ups and downs, *your journey has taught you that your capacity to love is way beyond anything you could ever have imagined it to be*. In the end, that love you feel in your heart will be the true gift, the promised boon, and the ultimate reward for having been a traveler on the sacred and mysterious path of Love.

Do not give up on Love, dear friends, no matter what.

BARBARA DE ANGELIS
February 27, 2001

Barbara De Angelis offers workshops and seminars throughout North America, and in her own unique, dynamic, and entertaining style, uplifts and motivates her audiences on the topics of love, relationships, and personal growth. She is also highly sought after for lectures, conferences, and speaking engagements throughout the world.

If you would like to receive a schedule of Barbara's personal seminars, or contact her to set up an event, please call or write:

Barbara De Angelis Seminars
12021 Wilshire Boulevard
Suite 607
Los Angeles, California 90025
Phone: (310) 535-0988
Fax: (310) 459-9472
E-Mail: AskBarbaraD@aol.com

For more information, and to purchase books, tapes, and videos, we invite you to visit Barbara's website:

Barbara-DeAngelis.com